Motivation and Delinquency

Volume 44 of
the Nebraska Symposium
on Motivation

University of Nebraska Press
Lincoln and London 1997

Volume 44 of the Nebraska Symposium on Motivation

Motivation and Delinquency

Richard A. Dienstbier
D. Wayne Osgood

Series Editor
Volume Editor

Presenters
Joan McCord

Professor of Criminal Justice, Temple University

Michael Rutter

Honorary Director of the MRC Child Psychiatry Unit and of the Social, Genetic & Developmental Psychiatry Research Centre, Institute of Psychiatry, London

Barbara Maughan

Career Scientist, MRC Child Psychiatry Unit and Social, Genetic & Developmental Psychiatry Research Centre, Institute of Psychiatry, London

Joanne Meyer

Senior Scientist, Statistical Genetics, Millenium Pharmaceuticals, Inc., Cambridge, Massachusetts

Andrew Pickles

Career Scientist, MRC Child Psychiatry Unit and Social, Genetic & Developmental Psychiatry Research Centre, Institute of Psychiatry, London

Judy Silberg

Assistant Professor of Human Genetics, Virginia Commonwealth University

Emily Simonoff

Clinical Scientist, MRC Child Psychiatry Unit and Social, Genetic & Developmental Psychiatry Research Centre, Institute of Psychiatry, London

Eric Taylor

Clinical Scientist, MRC Child Psychiatry Unit and Social, Genetic & Developmental Psychiatry Research Centre, Institute of Psychiatry, London

Gerald R. Patterson

Research Scientist, Oregon Social Learning Center, Eugene, Oregon

Karen Yoerger

Research Analyst, Oregon Social Learning Center, Eugene, Oregon

James T. Tedeschi

Professor of Psychology, University at Albany, State University of New York

Karen Heimer

Assistant Professor of Sociology, University of Iowa

Ross L. Matsueda

Professor and Chair of Sociology, University of Iowa

Motivation and Delinquency is Volume 44 in the series
CURRENT THEORY AND RESEARCH
IN MOTIVATION

© 1997 by the University of Nebraska Press
All rights reserved
Manufactured in the United States of America
International Standard Book Number
0-8032-3566-6 (Clothbound)

⊗ The paper in this book meets the minimum
requirements of American National Standard for
Information Sciences—Permanence of Paper for
Printed Library Materials, ANSI Z39.48-1984.

"The Library of Congress has cataloged
this serial publication as follows:"
Nebraska Symposium on Motivation.
Nebraska Symposium on Motivation.
[Papers] v. [1]–1953–
Lincoln, University of Nebraska Press.
v. illus., diagrs. 22cm. annual.
Vol. 1 issued by the symposium under
its earlier name: Current Theory and
Research in Motivation.
Symposia sponsored by the Dept. of
Psychology of the University of Nebraska.
1. Motivation (Psychology)
BF683.N4   159.4082   53-11655
Library of Congress

Preface

The volume editor for this 44th edition of the Nebraska Symposium on Motivation is Professor Wayne Osgood. Wayne selected and invited the contributors and coordinated all aspects of the editing of this volume. He has my gratitude for an excellent symposium and for the timely drawing together of the chapters.

With this volume, we have continued to employ procedures that were designed to facilitate the attendance at the symposium by scholars other than our main presenters. Specifically, to allow other scholars the opportunity to attend the symposium as participants, we invited posters on topics relevant to the main theme of the volume. Since this is a tradition we intend to continue, we urge you, our readers, to consider such poster submissions when you receive future announcements of the Nebraska Symposium.

This symposium series is supported largely by funds donated to the University of Nebraska Foundation by the late Professor Cora L. Friedline in the memory of Professor Harry K. Wolfe. This symposium volume, like those of the recent past, is dedicated to the memory of Professor Wolfe, who brought psychology to the University of Nebraska. After studying with Professor Wilhelm Wundt, Professor Wolfe returned to Nebraska, his native state, to establish the first undergraduate laboratory of psychology in the nation. As a student at Nebraska, Professor Friedline studied psychology under Professor Wolfe.

We are grateful to the late Professor Friedline for this bequest, and to the University of Nebraska Foundation for continued financial support for the series.

Richard A. Dienstbier
Series Editor

Contents

Introduction

D. Wayne Osgood
Pennsylvania State University

The 1996 Nebraska Symposium on Motivation addresses a timely issue: motivation and delinquency. Delinquency, in such forms as juvenile violence, drug abuse, and delinquent gangs, is one of the public's greatest concerns. The public's perceptions of ever-increasing rates of juvenile crime are often out of touch with the evidence (Bernard, 1992), and indeed, overall rates of delinquency appear to have changed little in recent years. Nevertheless, there have been dramatic increases in rates of some of the most serious forms of youth violence in recent years, and rates of substance use have increased for the past few years after an extended period of decline.

One key to the success of the Nebraska Symposium on Motivation is that motivation is relevant to explaining every type of behavior. Regardless of the behavior under study, it is difficult to imagine a satisfactory explanation that does not address the question of what motivates people to do this. What do they "get out of it"?

When applied to deviant behaviors such as delinquency, the topic of motivation takes an intriguing twist. Delinquency is defined as illegal behavior by minors, so our concern is with an activity that is distinct solely because it is prohibited by legal codes and (typically) by conventional standards of conduct. Thus, the question of motivation becomes, What motivates adolescents to do the very things that their elders have told them not to do?

Motivation has long been a key concept in the study of delinquency, and motivational themes play a central role in distinguishing among the classic theories of delinquency that play such a prominent role in every delinquency and criminology text. Indeed, Agnew (1995) recently argued that motivational concepts capture the most important differences between theories of delinquency and offer the best hope for a meaningful test of their validity. Many of the classic theories take conventional or conforming behavior for granted and therefore offer explanations of motivation away from conformity and toward deviance. For differential association theory (Sutherland & Cressey, 1955) deviance arises from associating with individuals or groups that support delinquency and oppose conventional standards of behavior. Thus, in this theory conformity is the motivation for delinquency, and delinquents are unique only in that they are conforming to a different standard of behavior. In a similar vein, social learning theory (Akers, 1977) portrays delinquency as motivated by reinforcement from peers and other associates. In another version of motivation toward delinquency, strain theories explain delinquency as a response to a disjunction between desire for material goods and access to those goods (e.g., Cloward & Ohlin, 1960).

Control theories take the opposite tack, assuming that delinquency requires no explanation because the motivation for delinquency inheres in the rewards of the delinquent acts themselves. Instead, conforming to standards that prohibit delinquency must be explained. Therefore, the motivational concepts in these explanations concern controlling forces that create conformity to the law, as in such social bonds as attachment to others and commitment to conventional lines of action in Hirschi's social control theory (Hirschi, 1969).

Though motivational concepts pervade the study of delinquency, they have seldom been the subject of explicit, systematic development in recent writings. The 1996 Nebraska Symposium on Motivation provided the occasion for this development, presenting the work of prominent scholars who are both well established in the field and active in developing important new directions for theory and research.

Though courses titled *juvenile delinquency* are most likely to be found in departments of sociology and criminal justice, the study of delinquency is spread across the full range of social and behavioral sciences and is found even in medical and biological research. Though many researchers appear to be comfortable limiting their attention to work within their own discipline, no one discipline owns this topic. The opposite is very much the case for the authors of the chapters that follow. Collectively they represent the fields of clinical psychology, social psychology, psychiatry, criminal justice, and sociology. More importantly, each author presents research that ignores the boundaries of academic disciplines, bringing together diverse perspectives to generate new insights.

The symposium volume begins with Joan McCord's chapter, which has the intriguing title "He Did It Because He Wanted To. . . ." McCord provides a good starting point by asking fundamental questions about what it means to be motivated to engage in delinquency and about the relationships between explanation, blame, and free will. She searches for suitable answers in the writings of philosophers. Working her way from the ancient Greeks to modern linguistic philosophers, she succeeds in developing a sound position for grounding meaningful theory and empirical research. Further, she uses this background as a base from which to pose her own Construct theory of motivation for crime, which gives a prominent role to linguistic socialization.

In the second chapter, Michael Rutter and his colleagues review findings from their program of research, which has spanned several decades. They show flagrant disregard for arbitrary disciplinary boundaries by developing a coherent framework that encompasses causal factors ranging from the social organization of communities and schools to behavioral genetics and hyperactivity. Throughout, they grapple with the complexity posed by the heterogeneous forms that delinquency takes, from minor misbehavior engaged in by most adolescents to persistent and serious violations associated with antisocial personality disorders.

Gerald Patterson and Karen Yoerger (1993) have proposed that age of onset constitutes a fundamental basis for distinguishing more serious delinquency from less. Together with Moffitt (1993), whose theoretical position has many similarities, they have inspired a wave of new research that is flooding the journals. In their symposium chapter, Patterson and Yoerger explore the causes of later-onset delinquency and demonstrate the close tie between the age of onset distinction and the elegant application of behaviorist psychology to delinquency that Patterson has been developing for over twenty years. They offer a thorough empirical investigation of late onset delinquency, using data from their Oregon Youth Study.

James Tedeschi's chapter applies his social interactionist theory of violence (Tedeschi & Felson, 1994) to juvenile delinquency, demonstrating an important new direction for research on crime and delinquency. Tedeschi applies the social psychology of interdependence to the problem of violence, construing violence as coercive attempts at social influence. In doing so, Tedeschi shows the relevance of interdependent interpersonal relationships, an element that has been all but ignored in established criminological theories and in psychological research on aggression, and shows how his theory applies to a variety of findings about delinquency.

In the final chapter, Karen Heimer and Ross Matsueda consider delinquency as it is viewed by the two social psychologies: psychological and sociological. Psychological researchers have considered delinquency mainly in terms of aggression, typically studied through laboratory experimentation. On the sociological side, Heimer and Matsueda concentrate on the application of Mead's symbolic interactionism that they have developed over the past several years. They demonstrate the value of that theory for integrating themes from many of the classic theories of delinquency and report findings from their program of research that support their approach.

It has been a privilege to serve as organizer for the 44th annual Nebraska Symposium on Motivation. Doing so has given me the opportunity to work with several of my favorite scholars in my own field and to preside over an exciting event highlighting their work. As organizer, I owe a debt of thanks to many people. First, thanks go to the symposium committee and the entire University of Nebraska–Lincoln psychology department for allowing me to serve as symposium organizer on the basis of my shirttail connection to the department as an adjunct member. (My home department was sociology.) Dick Dienstbier, the symposium series editor, was especially helpful in showing me the ropes. I owe even more gratitude to my wife, Jan Jacobs, a two-time symposium organizer, who not only offered sage counsel whenever asked, but who knows me well enough to give me a push when I needed it. My most heartfelt thanks go Claudia Price-Decker, the administrative secretary in the psychology department, and to all her staff. She made the job of symposium organizer a joy by managing the endless list of tasks that made the symposium a success. Finally, I feel very fortunate to have chosen such a fine group of authors/speakers. They gave excellent presentations and graciously interacted with everyone who came to the symposium. They produced excellent chapters, met deadlines without complaint, and were delightful companions. Thank you all.

REFERENCES

Agnew, R. (1995). Testing the leading crime theories: An alternative strategy focusing on motivational processes. *Journal of Research on Crime and Delinquency, 32*, 363–398.

Akers, R. L. (1977). *Deviant behavior: A social learning perspective*. Belmont CA: Wadsworth.

Bernard, T. J. (1992). *The cycle of juvenile justice*. New York: Oxford University Press.

Cloward, R. A., & Ohlin, L. E. (1960). *Delinquency and opportunity: A theory of delinquent gangs*. New York: Free Press.

Hirschi, T. (1969). *Causes of delinquency*. Berkeley: University of California Press.

Moffitt, T. E. (1993). Adolescence-limited and life-course-persistent antisocial behavior: A developmental taxonomy. *Psychological Review, 100*, 674–701.

Patterson, G. R., & Yoerger, K. (1993). Developmental models for delinquent behavior. In Sheilagh Hodgins (Ed.), *Crime and mental disorder*. Newbury Park CA: Sage.

Sutherland, E. H., & Cressey, D. R. (1955). *Principles of criminology* (5th ed.). Philadelphia: J. B. Lippincott.

Tedeschi, J. T., & Felson, R. B. (1994). *Violence, aggression and coercive actions*. Washington DC: American Psychological Association.

"He Did It Because He Wanted To . . ."

Joan McCord
Temple University

The Menendez brothers killed their parents. At their trial, two explanations competed for the endorsement of the jury. On the one side, the defense suggested that Lyle and Erik had been so emotionally and sexually abused that they were compelled to kill. On the other side, as the state argued, the brothers believed that they could become wealthy quickly by disposing of their parents. Cause versus motive. Lyle and Erik tried to show in their defense that they could not help doing what they did: their past experiences, over which they had no control, caused them to kill. The prosecution said, in effect, that these boys chose to kill, that they had motives for their crimes.

The defense lawyers tried to show that the past determined the acts for which the state attempted to hold the brothers responsible. Bit by bit, the defense filled in details of a past that might render murder the inexorable result of the boys' history. In doing so, they also hoped to show that the acts were explicable. The argument runs, as Nagel (1979) showed, toward shrinking the area of genuine agency. Thus, because the agent cannot be responsible for past conditions, "he cannot be responsible for their results" (p. 35).

What role does motivation play in crime? What makes an act—criminal or otherwise—intentional? How are motives related to intentional actions? And what, if anything, justifies punishment?

To address these questions, scholars must consider relations among such concepts as cause, responsibility, intent, and motivation. These concepts quite readily link with what Dennett referred to as an "undismissable philosophical question" (1984, p. 3) about free will.

Whether we like it or not, questions about free will are central to criminology. An intentional stance, wrote Dennett, "is a precondition of any moral stance, and hence if it is jeopardized by any triumph of mechanism, the notion of moral responsibility is jeopardized in turn" (1978, pp. 242–243).

Pragmatic reasons as well as justice require that society punish only those who are morally responsible for crimes. If people were equally liable to be punished whether they were or were not responsible, punishments would not deter them from committing crimes (see Hart, 1973).

On the other hand, crime prevention rests on knowing something about the factors that predict criminal behavior. Social scientists have shown that disorganized environments and dysfunctional families contribute to crime. Evidence indicates that some biological markers increase the probability of aggressive acts and impulsive behavior. Indeed, whether we are criminals or study criminals, whether we are saints or sinners, a case can be made that the type of person we are is at least largely dependent on factors outside our control.

Criminal acts can be distinguished from illegal behavior performed accidentally by their intentionality. Intentional actions are done knowingly and for reasons. One way of looking at motivation is to consider motives as the reasons a person has for intentional actions. Thus motivation plays a central role in criminal behavior.

Historically, the claim that a person's behavior is intentional has been a claim that the agent exercised free will, that the act was not "determined" by recognizable causes over which an individual has no control. I begin this chapter by inspecting the roots of what I take to be the mistaken idea that motivated, intentional actions cannot be both voluntary and subject to scientific scrutiny.

The roots of the idea of a contradiction between natural causes and voluntary actions lie deep in Western tradition, in the Greek philosophies of Plato and Aristotle from which so many modern theories in social and natural sciences have developed. Therefore, examination of the philosophic history of this idea provides an appropriate starting point for criticism.

After reviewing historical perspectives regarding the claim that some behavior is intentional, I examine the egoistic assumption underlying many current theories of motivation and theories of criminal behavior. I then sketch a theory about motives and how motives conducive to crime come to be. Finally, I discuss how the proposed Construct theory of motivation integrates what we know about the causes of criminal behavior, how it differs from traditional theories of crime, and what it suggests about crime prevention strategies.

Historical Perspectives on Intentional Action

Questions regarding motivation and responsibility for intentional action have posed puzzles for at least 2,000 years. To a large degree, current thinking about the issues is dependent upon the way in which they were addressed by the Greek philosophers Plato and Aristotle.

In the *Meno* (trans. 1949) and *Protagoras* (trans. 1956), Plato wrestled with the question whether virtue can be taught and, if so, how such teaching might affect responsibility for wrongdoing. In *The Republic* (trans. 1974), Plato claims that just action leads to happiness and that, therefore, wrongdoers act out of ignorance regarding their own well-being. In *Protagoras,* Socrates and his listeners agree that knowledge of virtue will lead to virtue and "that no one willingly does evil or what he thinks to be evil." Because he believed that neither ignorance nor accidents should be punished, Plato thought that punishments were not deserved. Punishments might, however, be necessary to affect future behavior. In *Laws* (trans. 1961), Plato specified punishments designed to teach those who had not learned proper behavior, advocating the death penalty for those who failed to learn.

Like Plato, Aristotle believed that conscious actions are aimed at the Good and that the Good is equivalent to happiness. Yet unlike Plato, Aristotle taught that, nevertheless, praise and blame were sometimes justified.

The *Nicomachean Ethics* (Aristotle, trans. 1962) explains the issue: "It is on account of the pleasure that we do bad things, and on account of the pain that we abstain from noble ones. Hence we ought to have been brought up in a particular way from our very youth, as Plato says, so as both to delight in and to be pained by the things that we ought" (Bk. 2, chap. 3). Aristotle added, "But if some one were to say that pleasant and noble objects have a compelling power, forcing us from without, all acts would be for him compulsory; for it is for these objects that all men do everything they do" (Bk. 3, chap. 1).

Rejecting the idea that all actions are necessitated by external causes, Aristotle identified voluntary actions as those for "which the moving principle is in the agent himself, he being aware of the particular circumstances of the action" (Bk. 3, chap. 1). Voluntary actions provide a foundation for virtues and vices for which praise or blame are deserved. Aristotle reasoned that praise and blame presuppose volitional action; that at least some voluntary actions involve choice; that choice requires deliberation; and that deliberation occurs only "about things that are in our power and can be done" (Bk. 3, chap. 2).

Aristotle set about providing an account of evildoing within a world in which causal chains that could be expressed through covering laws seemed to link choice to experiences. His account centered on the role of appetites. Appetites, Aristotle reasoned, were essential features in both voluntary actions and the covering laws that explained them. Responsibility could rest on the individual whose appetites were expressed in action.

Practical reason alone, Aristotle noted in *On the Soul*, does not always give an account of action. "Even when the mind does command and thought bids us pursue or avoid something, sometimes no movement is produced," he explained, continuing, "we act in accordance with desire, as in the case of moral weakness" (trans. 1941b, No. 433).

Practical reason requires choice. Yet the Aristotelian conception of causality as an object of speculative knowledge assumes necessary connections. Science, according to the *Analytic Posteriora*, provides knowledge of causes, including "an antecedent which necessitates a consequent" (trans. 1941a, Bk. 2, chap. 11). Aristotle presented a conundrum: If a science of man is possible, responsibility for action is impossible. Conversely, if responsibility for action is possible, actions must lie outside the range of science.

Two routes have traditionally been used to address this puzzle.

Along one, motives are conceived to lie outside of science. Such was the route described by Immanuel Kant (1704–1824) and adopted by many psychologists.

Along the other route, the voluntary nature of actions is subsumed under interpretations of causal relations, and voluntary actions are seen to be subject to causal laws. Thomas Hobbes (1588–1679), for example, defined actions as voluntary when they were free from external force. Yet Hobbes believed that all voluntary actions were motivated by self-interest, writing in *Leviathan* (1651/1975), "of the voluntary acts of every man, the object is some *Good to Himselfe"* (Bk. 1, chap. 14; italics in original). Free will "consisteth in this, that he finds no stop, in doing what he has the will, desire, or inclination to doe" (Bk. 2, chap. 21). Consistent with his view of motivation and voluntary actions, Hobbes believed that punishments were justified only in order for "the disposing of men to obey the Law" (Bk. 2, chap. 28).

David Hume (1711–1776), following Bishop Butler, argued against Hobbes that motives could not be solely self-interested. He noted the implausibility of attributing all acts of kindness to self-interest, the confusion embodied in attributing satisfaction from achieving a goal with satisfaction as a goal, and the difficulty of accounting for differences in behavior with an assumption that everyone seeks only self-interest. Rather, Hume proposed, we should consider the influencing motives of the will (1739/1888, Bk. 2, sect. 3).

All intentional action, according to Hume, requires passion of some kind. He wrote that "reason alone can never be a motive to any action of the will" (1739/1888, p. 413). Suppose, for example, that two people agree that a third person needs help, but only one of them wants to give help. According to Hume's thesis, only the one who wants to can voluntarily do so. Alternatively, Hume might point out, many know that people leaving automated teller machines often have a lot of money and are likely to be vulnerable to pickpockets, but only a few people pick pockets. Unless a person wants to pick pockets, according to the argument, he or she will not voluntarily do so. Hume therefore believed "Reason is, and ought only to be the slave of the passions," (p. 415).

As an empiricist, Hume distinguished between the constant conjunction of causal relations and necessary connections between events. Because causes do not necessitate effects, a causal relation for action does not restrict the agent. Hume urged, "We cannot surely mean that actions have so little connection with motives, inclinations, and circumstances that one does not follow with a certain degree of uniformity from the other. . . . By liberty, then, we can only mean a power of acting or not acting according to the determinations of the will; that is, if we choose to remain at rest, we may; if we choose to move, we also may" (1748/1955, Vol. 7, pt. 1).

Hume's positions regarding intentional actions and causes have been tenacious. Hume claimed three things: intentional action requires desires; causes are evidenced in the constant conjunction with specific effects; and causes do not compel.

As one of the proponents for these ideas, Moritz Schlick, wrote, "Since natural laws are only descriptions of what happens, there can be in regard to them no talk of 'compulsion'" (1939, p. 147). According to Schlick, compulsion, not necessity, is the proper contrast to freedom. Schlick argued, as had Aristotle, that people are responsible for their actions when the moving principle is within them. Schlick concurred with Hume, however, in claiming that responsibility for action requires only that someone could have done otherwise *had he wanted to*.

Intentional actions could be explained scientifically if motives could be subsumed under covering laws. According to Carl Hempel (1942), social science consists in providing "explanation sketches." Such sketches indicate the nature of evidence that would be necessary to construct general laws from which actual events could be deduced. Nowell-Smith (1954) elaborated on this perspective for explaining an action: "The very fact that the particular proposition is given as an explanation contextually implies that there is such a general rule; for only so could the particular fact alleged be an explanation" (p. 117). Nowell-Smith considers a case in which Jones was asked why he helped a man cross the road. Jones answered, "because he is blind." Such an answer would be proper, Nowell-Smith suggested, only because "a pro-attitude toward helping the blind is so common that it can be taken as understood" (pp. 117–118). A more complete explanation would specify the generality of the pro-attitude that Jones had toward helping people who are blind.

Many current theories of motivation assume the premise that voluntary actions depend on finding a moving principle in the agent and attributing actions to reasons plus pro-attitudes, wants, or drives. These include theories that rely on desires for attachment, approval, autonomy, self-esteem, control, or self-efficacy and that attribute action to such drives as thirst or hunger.

Philosophers, too, continue to work with the notion that motivation requires both reason and passion. Harking back to Aristotle, for example, Fred Dretske (1991) concludes that intentional behavior can be distinguished from mere happenings by determining whether "internal factors can be given credit—remote but nonetheless *primary* credit—for the effect" (p. 27; italics in original). Dretske added, "Without pure desires, . . . [there can be] no motivation, no purpose, no behavior explicable in terms of an agent's *reasons*" (p. 111).

Twenty years earlier, John Hospers had drawn what seems to be a reasonable conclusion from this line of thought: "Let us note that the more *thoroughly* and *in detail* we know the causal factors leading a person to behave as he does, the more we tend to exempt him from responsibility" (1961, p. 133; italics in original). An unhappy consequence of Hospers's observation seems to be that those who hold criminals responsible for their misdeeds do so only because they lack an understanding of why the crimes were committed.

Most contemporary theories that attempt to explain motivation for delinquent behavior rely on assumptions about drives and needs designed to provide the moving principle of action. (See Farrington, 1993, for a summary.) Such internal forces as drives or needs, however, have little explanatory power. If Alfred goes to the refrigerator and takes out a soft drink, we may claim he does so because he is thirsty. But he may take the beverage to his wife or place it on the table. Then we doubt that Alfred took the drink from the refrigerator because he was thirsty.

What grounds are there for believing that thirst is a drive necessary to explain drinking? Certainly Alfred does not drink every time he is thirsty. Nor is he thirsty every time he drinks. Insufficient regularities linking behavior to claimed drives and needs should make it clear that these theories are not the product of perceived covariation. Evidence for the drives or needs in question consists, rather, in pointing to the behaviors that the drives and needs purport to explain.

Theories that drives or passions account for morally relevant motivations provided one type of solution to the apparent conflict between a science of individual action and having responsibility for actions. They did so by defining morally relevant actions in relation to those actions people want to do, raising doubt that anyone could want a freedom beyond that implied by absence of coercion. Critics, however, considered actions caused by emotions to be dubious candidates for voluntary virtues. Reasons, not passions, they argued, account for morally responsible behavior. This line of thought, as noted above, considers voluntary action outside the range of science. Durkheim (1895/1938), for sociology, and Skinner (1953), for psychology, accepted this view. But back to foundations.

In his *Critique of Pure Reason* (1781/1929), Immanuel Kant presented the Thesis to the Third Antinomy: "Causality in accordance with laws of nature is not the only causality . . . it is necessary to assume that there is also another causality, that of freedom." The Antithesis claims, "There is no freedom; everything in the world takes place solely in accordance with laws of nature."

Like many contemporary thinkers, Kant had no doubt that freedom and causality must be compatible. "Philosophy must . . . assume that no true contradiction will be found between freedom and natural necessity in the same human actions," he wrote in *Foundations of the Metaphysics of Morals*, "for it cannot give up the concept of nature any more than that of freedom" (1785/1959, No. 456).

Kant reconciled moral responsibility with a world of necessary connections by creating a chasm between the scientific world that can be perceived and the noumenal world of the acting agent. Moral action consists in acting for the sake of the categorical (unconditional) imperative, the moral law that one can will universally. Freedom, according to Kant, is obeying the law that one issues to oneself in defining right action.

In his *Critical Examination of Practical Reason* (1788/1873), Kant integrated freedom of action with universal causality by invoking the idea that acting agents create descriptions under which they choose to act. An action that is caused when perceived externally is free when chosen through self-regulating laws.

Kant conceived the world of appearance as a way of organizing events that have a different set of attributes when viewed from the perspective of intelligent agency. He explained:

There is no real contradiction when the events and even the world in which they occur are regarded (as they ought to be) merely as appearances; since one and the same acting being, *as an appearance* (even to his own inner sense), . . . has a causality in the world of sense that always conforms to the mechanisms of nature, but with respect to the same events, so far as the acting person regards himself at the same time as a noumenon. . . , he can contain a principle by which that causality acting according to laws of nature is determined, but which is itself free from all laws of nature (1788/1873, No. 252; italics in original).

The Kantian solution had two results: it removed motives, intentions, and values from scientific scrutiny; and it bifurcated explanations for actions into those based on reasons and those based on causes. Although Kant did not argue that any event might be otherwise than it was, his theory rendered motives central to understanding actions.

Kant had argued that scientific explanations were causal and belonged to the world as perceived, but that things in themselves— *ding an sich*—were not perceivable. This other world, so to speak, included actions for reasons. The private, personal, mental world of Kant lay outside the reach of science.

Many contemporary philosophers, too, have suggested that free action, morally relevant action, depends on describing behavior in a certain way. These compatibilists accept the idea that causes necessitate consequences, that they stand in relation to their consequences as sufficient conditions. They add, however, that motives for voluntary actions are not causes.

Friedrich Waismann explained the point by way of analogy. A sentence can be viewed "as a series of noises produced by a human agent; or as a vehicle of thought. For a series of noises there may be causes but no reasons; for a series of words expressing thought there may be reasons but no causes" (1953, p. 31).

This view places the descriptions under which people act voluntarily outside the realm of causality. Though bodily processes may be responsive to causal antecedents, actions are not rightly described in causal terms. Actions are attributable to motives, but motives ought not be considered causes.

Vendler exemplifies the position by contrasting the rising of an arm—which is not an action—with raising an arm. "What is an action is the *raising* of the arm: this is done by John, and not caused by anything" (1984, p. 372; italics in original). Claiming "An agent is not a member of the causal chain" (p. 380), Vendler acknowledges the cause-like role of motives. He distinguishes the role of motives, however, from the determinative role of real causes. Motives cause actions in the sense of influencing them, "not by necessitating as real causes do but by providing a reason" (p. 382).

In a book called *Free Action*, A. I. Melden states the case against actions having causes: if actions are caused by inclinations, desires, and motives, and these are results of antecedent psychological or social factors, "then whatever happens is none of my doing but of these very psychological factors, themselves" (1961, p. 8). Melden denied that causality, as used by social scientists, could account for actions. Actions, according to Melden, cannot be physical events plus motives because motives explain actions, and an explanation cannot be a part of that which is explained. Put somewhat differently, Meldon argued that motives presuppose actions and cannot, therefore, be their cause.

Motives, according to this view, provide descriptive material that puts actions into contexts. The theory places motives "in the public arena of human action, rather than in the hidden recesses of one's mind" (p. 91). Melden saw motives as ways of explaining what actions were being done. As explanations, they provide answers to questions about *what* a person is doing rather than *why* a person is doing it. A motive, therefore, "provides us with a better understanding of the action itself by placing it with its appropriate context" (p. 102).

On this view, the prosecution for the Menendez brothers set a scene for the jury, a scene in which the jury could understand the killing as a murder for profit. Because motives lie outside scientific scrutiny, however, setting a scene may be only tenuously related to describing scientific facts.

H. L. A. Hart, the legal philosopher, legitimized this approach in "The Ascription of Responsibility and Rights": "Sentences of the form 'He did it' have been traditionally regarded as primarily descriptive whereas their principal function is what I venture to call *ascriptive*, being quite literally to ascribe responsibility for actions much as the principal function of sentences of the form 'This is his' is to ascribe rights in property" (1951, p. 145; italics in original).

Rules for ascribing responsibility might, but need not, include evidence about having done particular things in particular places. They might, but need not, include having motives of a particular type.

Kant's arguments segregating the world of science from that of action put social science on the defensive. In *The Idea of a Social Science*, Peter Winch argued specifically "that the conceptions according to which we normally think of social events are logically incompatible with the concepts belonging to scientific explanation" (1958, p. 95). On the grounds that social relations are fundamentally based on ideas, Winch argued that social relations must be an "unsuitable subject for generalizations and theories of the scientific sort to be formulated about them" (p. 133). If he were right, then attempts to understand criminal behavior through searching for its causes would be useless.

Although demurring from Winch's strong position against social science, the British criminologist Nigel Walker asserted that social science was more useful to understanding normal behavior than to understanding misbehavior. Walker wrote that criminology could be valuable only if it turned to "introspectibles—motives, reasons and such-like" (1977, p. 142). The study of these introspectables, according to Walker, would help to explain actions without abolishing "the basis for moral praise or blame" (p. 5).

Thus, the Kantian move to preserve both scientific cause and free action had two conflicting consequences regarding motives: it privatized feelings, beliefs, and attitudes constituting motives; and it depicted motives as entirely public but disconnected from the feelings, beliefs, and attitudes of the acting agents.

Two Aristotelian assumptions had led to the Kantian position. The first assumption is that causality implies necessity and necessity requires constant conjunction between causes and their effects. In the words of John Stuart Mill describing the law of universal causation, "Every phenomenon is related, in an uniform manner, to some phenomena that coexist with it, and to some that have preceded and will follow it" (1843/1973, p. 323). The second assumption is that there is a private world of ideas to which each individual has unique access. This private world contains our beliefs, thoughts, and desires. Both assumptions have been undermined by recent critical examination.

Causes were thought to be sufficient conditions for their consequences. Thus, causes and their effects implied constant conjunction. If A causes B, then whenever A occurs, B does so as well. In linguistic terms, causal claims were required to support the counterfactual that if not-B, then not-A.[1] Science was thought to consist in gathering evidence regarding universal laws, laws determined by causes and their effects. Scientists were to evaluate theories that contained clear definitions and hypotheses that could be tested through observation or experiments.

Problems related to this conception of science had been cited in relation to specifying the types of evidence one should accept as confirmation of a theory. Hempel (1945) referred to these problems as "paradoxical instances" of confirmation. For example, according to the rules of confirmation in the counterfactual, every instance of a nonblack nonraven would seem to confirm an inference that all ravens are black. Those rules would allow a claim that all ravens are black to gain credibility from recognition of white (i.e., nonblack) tennis shoes (i.e., nonravens). Attempts to set limits of relevance failed.

Failure to establish solid grounds for boundaries to indicate what evidence should be considered relevant for testing scientific hypotheses undermined confidence in the relation between empirical claims and supporting evidence. The presumptive relation between inference and evidence took a blow from a different direction when Nelson Goodman (1955) showed that the decision to couple evidence with a particular theory rested only on convention. Identifying what he called "the new riddle of induction," Goodman crippled what had become known as confirmatory theory by showing that evidence to support one claim may simultaneously support alternative incompatible claims. Without a clear link between evidence and theory, a fact can be subsumed under any number of theories, theories that need not be consistent with one another. Yet evidence, of course, does not come clearly linked with a particular theory.

Take as an example the theory that lack of parental control causes delinquency. Our search for evidence turns up two groups of children, one whose parents exert little control over their behavior and one whose parents impose strong controls. Ten years later, we find that those whose parents exerted little control were more likely to become delinquents. That evidence confirms the theory that lack of parental control causes delinquency. But when we consider the matter further, the same evidence confirms a theory that children who are hard to control are likely to become delinquent. It also confirms a theory that parents who care enough to exert control reduce the tendency toward delinquency. It also confirms a theory that parents who exert control model the behavior their children display when they resist enticements to commit crimes. The list could continue, but I assume the point is clear.

What appears to convert evidence into confirmation of a particular theory actually turns out to be willingness to accept a narrow view. Goodman noted, "What we often mistake for the actual world is one particular description of it" (1955, p. 56). Evidence becomes evidence for a particular theory, Goodman explained, only after a judgment of relevance has been made. The judgment of relevance, in turn, seems to depend on commitment to a theory. Therefore, theories do not become credible through the support of evidence but, rather, acquire their support through having become well entrenched through use.

Thinking along similar lines, William Dray identified three types of tests for theories regarding causes: manipulation, deduction from covering laws, and the exercise of evaluative judgments. Because manipulation cannot be used to study historical events, and because empirical investigations would be unnecessary if covering laws were already known, Dray argued that historical analyses depend on the exercise of evaluative judgments. Dray believed that attribution of responsibility provided the underpinning for assigning causal status to an agent. "Unless we are prepared to hold the agent responsible for what happened," he claimed, "we cannot say that his action *was* the cause" (1957, p. 100; italics in original).

Around the same time that causal claims were being criticized, Gilbert Ryle (1949) destroyed the Cartesian notion that mental states or happenings occur inside physical bodies. Labeling the conventional theory a "dogma of the Ghost in the machine," Ryle suggested that people can be mistaken about their own beliefs even as they can be mistaken about those of others, that talk of mental processes and talk of physical processes are two languages, and that confusing the two processes is a category mistake, like asking whether someone left in a huff or in a taxi. Ryle argued that ordinary people do not experience volitions. Actions are the sorts of things people do, and motives are expressions of their disposition to behave in certain ways.

Georg Henrik von Wright suggested that the essential feature of causality consists in the connection and not in universality. "Actions are prompted by motives; the force of motives lies in the fact that agents are disposed to follow characteristic patterns of behavior; such patterns (dispositions) provide the 'laws' linking the motives to the action in the individual case" (1971, p. 23).

Doubts about traditional notions of causality and the privileged privacy of beliefs gave impetus to a series of questions related to language and its learning. These questions provoked new looks at motives and causes as well as beliefs and actions. If language was not based on reference to private objects, then the traditionally privileged position of motives might also be subject to scrutiny.

Philosophers as varied as Plato and Aristotle, Descartes, Hobbes, Locke, Berkeley, and Hume had assumed that language was learned ostensively, by pointing. Whereas Plato had judged that language referenced ideas or forms, and Aristotle assumed that words denoted objects in the world, the empiricists believed that language denoting sensations referred to private experiences, to sense data for which individuals had privileged access. These sense data provided a foundation, securing knowledge through the certainty that, for example, C. I. Lewis thought necessary when he claimed, "If anything is to be probable, then something must be certain" (1946, p. 186).

Logical positivists added a claim that meaningful sentences necessarily referenced experiences and were either true or false. Although problems arose because the move from private sensation to public objects posed what sometimes seemed to be insurmountable obstacles, the underlying theory of language remained dominant until roughly the middle of the twentieth century. At that point, J. L. Austin mounted concerted attacks on the use of sense data to explain phenomena (attacks that appeared in *Sense and Sensibilia,* published posthumously). The major thrust of Austin's attack was on the separation between a "material world" that is perceived and the perceptions themselves. A. J. Ayer (1940) had argued in *The Foundations of Empirical Knowledge* that sense data were the objects of all perceptions, to which Austin parried: "If one has already been induced to swallow the idea that every case . . . supplies us with 'percep-tions', one is only too easily going to be made to feel that it would be straining at a gnat not to swallow sense-data in an equally compre-hensive style. . . . the assumption of their ubiquity has been slipped in without any explanation or argument whatever" (1962b, p. 47).

In *Philosophical Investigations,* Ludwig Wittgenstein invited readers to perform experiments to demonstrate the impossibility of "mental processes" and "private meanings." He showed that pains and perceptions depend on rules or conventions. When I describe my intentions to someone, Wittgenstein explained, I do so "because I want to tell him something about *myself,* which goes beyond what happened at that time" (1953, No. 659; italics in original).

In 1953, Willard Van Orman Quine administered what some have taken to be the *coup de grâce* to empiricism as it had been devel-oped by the Vienna School. Language is so closely tied to experi-ence, he argued, that the idea of testing propositions derived from general theory misleadingly represents both language and experi-ence. "It becomes folly to seek a boundary between synthetic state-ments, which hold contingently on experience, and analytic state-ments, which hold come what may. Any statement can be held true come what may, if we make drastic enough adjustments elsewhere in the system" (1961, p. 43).

To Quine's attack on the linguistic assumptions of empiricism, J. L. Austin (1962a) added analyses of the many meaningful uses of language, uses such as requesting, describing, welcoming, per-suading, and performing. These analyses showed that language could not rest on ostensive grounds.

In a similar vein, Wilfrid Sellars attacked the idea that knowl-edge of a public world could ever be acquired with a framework that started from sensing any kind of object "directly." A behaviorist psy-chology, he noted, need not require physiological identification of fundamental concepts. He counseled: "For empirical knowledge, like its sophisticated extension, science, is rational, not because it has a *foundation* but because it is a self-correcting enterprise which can put *any* claim in jeopardy, though not *all* at once" (1963, p. 170; italics in original).

Most contemporary philosophic efforts to explicate the relations between motivation and action have built on the postempiricists whose work is described above. My theory is heavily influenced by their analyses. Before turning to it, I consider some of the ways in which theories of motivation can account for crime and in which theories of crime have involved motives.

Theories of Motivation and Motivational Theories of Crime

Motivational theories in contemporary psychology, harking back to Hobbes and William James (1890), have typically been constructed on the egoistic assumption that voluntary actions necessarily aim at satisfying a desire to maximize one's own satisfactions. Some of these theories assume specific drives, such as hunger, needs for affection and self-esteem, or self-efficacy, the satisfaction of which account for motivated action.

In 1986, for example, the psychologist Albert Bandura wrote, "In the social cognitive view, self-efficacy judgments enter into the regulation of all types of performances, except for habitual patterns that have become routinized" (p. 411). These self-regulatory judgments influence the goals people select, Bandura explained in 1989, and "goals create motivating involvement in activities by specifying the conditional requirements for positive self-evaluation" (p. 1180).

Many theories of crime have relied on psychological egoism for their explanatory power. Strain theories, for example, refer to barriers between an individual's desire for personal success and its achievement. Control theories propose that well-socialized behavior relies on trades between satisfaction of immediate desires and presumed self-interested benefits from delays in gratification. Opportunity theories define targets in terms of available opportunities for gaining satisfaction at minimum risk. Michael Gottfredson and Travis Hirschi claim that nothing but personal gain motivates all crime: "The motive to crime is inherent in or limited to immediate gains provided by the act itself. There is no larger purpose behind rape, or robbery, or murder, or theft, or embezzlement, or insider trading" (1990, p. 256). Because Gottfredson and Hirschi opine that criminals and noncriminals differ only with regard to their impulse control, one can assume they believe that all people seek to avoid their own pain and to increase their own pleasure.

C. D. Broad, in his famous exposition of ethical theories, described this Hobbesian view as one "not without a certain superficial plausibility" (1930, p. 54). Nevertheless, Hume had pointed out that doing things for the pleasures they bring presupposes having prior propensities in their favor. "Nature must, by the internal frame and constitution of the mind, give an original propensity to fame, ere we can reap any pleasure from that acquisition, or pursue it from motives of self-love and desire of happiness. If I have no vanity, I take no delight in praise; if I be void of ambition, power gives me no enjoyment; if I be not angry, the punishment of an adversary is totally indifferent to me" (1777/1960, p. 144).

The egoistic assumption deserves to be excoriated for four reasons: it blurs the boundaries between actions having very different motives; it encourages acceptance of a sophisticated fiction in lieu of corrigible judgments; psychological egoism fails to yield either predictions or explanations for action; and the egoistic theory runs in the face of reasonable evidence that altruism without self-interest is possible.

BLURRING THE BOUNDARIES AMONG DIFFERENT TYPES OF ACTIONS

In his defense of free action, Kant had recognized the popularity of using the incentive that moral actions bring happiness. He objected. Among his arguments was the fact that the principle of one's own happiness "puts the motives to virtue and those to vice in the same class, teaching us only to make a better calculation while obliterating the specific difference between them" (1785/1959, p. 61).

As noted by David Hume (1777/1960), the differences between a person whose actions bring him to take into account the welfare of others and one who always seems to be seeking to gain things only for himself is the difference between deserving esteem or disdain. The differences appear, furthermore, to be enduring parts of character. It is unlikely, Hume remarked, that the difference in motivation is attributable to a minute metaphysical difference in self-love.

Thought by many to be the "father" of deterrence theory in criminology, Jeremy Bentham, like Hume, believed that some motives were benevolent. Similar motives, he noted, might explain very different actions. These might be "the most laudable, or the most criminal." He continued,

However, in considering the whole catalogue of motives, that is, the whole catalogue of pleasures and pains, we may classify them according to the tendency which they seem to have to unite or to disunite the interests of the individual and of the community. Upon this plan, motives may be distinguished into four classes,—the *purely social motive*, benevolence; *semi-social motives*, the love of reputation, the desire of friendship, religion; *anti-social motives*, antipathy in all its branches; *personal motives*, pleasures of sense, love of power, pecuniary interest, the desire of self-preservation. (1882, p. 254; italics in original).

The nature of friendship raises additional problems for psychological egoism. My friend is someone whose well-being pleases me. The psychological hedonist might argue that it is for the sake of that pleasure that I do something for my friend. A psychological egoist cannot distinguish between doing something for my friend and doing something so that my friend will help me. Yet there seems to be a clear difference between what I do for my friend in order to benefit myself and what I might do for my friend for her sake. The differences are recognized both in the conditions under which I act and the way I feel about the action. My giving money to my friend so that she will provide me with goods or services, for example, differs from my giving money to a friend because she seems to need it. Though both might give me pleasure, the first does so as consequence of my receiving something, whereas the second does not.

ENCOURAGING ACCEPTANCE OF A SOPHISTICATED FICTION

There are countless incidents in everyday life that seem to have resulted from people doing things from many different motives. For example, I ask the time of day, and a gentleman sitting next to me informs me of it. It seems to me that his motive could have been as simple as wanting to be courteous. Surely being courteous does not generally bring pleasure, so if psychological egoism is correct, I must also assume that he is one of those peculiar people who takes pleasure from telling people time or from being courteous, or I must invent a story that involves aversive consequences should he fail to respond to my request.

Perhaps a clearer example of the use of fiction to preserve psychological egoism comes from instances of sacrifice. A soldier throws himself on a mine to save his buddy. The dead soldier, it might be said, could not stand the idea of going back to the barracks and having to admit that it was his buddy who died. A mother with very little money goes hungry most of the time in order to feed her children. The mother, it might be said, wants to be entertained by the children or is pained by the crying they would do if they were not fed.

The claims regarding self-interested motives, it should be noted, have no supporting evidence. Other soldiers return to the barracks and acknowledge that a buddy has died. It might be unlikely that there even was time to consider options before the altruistic deed was done. The children may not cry when they are hungry, and the mother might not be entertained by their presence. But data are not relevant to claims that every action must have self-interested motives. Hume makes this point: "A man that has lost a friend and patron may flatter himself that all his grief arises from generous sentiments, . . . but a man that grieves for a valuable friend who needed his patronage and protection, how can we suppose that his passionate tenderness arises from some metaphysical regards to a self-interest which has no foundation or reality?" (1777/1960, p. 273).

FAILING TO EXPLAIN OR PREDICT

What is ordinarily thought of as the motive for an action, at a minimum, helps to describe the action by placing it in context. I raise my hand with a paper in it. You ask me why. I tell you my motive: "I wanted to attract the attention of my friends." Or, perhaps, I say, "because the papers belong to you and I thought you had forgotten them." My motives for waving the papers are different in the two instances. Your knowledge of the motive justifies you in thinking—in the first case—that I might have plans to do something with my friends. Perhaps you want to join me. These thoughts would not be justified through knowledge of the motive in the second case. Whereas the motives given above provide information about me and what to expect, an answer stating that it pleases me to do so is uninformative.

For a second type of instance, let me return to the case presented above from Nowell-Smith (1954). Jones helped a man cross the road. We know he did so because the man he helped was blind. Faced, now, with finding someone to help Baker who is blind, it is reasonable to believe we have grounds for calling on Jones for help. He is the sort of man who does things to help the blind.

Suppose the egoist insists we cut to the quick. Jones helped a man cross the road. He did so, the egoist claims, because it gave him pleasure. Suppose he had a bet with his friend that he could help someone cross the road, and if he did so within the half hour, he would win $10. Of course it gave him pleasure to help a man cross the road. The claim that the action was motivated by a desire for pleasure does not, however, give us any grounds whatsoever for believing Jones is the sort of man who usually helps the blind, helps people cross the road, or even is the sort of person who takes bets.

During the coldest day of winter, Elvira is out shoveling the walk of her neighbor. I ask her why she is doing it. She explains that the couple who live in the house are elderly and really no longer able to shovel for themselves. "But why you?" I persist. With a slight shrug, she continues, "I guess I was brought up to believe I ought to do things that help my neighbors." "Aha," say I. "Now I know why you did it. You shoveled the walk in the very cold weather because you would rather be cold and risk hurting your back than stay warm by the fire in your own home and have your conscience bother you."

What evidence do I have that this is Elvira's preference? True, she often does nice things for other people. She may hate cold weather and may almost never voluntarily spend time outside in winter when she can avoid it. My evidence that Elvira shoveled the walk of her neighbor for self-serving reasons consists in this: she did it, and my theory says that everything anyone voluntarily does is done for self-serving reasons. This is circular reasoning.

DENYING EVIDENCE THAT TRUE ALTRUISM IS POSSIBLE

Despite the popularity of assumptions that self-interest is a natural motive and that other interests must be taught, altruistic behavior seems as natural as self-interested behavior. As noted above, one can invent an egoistic explanation for any particular altruistic act. Yet, such merely postulated motivations ought not be taken as evidence.

Under some circumstances, for instance, self-consciousness does tend to increase helpfulness (Berkowitz, 1987; Duval, Duval, & Neely, 1979; Gibbons & Wicklund, 1982; Wicklund, 1975). Yet the degree to which becoming self-conscious increases altruistic behavior has sometimes mistakenly been interpreted as showing that altruism is egoism in disguise.

Attribution theory, for example, interprets altruism as a means by which to attribute socially desirable characteristics to oneself (Berkowitz, 1965; Grusec & Dix, 1986; Heider, 1946). Reactance theory considers altruistic behavior as a quest for perceived freedom (Brehm & Brehm, 1981). Reciprocity theories, including those that claim self-rewards motivate altruistic acts, merely assume—without evidence—that giving depends on expectations for receiving benefits (Baumann, Cialdini, & Kenrick, 1981; Cialdini et al., 1987; Hatfield, Walster, & Piliavin, 1978; Hinde, 1979; Hoffman, 1980; Rosenhan, 1978).

Evidence favoring the reality of altruistic motivations includes studies of twins and young children. The evidence also includes experimental studies for which the incentives were reducing the pain of someone else. Studies of twins indicate that correlations of measures of altruism between monozygotic (identical) twins are about twice those found between dizygotic (fraternal) twins (Rushton, Fulker, Neale, Nias, & Eysenck, 1986). This evidence suggests that there may be a genetic component to altruism. Altruistic and supportive parents tend to have altruistic children (London, 1970; Miller & Eisenberg, 1988), and altruism appears to be about as stable a characteristic as aggression (Cummings, Hollenbeck, Iannotti, Radke-Yarrow, & Zahn-Waxler, 1986).

Those who study infants have found social interests in very young children (Caplan, 1993; Harris, 1994; Hay, 1994; Rheingold & Emery 1986; Zahn-Waxler & Radke-Yarrow, 1982; Zahn-Waxler, Radke-Yarrow, Wagner, & Pyle 1988). In one study, mothers displayed happiness, sadness, and anger. Their 10-week-old infants responded with interest and apparent pleasure when the mothers displayed happiness. They looked down at the floor or sucked when their mothers looked sad. They cried or averted their mothers' gaze when the mothers displayed anger (Haviland & Lelwica, 1987).

Between 12 and 18 months, the level of altruistic behavior seems to stabilize (Cummings, Hollenbeck, Iannotti, Radke-Yarrow, & Zahn-Waxler, 1986). Many children show patterns of nurturance toward particular others by 18 months (Rheingold & Emery, 1986). By the time children are three to four years old, their friendship choices reflect preferences for others who evidence prosocial behavior (Denham, McKinley, Couchoud, & Holt, 1990). At these ages, normal behavior includes sharing toys without self-interested arguments (Killen, 1989).

Social learning provides an account of altruism not dissimilar to that for aggression. Surroundings suggesting that helpful behavior is appropriate seem to increase altruism (Eron & Huesmann, 1986; Friedrich & Stein, 1973; Yarrow, Scott, & Waxler, 1973). Physical abuse, on the other hand, appears to decrease altruism (Eisenberg & Mussen, 1989).

An intriguing cross-national study yields evidence to suggest that people generally consider altruistic actions in terms related to other-oriented and task-oriented reasons rather than in relation to self-interest (Boehnke, Silbereisen, Eisenberg, Reykowski, & Palmonari, 1989).

If giving help were a self-interested action designed to elicit approval of others, one would expect to find more instances of giving help when the act is public. In fact, however, giving help is reduced when others are present (Clark & Word, 1972; Latané & Dabbs, 1975; Latané & Darley, 1968; Levy et al., 1972).

Experimental approaches test some of the hedonistic accounts of altruistic behavior. In one study, experimenters used only the relief of a stranger's pain as motivation (Weiss, Boyer, Lombardo, & Stich, 1973). Subjects, who were college students, had been told they were to evaluate the tracking performance of an older student (a confederate in the experiment) who was performing under the stress of shocks. Shocks were apparently administered to the confederate until the six evaluation buttons had been pressed. Thus the subjects believed that the faster they performed their evaluation tasks, the less the older student would be shocked. After the sixth "evaluation" for each of fifteen trials, a sign reading "shock off" lit up and the older student sighed with relief. A comparison group performed the same task except that shock to the confederate was seemingly continued throughout the series of trials. Response speed increased only for the altruistic-reward group. The experimenters repeated the experiment, introducing a third condition: the shock was reduced (rather than eliminated) between trials. Response time curves reflected the degree of altruistic motivation, with greatest decreases when shocks were eliminated after the sixth button had been pushed, slower decreases with reduced shocks, and no slope for response time in the absence of altruistic rewards.

In a series of experiments on altruism, C. Daniel Batson and his co-workers incorporated measures of mood as the dependent variable, with manipulations based on the need to perform altruistic acts. The experimenters reasoned that if helping actions provided self-rewarding relief, subjects would be disappointed by losing an opportunity to help. On the other hand, if altruism motivated help giving, relief should be equally great whether or not it was the subject who did the helping.

The experimenters manipulated a situation so that it looked as though correct answers by college students who were the subjects of the study could relieve a partner from the pain of being shocked. The subjects' empathy and mood were measured. Then half were told that plans had changed, and that the partner would not receive shock for making errors after all. The remaining subjects went on to relieve their partners from shocks. Empathy and mood were again measured. The authors found that there was as much relief for those subjects who believed their actions would not be required in order to relieve pain as for the subjects who believed their actions did relieve pain. The researchers therefore concluded that true altruism motivated at least some of those in the study.

Other studies in the series may be even more convincing. In one study, students were randomly assigned to listen to either of two sets of directions for listening to a taped interview of Katie, presumably a fellow student whose parents and sister had recently been killed in an auto crash. In one set of directions, students were directed to attend to the technical aspects of the interview in terms of its audience impact; in the other, they were asked to imagine how the person interviewed on the tape was feeling. After listening to the tape, every student read two letters, one from Katie and one from her professor. Both letters solicited help for Katie, such as baby-sitting her younger brother and sister while Katie attended night classes, fixing things around the house, providing transportation, and helping with fund-raising projects.

Conditions also varied in terms of justification for not giving help. This manipulation was handled by having a sign-up sheet with seven of eight spaces already filled out by (fictitious) students who presumably had heard the tapes. Half the subjects in each attention group were presented lists with high justification for *not* participating; that is, only two of the prior seven students had volunteered according to the sign-up sheet. On the lists for the other half, all prior students had volunteered help. The students in the study were last to sign the sheets, thus reducing the likelihood that they would believe others would see their responses.

Among the students who listened for content and presumably recognized Katie's need, justification for not volunteering had little effect: 60% of those with high justification for not helping and 70% of those with low justification offered their time to help Katie. On the other hand, those who had listened to the tape for technical factors were influenced by the manipulated grounds for justifying failure to volunteer. Whereas 55% of those in the low justification condition (despite having attended to technical features of the tape) volunteered, only 15% of those with high justification for not helping signed on to volunteer their help. Thus Bateson and his co-workers not only showed that help could be elicited without direct offers of reward to the helper, but also indicated a psychological mechanism that tends to increase altruism: empathy.

A reaction-time experiment confirmed the link between altruism and empathy. The Stroop task used showed that delay in recognition of simple colors differentiated students high in empathy from those low in empathy for words relevant to altruism, though not for neutral words or those related to social rewards or to punishments. Their own experimental studies convinced the researchers that "the motivation to help evoked by feeling empathy is at least partly altruistic. If it is, then psychologists will have to make some fundamental changes in their conceptions of human motivation and, indeed, of human nature" (Batson et al., 1988, pp. 75–76).

Jane A. Piliavin and Hong-Wen Chaing reached a similar conclusion regarding sociologists. They note the insufficiency of alternative explanations for altruism and conclude that "there is an altruistic motivation behind prosocial behavior when empathy is aroused" (1990, p. 37).

CONCLUSION

The stimulus for claims that all voluntary actions depend on desires for one's own pleasure and avoidance of pain seems to come from a mistaken assumption of simplicity inappropriate to understanding the diversity of human behavior. Not only does psychological egoism fail to explain diversity of behavior; it also adds complexity by introducing a superfluous self-reference.

The mistaken assumption rests on a common error of reasoning, what some logicians call a quantification error. The quantification error is one that occurs when jumps are made from the fact that a) every instance of a particular type is accompanied by some instance of another type to b) the conclusion that there is a type of the second kind that accompanies every instance of the first type. An example of the fallacy would be reasoning from the true premise that every flower requires some amount of sunshine and water to the false conclusion that a prescribed amount of sunshine and water can be found that would be suitable for every flower. Perhaps the clearest way to show that the reasoning *is* fallacious is to consider numbers. For every number, there is a larger number. That is fact. It is false, of course, that there is a number that is larger than every number.

Those who espouse a theory of universal egoistic motivation confuse the fact that there are motives for every voluntary action with the claim that there must be a single motive for every voluntary action. Those who insist that motives are fundamentally self-interested confound the grounds for claiming that an action is voluntary with the motives necessary to voluntary acts. When an action is voluntary, the agent must want to do what he does voluntarily (under some description), but the agent's wants need not be self-directed at all. In fact, for good reason, some contemporary philosophers suggest that wanting, as used for voluntary actions, acts as a placeholder rather than as a designation for a state or process (e.g., Davidson, 1980).

The fact that not all motives are self-interested opens the way for distinguishing people whose motives are primarily self-interested from others. Predatory criminals, one can suppose, are among those most likely to have egoistic motives for their actions.

Sketch of a Theory about Motives Conducive to Crime

The demise of radical empiricism at the hands of linguistic analysis gave a new twist to the investigation of old problems in the analysis of motivation. Prior theories, based on an assumption that language was fundamentally denotational, had assumed that whatever else motives were, they were countable among the objects in the universe. That is, they had a metaphysical reality.

G. E. M. Anscombe, however, suggested that such emotions as revenge and gratitude are motives because they serve to explain action; they are not some "further thing" apart from the action they explain. Elaborating, Anscombe wrote: "If an action has to be thought of by the agent as doing good or harm of some sort, and the thing in the past as good or bad, in order for the thing in the past to be the reason for the action, then this reason shews [sic] not a mental cause but a motive" (1958, p. 22). In other words, according to Anscombe, motives are descriptions of a certain class of reasons.

Anscombe led the way to showing what, in my opinion, can be done to understand motivation. I suggest that an adequate motivational theory must satisfy three criteria:

- It must be able to show that socialization practices influence action.
- It must account for why valid descriptions of motives make a difference in terms of predictions and expectations about the behavior of a motivated individual.
- It must give a plausible account of criminal behavior as voluntary action.

Let me begin with a brief review of features of the theories discussed above and how they hold up against the three criteria. The Humean tradition assumed that passions ruled behavior. According to this perspective, motivation required some form of desire. Motives can be influenced by socialization practices because the family can influence what a person wants. This tradition can also provide an account of constancy in action by noting that desires and habits tend to remain stable, once formed. But because of the primary role it assigns to emotions over which reason has no control, the Humean type of theory fails to give a plausible account of criminal behavior as voluntary.

The Kantian tradition assumed that reasons can motivate, without benefit of desire. Reasons, in Kant's opinion, are not influenced by socialization. Therefore, anyone could have access to free action simply by using the categorical imperative to test a judgment. Kantian theories do not address the question of behavioral expectations, though one might come to know that certain people are more likely than others to fulfil their obligations. To the extent that criminal actions are objects of scientific study at all, they would not be considered voluntary. But under the description of being actions of free agents, the criminal would be accountable.

Criminological and psychological theories that attribute all voluntary behavior to psychological egoism can accommodate the influence of socialization by showing that what gives pleasure and pain is influenced by earlier experience. These theories, however, fail to provide a basis for expectations about the behavior of motivated individuals. Furthermore, as noted above, they rest on false assumptions. Nevertheless, these theories may yield more suitable accounts of at least some voluntary criminal behavior than of voluntary behavior in general.

The theory I propose rests heavily on the work of Donald Davidson. In what continues to be an extremely influential assault on problems in understanding motivation, Davidson (1980c) linked motives to causal claims by appeal to relatively stable desires and beliefs of an agent. Desires and beliefs, Davidson reasoned, should be considered dispositional, as tendencies to act in certain ways. Like solubility and breakability, they contain something like a promise that causal laws are available. On Davidson's view, "motives explain an action only if they cause it" (p. 264). He added, "the laws that are implicit in reason explanation . . . concern only individuals—they are the generalizations embedded in attributions of attitudes, beliefs, and traits" (p. 274). On this view, reasons help to place actions in broader contexts. Davidson (1980b) noted, however, that identifying the correct event as a cause was not the same as describing it in such a way as to display the causal law.

Thomas Nagel (1970) pointed out that the attribution of desires to people who act for reasons is grounded in logical, but not empirical, necessity. My theory claims that motivation arises as children begin to use language to describe the reasons they have for doing what they do. The reasons they are taught to use in justifying actions will become, according to my theory, *potentiating reasons*. In other words, I believe Kant was correct in stating that reasons can be motivating.

Motives are not something extra—some pro-attitude, disposition, or desire—inside the individual. We attribute particular desires and dispositions to people in virtue of the choices that they make. These attributions are defeasible by reference to patterns of behavior. In my opinion, motives are supervenient properties of the descriptions suitable for linking potentiating reasons to an action.

Desires and emotions, though partly private, have a public face. We can learn that we want revenge, for example, because we are pleased when our enemies are injured. We are taught what it means to love by the use of the words, with some believing it requires injuring ("we always hurt the ones we love") while others believe that love implies only desiring companionship and the well-being of another.

We know what it means to want something to drink, to eat, to excite us. That is, we have an idea of the sort of thing that will alleviate thirst, hunger, boredom. But what is it to "want" to do something? That wanting is far from clear—because there is no set of circumstances that can be identified as that sort of wanting, no "cash value" to the claim.

Potentiating reasons serve for action as arguments do for belief. That is, we believe on the basis of convincing arguments, even when what we believe is not what we would like to believe. Different people have different capacities to be persuaded against what they hope is true. Similarly, potentiating reasons lead to actions without regard to a "pro-attitude." The degree to which different people have potentiating reasons that are or that are not self-serving varies from one individual to another and within individuals through time.

Socialization affects behavior by influencing the identification of potentiating reasons. Once an individual has developed a set of potentiating reasons, that individual will use the set to organize the environment and to act upon it. Therefore, the actions of an individual tend to be predictable. Motivated action, on this theory, is action for a reason (or set of reasons) and is therefore plausibly considered to be voluntary.

This theory rests on two assumptions: that people are born with the capacity to reason and to respond to their environments, and that language, values, and actions are learned in conjunction with one another.

THE ASSUMPTION OF AGENCY

My theory begins with the assumption that neonates are capable of responding to their environments and affecting them. That is, "agency" begins at birth. Babies act, think, respond, and choose. These are not derivative or learned behaviors. Some babies cry more than others, some suck more forcefully, and some are more alert than others. Very early, babies differentiate the smell of their mother's milk from that of other mothers; they turn to light and otherwise indicate that they are thinking beings.

Some psychologists have argued that babies must learn to differentiate themselves from their environments. This theory, like any other about what a newborn knows or believes, cannot be tested empirically. That neonates have agency from birth seems to me no more strange than that agency appears at some later time. In view of the central nature of agency to all voluntary actions, it seems *more* peculiar to assume that agency subsequently appears unannounced and in all of us. I take it that William Lycan (1987) has argued for a similar position in defending the notion of "Homunctionalism." I am certainly not arguing against a biological theory in claiming this. Rather, it seems to me perfectly natural that people think and choose and that these features have been part of natural selection processes. As Lycan points out, "the mystery of the mental is no greater than the mystery of the heart, the kidney, the carburetor or the pocket calculator" (p. 44). Or again, from Daniel Dennett (1984): "Whatever 'genuine consciousness' or 'real intentionality' comes to, it must lie at the reachable top of that pyramid of natural physical processes" (p. 37).

Newborn babies begin to learn from their environments as soon as they are born. Environments affect early behavior regarding even such a simple thing as crying. Thoman, Korner, and Benson-Williams (1977) randomly assigned 18 healthy neonates to one of three conditions. In one, the infant was held on the shoulder while a recording of a woman's soothing sounds was played; in another, the recording was played but the infant was not held; in the control group, the infant was neither held nor presented with the recording. The experiment lasted 48 hours. As anticipated, the babies who were held subsequently spent more time with their eyes open. Unexpectedly, after the experiment ended, they also spent more time crying. The experimenters reasoned that the infants had learned to cry in order to be held.

THE ASSUMPTION OF LINGUISTIC CONNECTION

As noted above, empiricists had claimed that language referred to private objects, objects that appeared "in the mind." These private mental objects seemed to be incorrigible. The nemesis for empiricists turned out to be their inability to show how private experiences could be linked with public objects. Empiricists could provide no satisfactory theory of meaning (Frege, 1892/1960).

In developing the field of semantics, Alfred Tarski (1949) suggested a definition of truth that linked the private world of ideas to the public world of reference. Tarski's semantic definition of truth claimed that a statement is true just in case the world is as the statement claims.

In an article published in 1967, Davidson suggested that Tarski's definition of truth could be converted to a sound theory of meaning: "It is a misfortune that dust from futile and confused battles . . . has prevented those with a theoretical interest in language . . . from recognizing in the semantical concept of truth (under whatever name) the sophisticated and powerful foundation of a competent theory of meaning" (p. 310). Davidson subsequently explained the connection as one in which truth conditions provided meaning. "The truth of an utterance depends on just two things: what the words as spoken mean, and how the world is arranged" (1986, p. 309).

When children learn a language, they learn the meanings of words and sentences. They learn these, as Davidson suggested, by recognizing how to use words and be understood. The utterances of two people can, on this view, mean the same thing when "belief in its truth is systematically caused by the same events and objects" (p. 318).

Language is used to make promises and requests and to ask questions. Language can be used to give reasons for actions as well as beliefs. Children learn all these uses of language from the rules of application that provide meaning to our utterances.

"Language is a social art," wrote Quine (1960, p. ix). "In acquiring it we have to depend entirely on intersubjectively available cues as to what to say and when." More than 30 years after Quine said that, Jerry Fodor put the point like this: "The content of a thought depends on its *external* relations; on the way that the thought is related to the world, *not on the way that it is related to other thoughts*" (1994, p. 4; italics in original).

Learning a language involves proper categorization. This idea is not a novel one. In "Cratylus," Plato (trans. 1937) has Socrates report that speaking is a kind of action involving placing things in their proper classes in order to communicate about them. The dialogue suggests that truth therefore depends on both convention and reality.

Learning how to use a language requires learning how to follow appropriate linguistic rules. A contemporary postempiricist philosopher described learning language skills in this way: "The special power of language in these matters derives from the fact that linguistic behaviour is behaviour which obeys rules correlating performances with empirical states of affairs" (Bennett, 1989, pp. 87–88).

Socialization is the means by which children acquire the habits of a culture and learn the rules of that culture. Some rules inform children how to map sounds onto the things they see: these rules are linguistic. Other rules require learning how to describe the conditions under which it is permissible to do certain things. These rules serve to identify proper motivations.

A CONSTRUCT THEORY OF MOTIVATION

Construct theory (McCord, 1993) postulates that children learn by constructing categories organized by the concepts of the language in their culture. These categories can be identified by descriptions, much as one might identify folder labels in a filing system. One set of categories contains what I have called potentiating reasons. These are the reasons that can provide grounds for action. When they are used in connection with actions, they are motives.

Different people learn different potentiating reasons. One child might learn that seeing another child without a crayon is a good reason to offer to share. Another child learns that having something others do not have is good reason to brag. Reasons and actions come together even as sounds and meanings join—in virtue of the way in which others act and respond to action.

Potentiating reasons are learned from the explanations that people give for what they do. For example, let us assume that Jamie hits Jackson. When asked why he did so, Jamie says Jackson has a toy Jamie wants. If Jamie is told that he should not hit Jackson because he wants Jackson's toy, Jamie learns that this is not supposed to be a potentiating reason. If, however, Jamie gets the toy (perhaps when no one is watching), Jamie is likely to classify wanting a toy as a potentiating reason for hitting.

Learning a language and learning how to act are intricately connected through the logical connective "if . . . then." This connective gives linguistic expression to what a neonate learns when he or she cries and gets a response (for example, if I cry, then I will be held), what an infant learns by shaking a rattle (if I shake it, then it will make noise), and what the child learns when discovering natural consequences in the physical world.

What to count as pleasurable and what to consider painful are, according to Construct theory, largely set by socialization practices. If children are rewarded by being allowed to stay up late, they are likely to come to value late bedtimes. Parents and teachers who assign tasks as punishment convey the impression that being helpful must be painful. Reporting on his reluctance to see rewards and punishments employed in educating children, John Locke recounted how he had helped a friend whose younger son "was not easily brought to his book." Locke and his friend, "in a discourse on purpose amongst ourselves, in his hearing, but without taking any notice of him, declared that it was the privilege and advantage of heirs and elder brothers, to be scholars. . . . and that for younger brothers, it was a favour to admit them to breeding; to be taught to read and write, was more than came to their share." The result was that the child "would come himself to his mother to learn; and would not let his maid be quiet, till she heard him his lesson" (1693/1794, No. 148).

Whether to count one's pleasure and pain as grounds for action—as potentiating reasons—also depends on socialization. Some people seem barely to notice when they are severely injured, while others nurse the slightest wound. Athletes in contact sports clearly do not make their choices in the light of avoiding pain. Daily routines, for the most part, are chosen for reasons other than the pleasures that they bring.

Environments unresponsive to a child's physical requirements teach children to pay little attention to pain and are likely to teach them to classify themselves among things of little value. Children learn to notice what to consider painful. Goldfarb's (1945, 1958) studies of institutionalized infants indicate the degree to which caring about pains is a function of experience. One institutionalized child who received little attention sat on a radiator too hot for the teacher to touch. Another cut the palm of his own hand with sharp scissors. Another closed a door on her hand, injuring her finger so severely that it turned blue, but she did not cry or otherwise show pain. Another had not complained of pain although a steel splinter had been lodged in her cornea for two days. All the children gave pain responses to a pin prick, so that it was clear they had normal pain receptors. They simply had not learned to use their own pain as grounds for action.

We know that persistent criminals are relatively unresponsive to physical pains (Farrington, 1988; Hare, 1978; Mednick, 1977; Satterfield, 1987; Siddle, 1977; Wadsworth, 1976). Children who come from backgrounds where injuries are given scant attention are likely to have few potentiating reasons for changing courses of action that are based on injuries to themselves or others.

The rules of rewards and punishments teach children what to value. Children recognize that what is used for a reward must be more valuable than that which is rewarded (Boggiano & Main, 1986; Greene & Lepper, 1974; Lepper, Greene, & Nisbett, 1973; Lepper, Sagotsky, Defoe, & Greene, 1982; Ross, Karniol, & Rothstein, 1976). Something given as a punishment must not be as desirable as what is being punished (Aronson & Carlsmith, 1963). They learn, too, that being threatened with a punishment is a potentiating reason not to do something that otherwise might be done.

When rewards and punishments are used to teach children what to do, they also indicate that the children ought to value their own pleasure and attempt to reduce their own pain. Punishments and rewards teach children to focus on themselves in deciding how to act. Children who are offered rewards for doing what their parents want them to do learn that getting a reward is a potentiating reason for acting. That is, getting something pleasurable is a ground for acting. Similarly, children threatened with punishments learn that avoiding pain is a legitimate reason for action. Through their use, rewards and punishments create potentiating reasons for seeking pleasure and avoiding pain.

We know that neglect, rejection, and abuse foster misbehavior (Lewis, Mallouh & Webb, 1989; McCord, 1983; Widom, 1989). Abusing parents spend little time communicating with their children (Kavanagh, Youngblade, Reid, & Fagot, 1988), so that the children are likely to have little understanding of the thoughts or feelings of others (Camras et al., 1990; Perry & Perry, 1974). In the absence of communication about feelings, it is likely that few potentiating reasons based on how others feel will be learned.

Children who become criminals have typically come from families that give them little supervision (Loeber & Stouthamer-Loeber, 1986; McCord, 1979). Therefore, they may learn to take what seems appealing. The potentiating reason for many of their actions seems to be simply that something is appealing.

If, as is often the case for juvenile delinquents, a child sees that parents are mean to one another when anything goes wrong, the child learns that many types of problems are potentiating reasons for giving injuries to others.

People holding very different moral beliefs may commit similar crimes. One person steals from a department store to give a muff to his girlfriend, reasoning that there is nothing wrong with taking goods from a store. Another, perhaps stealing from the same store and giving to the same girl, argues that the taking is appropriate. There are a number of scenarios that could make this plausible: for example, the man has been promised wages that have not been paid; the store regularly discriminates against a group to which the thief belongs; Mimi is on her deathbed and only the muff can let her die with relative serenity.

Reasoning styles can give a handle to understanding intentional action. Morally relevant reasoning is likely to be particularly important for understanding criminal behavior.

The Construct theory of motivation merges the concepts of cause with those of a certain type of reasons, potentiating reasons. In doing so, the Construct theory differs from cognitive theories that rely on actors' judgments regarding what are presumed to be the private world of motives, justifications, and values.

Potentiating reasons are grounds for action. These differ among individuals and sometimes change through time. Just as we come to understand a language by watching and listening, it is possible to discover the potentiating reasons of others by watching how they act and the conditions under which they act. Bennett wrote that "one's entitlement to believe that one shares with others a common understanding of a language is answerable to criteria concerning the relationship between what is said in the language and what is the case about the world" (1989, p. 64). Similarly, the Construct theory of motivation claims that entitlement to believe that we understand why a person acts in particular ways depends on the relation between the actions and the situational cues that evoke the actions.

Because potentiating reasons are useful organizing categories, they tend to be stable. Yet experiences can alter intentional behavior through changing what a person believes about the world.

The Construct theory of motivation implies that interventions need not be directed at deep-seated emotions. Rather, behavioral change can be expected as a consequence of changing grounds for action. Such changes come about in a variety of ways, sometimes indirectly through the acquisition of loves or friendships and sometimes through direct (possibly traumatic) experiences.

As the theory would predict, behavior changes can be generated by altering cues for action without altering emotions. Hudley and Graham (1993) randomly assigned aggressive, unpopular boys in 4th through 6th grades to a group in which they were trained to recognize the nonhostile intentions of others. These boys were compared with a control group, also randomly assigned, that was trained to increase attention spans. Teachers blind to which type of training the boys had received rated the boys on aggression and prosocial behavior both before and after treatment. Had some fundamental personality shift been responsible for change in behavior, one would expect to find both ratings changed. Those who received the nonhostile cue training were rated as less aggressive, though not more prosocial. The boys rated themselves in terms of how angry they would feel if described frustrating events happened to them. There was no indication that the boys who acted less aggressively were less angry in response to frustration.

One month after treatment ended, the boys participated in an experimental, frustrating task. They were told they could win prizes if they followed directions correctly, directions given by another boy, seated behind a barrier. Both boys believed they had the same map, but in fact they did not. Thus, success was impossible. None of the boys trained to recognize nonhostile intentions insulted their partners, though boys in the other group did so. The boys' verbal behavior was scaled for injurious comments. Those boys trained to recognize nonhostile intentions were significantly less likely to use hurtful comments. In sum, the boys who had been taught new grounds for action seem to have changed their behaviors without changing their emotions.

The Construct theory of motivation differs from other theories purporting to explain criminal behavior by specifically recognizing that actions are not "naturally" self-interested. It provides a theory of volitional action without postulating the existence of mysterious entities ("volitions"). The Construct theory of motivation is empirical and seems to provide an account of what we know about relative risks for criminal behavior.

The Construct theory of motivation shows that socialization practices influence action by teaching children what to count as potentiating reasons. It accounts for why valid descriptions of motives make a difference in terms of expectations about the behavior of a motivated individual. It does so by assimilating potentiating reasons to motives for action. Finally, the Construct theory of motivation gives a plausible account of how criminal behavior can be voluntary action by showing potentiating reasons in their roles as causes for motivated actions.

NOTE

1. A complete causal account of B would yield both necessary and sufficient conditions, A', so that if not-A', then not-B as well.

REFERENCES

Anscombe, G. E. M. (1958). *Intention*. London: Basil Blackwell.

Aristotle. (1941a). Analytic Posteriori (G. R. G. Mure, Trans.). In R. McKeon (Ed.), *The basic works of Aristotle*. New York: Random House.

———. (1941b). On the soul (J. A. Smith, Trans.). In R. McKeon (Ed.), *The basic works of Aristotle*. New York: Random House.

———. (1962). *Nicomachean ethics* (Martin Ostwald, Trans.). New York: Macmillan.

Aronson, E., & Carlsmith, J. M. (1963). Effect of the severity of threat on the devaluation of forbidden behavior. *Journal of Abnormal and Social Psychology, 66*(6), 584–588.

Austin, J. L. (1962a). *How to do things with words*. Oxford: Clarendon Press.

———. (1962b). *Sense and sensibilia* (Reconstructed from manuscript notes by G. J. Warnock). Oxford: Clarendon Press.

Ayer, A. J. (1940). *The foundations of empirical knowledge*. London: Macmillan.

Bandura, A. (1986). *Social foundations of thought and action: A social cognitive theory*. Englewood Cliffs NJ: Prentice-Hall.

———. (1989). Human agency in social cognitive theory. *American Psychologist, 44*(9), 1175–1184.

Batson, C. D., Dyck, J. L., Brandt, J. R., Batson, J. G., Powell, A. L., McMaster, M. R., & Griffitt, C. (1988). Five studies testing two new egoistic alternatives to the emphathy-altruism hypothesis. *Journal of Personality and Social Psychology, 55*(1), 52–77.

Baumann, D. J., Cialdini, R. B., & Kenrick, D. T. (1981). Altruism as hedonism: Helping and self-gratification as equivalent responses. *Journal of Personality and Social Psychology, 40*(6), 1039–1046.

Bennett, J. (1989). *Rationality: An essay towards an analysis*. Cambridge: Hackett. (Originally published 1964)

Bentham, J. (1882). *Theory of legislation* (4th ed.). London: Trubner.

Berkowitz, L. (1965). The concept of aggressive drive: Some additional considerations. In L. Berkowitz (Ed.), *Advances in experimental social psychology* (Vol. 2, pp. 301–329). New York: Academic Press.

———. (1987). Mood, self-awareness, and willingness to help. *Journal of Personality and Social Psychology, 52*(4), 721–729.

Boehnke, K., Silbereisen, R. K., Eisenberg, N., Reykowski, J., & Palmonari, A. (1989). Developmental pattern of prosocial motivation: A cross national study. *Journal of Cross-Cultural Psychology, 20*(3), 219–243.

Boggiano, A. K., & Main, D. S. (1986). Enhancing children's interest in activities used as rewards: The bonus effect. *Journal of Personality and Social Psychology, 31*(6), 1116–1126.

Brehm, S. S., & Brehm, J. W. (1981). *Psychological reactance: A theory of freedom and control*. New York: Academic Press.

Broad, C. D. (1930). *Five types of ethical theory*. London: Routledge & Kegan Paul.

Camras, L. A., Ribordy, S., Hill, J., Martino, S., Sachs, V., Spaccarelli, S., & Stefani, R. (1990). Maternal facial behavior and the recognition and production of emotional expression by maltreated and nonmaltreated children. *Developmental Psychology, 26*(2), 304–312.

Caplan, M. (1993). Inhibitory influences in development: The case of prosocial behavior. In D. F. Hay & A. Angold (Eds.), *Precursors and causes in development and psychopathology* (pp. 169–198). Chichester, England: Wiley.

Cialdini, R. B., Schaller, M., Houlihan, D., Arps, K., Fultz, J., & Beaman, A. (1987). Empathy-based helping: Is it selflessly or selfishly motivated? *Journal of Personality and Social Psychology, 52*(4), 749–758.

Clark, R. D., III, & Word, L. E. (1972). Why don't bystanders help? Because of ambiguity? *Journal of Personality and Social Psychology, 24*(3), 392–400.

Cummings, E. M., Hollenbeck, B., Iannotti, R., Radke-Yarrow, M., & Zahn-Waxler, C. (1986). Early organization of altruism and aggression: Developmental patterns and individual differences. In C. Zahn-Waxler, E. M. Cummings, & R. Iannotti (Eds.), *Altruism and aggression: Biological and social origins* (pp. 165–188). Cambridge: Cambridge University Press.

Davidson, D. (1967). Truth and meaning. *Synthese, 17*(3), 304–323.

———. (1980a). Actions, reasons, and causes. In D. Davidson (Ed.), *Essays on actions and events* (pp. 3–19). Oxford: Oxford University Press. (Reprinted from *The Journal of Philosophy, 60*(23), 1963, 691–700)

———. (1980b). Causal relations. In D. Davidson (Ed.), *Essays on actions and events* (pp. 149–162). Oxford: Oxford University Press. (Reprinted from *The Journal of Philosophy, 64*(21), 1967, 691–703)

———. (1980c). Hempel on explaining action. In D. Davidson (Ed.), *Essays on actions and events* (pp. 261–275). Oxford: Oxford University Press. (Original essay published 1976)

———. (1986). A coherence theory of truth and knowledge. In E. LePore (Ed.), *Truth and interpretation: Perspectives on the philosophy of Donald Davidson* (pp. 307–319). Oxford: Basil Blackwell.

Denham, S. A., McKinley, M., Couchoud, E. A., & Holt, R. (1990). Emotional and behavioral predictors of preschool peer ratings. *Child Development, 61*(4), 1145–1152.

Dennett, D. C. (1978). Mechanism and responsibility. In D. Dennett (Ed.), *Brainstorms* (pp. 233–255). Cambridge: Bradford Books, MIT Press. (Original essay published 1973)

———. (1984). *Elbow room: The varieties of free will worth wanting.* Cambridge: MIT Press.

Dray, W. (1957). *Laws and explanation in history.* London: Oxford University Press.

Dretske, F. (1991). *Explaining behavior: Reasons in a world of causes.* Cambridge: MIT Press. (Originally published 1988)

Durkheim, E. (1938). *The rules of sociological method* (S. A. Solovay & J. H. Mueller, Trans.). Chicago: University of Chicago Press. (Originally published in French 1895)

Duval, S., Duval, V. H., & Neely, R. (1979). Self-focus, felt responsibility, and helping behavior. *Journal of Personality and Social Psychology, 37*(10), 1769–1778.

Eisenberg, N., & Mussen, P. H. (1989). *The roots of prosocial behavior in children.* Cambridge: Cambridge University Press.

Eron, L. D., & Huesmann, L. R. (1986). The role of television in the development of prosocial and antisocial behavior. In D. Olweus, J. Block, & M. Radke-Yarrow (Eds.), *Development of antisocial and prosocial behavior* (pp. 285–314). New York: Academic Press.

Farrington, D. P. (1988). Social, psychological and biological influences on juvenile delinquency and adult crime. In W. Buikhuisen & S. A. Mednick (Eds.), *Explaining criminal behaviour: Interdisciplinary approaches* (pp. 68–89). New York: E. J. Brill.

———. (1993). Motivations for conduct disorder and delinquency. *Development and Psychopathology, 5,* 225–241.

Fodor, J. A. (1994). *The elm and the expert: Mentalese and its semantics.* Cambridge: MIT Press.

Frege, G. (1960). On sense and reference. In P. Geach & M. Black (Eds.), *Translations from the philosophical writings of Gottlob Frege* (pp. 56–78). Oxford: Basil Blackwell. (Original essay published 1892)

Friedrich, L. K., & Stein, A. H. (1973). Aggressive and prosocial television programs and the natural behavior of preschool children. *Monographs of the Society for Research in Child Development, 38*(4, Serial No. 151), 1–64.

Gibbons, F. X., & Wicklund, R. A. (1982). Self-focused attention and helping behavior. *Journal of Personality and Social Psychology, 37*(10), 1769–1778.

Goldfarb, W. (1945). Psychological privation in infancy and subsequent adjustment. *American Journal of Orthopsychiatry, 15,* 247–255.

———. (1958). Pain reactions in a group of institutionalized schizophrenic children. *American Journal of Orthopsychiatry, 28,* 777–785.

Goodman, N. (1955). *Fact, fiction & forecast.* Cambridge: Harvard University Press.

Gottfredson, M. R., & Hirschi, T. (1990). *A general theory of crime.* Stanford: Stanford University Press.

Greene, D., & Lepper, M. R. (1974). Effects of extrinsic rewards on children's subsequent intrinsic interest. *Child Development, 45,* 1141–1145.

Grusec, J. E., & Dix, T. (1986). The socialization of prosocial behavior: Theory and reality. In C. Zahn-Waxler, E. M. Cummings, & R. Iannotti (Eds.), *Altruism and aggression: Biological and social origins* (pp. 218–237). Cambridge: Cambridge University Press.

Hare, R. D. (1978). Electrodermal and cardiovascular correlates of psychopathy. In R. D. Hare & D. Schalling (Eds.), *Psychopathic behaviour* (pp. 107–143). Chichester, England: John Wiley.

Harris, P. L. (1994). The child's understanding of emotion: Developmental change and the family environment. *Journal of Child Psychology and Psychiatry and Allied Disciplines, 35*(1), 3–28.

Hart, H. L. A. (1951). The ascription of responsibility and rights. In A. Flew (Ed.), *Logic and language* (1st series, pp. 145–156). Oxford: Basil Blackwell.

———. (1973). *Punishment and responsibility.* Oxford: Oxford University Press.

Hatfield, E., Walster, G. W., & Piliavin, J. A. (1978). Equity theory and helping relationships. In L. Wispé (Ed.), *Altruism, sympathy, and helping* (pp. 115–139). New York: Academic Press.

Haviland, J. M., & Lelwica, M. (1987). The induced affect response: 10-week-old infants' responses to three emotional expressions. *Developmental Psychology, 23,* 97–104.

Hay, D. F. (1994). Prosocial development. *Journal of Child Psychology and Psychiatry and Allied Disciplines, 35*(1), 29–71.

Heider, F. (1946). Attitudes and cognitive organization. *Journal of Psychology, 21,* 107–112.

Hempel, C. G. (1942). The function of general laws in history. *The Journal of Philosophy, 39,* 35–48.

———. (1945). Studies in the logic of confirmation. *Mind, 54,* 1–26, 97–121.

Hinde, R. A. (1979). *Towards understanding relationships.* London: Academic Press.

Hobbes, T. (1988). *Leviathan.* Buffalo: Prometheus. (Originally published 1651)

Hoffman, M. L. (1980). Moral development in adolescence. In J. Adelson (Ed.), *Handbook of adolescent psychology* (pp. 295–343). New York: John Wiley.

Hospers, J. (1961). What means this freedom? In S. Hook (Ed.), *Determinism and freedom in the age of modern science* (pp. 126–142). New York: Collier.

Hudley, C., & Graham, S. (1993). An attributional intervention to reduce peer-directed aggression among African-American boys. *Child Development, 64*(1), 124–138.

Hume, D. (1888). *A treatise of human nature* (L. A. Selby-Bigge edition). Oxford: Clarendon Press. (Originally published 1739)

———. (1955). *An inquiry concerning human understanding.* Indianapolis: Bobbs-Merrill. (Originally published 1748)

———. (1960). *An enquiry concerning the principles of morals.* La Salle IL: Open Court. (Originally published 1777)

James, W. (1890). *The principles of psychology.* New York: Henry Holt.

Kant, I. (1873). Critical examination of practical reason. In *Critique of practical reason* (T. K. Abbott, Trans.). London: Longmans, Green. (Originally published 1788)

———. (1929). *Critique of pure reason* (N. K. Smith, Trans.). London: Macmillan. (Originally published 1781)

———. (1959). *Foundations of the metaphysics of morals* (L. W. Beck, Trans.). Indianapolis: Bobbs-Merrill. (Originally published 1785)

Kavanagh, K. A., Youngblade, L., Reid, J. B., & Fagot, B. I. (1988). Interactions between children and abusive versus control parents. *Journal of Clinical Child Psychology, 17*(2), 137–142.

Killen, M. (1989). Context, conflict, and coordination in social development. In L. T. Winegar (Ed.), *Social interaction and the development of children's understanding* (pp. 119–146). Norwood NJ: Ablex.

Latané, B., & Dabbs, J. M. (1975). Sex, group size, and helping in three cities. *Sociometry, 38*(2), 180–94.

Latané, B., & Darley, J. M. (1968). Group inhibition of bystander intervention in emergencies. *Journal of Personality and Social Psychology, 10*(3), 215–221.

———. (1975). Sex, group size, and helping in three cities. *Sociometry, 38*(2), 180–194.

Lepper, M. R., Greene, D., & Nisbett, R. E. (1973). Undermining children's intrinsic interest with extrinsic rewards. *Journal of Personality and Social Psychology, 28*(1), 129–137.

Lepper, M. R., Sagotsky, G., Dafoe, J. L., & Greene, D. (1982) Consequences of superfluous social constraints: Effects on young children's social influences and subsequent intrinsic interest. *Journal of Personality and Social Psychology, 41*(1), 51–65.

Levy, P., Lundgren, D., Ansel, M., Fell, D., Fink, B., & McGrath, J. E. (1972). Bystander effect in a demand-without-threat situation. *Journal of Personality and Social Psychology, 24*(2), 166–171.

Lewis, C. I. (1946). *An analysis of knowledge and valuation*. LaSalle IL: Open Court.

Lewis, D. O., Mallouh, C., & Webb, V. (1989). Child abuse, delinquency, and violent criminality. In D. Cicchetti & V. Carlson (Eds.), *Child maltreatment: Theory and research on the causes and consequences of child abuse and neglect* (pp. 707–721). Cambridge: Cambridge University Press.

Locke, J. (1794). *Some thoughts concerning education: Vol. 8. Collected works* (9th ed.). London: T. Longman. (Originally published 1693)

Loeber, R., & Stouthamer-Loeber, M. (1986). Family factors as correlates and predictors of juvenile conduct problems and delinquency. In M. Tonry & N. Morris (Eds.), *Crime and justice* (Vol. 7, pp. 29–149). Chicago: University of Chicago Press.

London, P. (1970). The rescuers: Motivational hypotheses about Christians who saved Jews from the Nazis. In J. Macaulay & L. Berkowitz (Eds.), *Altruism and helping behavior* (pp. 241–250). New York: Academic Press.

Lycan, W. G. (1987). *Consciousness*. Cambridge: MIT Press.

McCord, J. (1979). Some child-rearing antecedents of criminal behavior in adult men. *Journal of Personality and Social Psychology, 37*, 1477–1486.

———. (1983). A forty year perspective on effects of child abuse and neglect. *Child Abuse & Neglect, 7*, 265–270.

———. (1993). Crime, conscience, and family. In B. Forst (Ed.), *The socioeconomics of crime and justice* (pp. 65–87). New York: M. E. Sharpe.

Mednick, S. A. (1977). A bio-social theory of the learning of law-abiding behavior. In S. A. Mednick & K. O. Christiansen (Eds.), *Biosocial bases of criminal behavior* (pp. 1–8). New York: Gardner.

Melden, A. I. (1961). *Free action*. London: Routledge & Kegan Paul.

Mill, J. S. (1973). *A system of logic ratiocinative and inductive*. Toronto: University of Toronto Press. (Originally published 1843)

Miller, P. A., & Eisenberg, N. (1988). The relation of empathy to aggressive and externalizing/antisocial behavior. *Psychological Bulletin, 103*, 324–344.

Nagel, T. (1970). *The possibility of altruism*. Princeton: Princeton University Press.

———. (1979). *Mortal questions*. Cambridge: Cambridge University Press.

Nowell-Smith, P. H. (1954). *Ethics*. Middlesex, England: Penguin.

Perry, D. G., & Perry, L. C. (1974). Denial of suffering in the victim as a stimulus to violence in aggressive boys. *Child Development*, 45(1), 55–62.

Piliavin, J. A., & Chaing, H. W. (1990). Altruism: A review of recent theory and research. *Annual Review of Sociology, 16*, 27–65.

Plato. (1937). Cratylus (B. Jowett, Trans.). In B. Jowett (Ed.), *The dialogues of Plato* (Vol. 1, pp. 173–229). New York: Random House.

———. (1949). *Meno* (B. Jowett, Trans.). New York: Liberal Arts Press.

———. (1956). *Protagoras* (B. Jowett, Trans.; revised by M. Ostwald). Indianapolis: Bobbs-Merrill.

———. (1961). Laws (A. E. Taylor, Trans.). In E. Hamilton & H. Cairns (Eds.), *The collected dialogues of Plato* (pp. 1225–1513). New York: Random House.

———. (1974). *The republic* (G. M. A. Grube, Trans.). Indianapolis: Hackett.

Quine, W. V. O. (1960). *Word and object*. Cambridge: Harvard University Press.

———. (1961). *From a logical point of view* (Rev. ed.). Cambridge: Harvard University Press. (Original work published 1953)

Rheingold, H., & Emery, G. N. (1986). The nurturant acts of very young children. In D. Olweus, J. Block, & M. Radke-Yarrow (Eds.), *Development of antisocial and prosocial behavior* (pp. 75–96). New York: Academic Press.

Rosenhan, D. L. (1978). Toward resolving the altruism paradox: Affect, self-reinforcement, and cognition. In L. Wispé (Ed.), *Altruism, sympathy, and helping: Psychological and sociological principles* (pp. 101–113). New York: Academic Press.

Ross, M., Karniol, R., & Rothstein, M. (1976). Reward contingency and intrinsic motivation in children: A test in the delay of gratification hypothesis. *Journal of Personality and Social Psychology, 33*, 442–447.

Rushton, J. P., Fulker, D. W., Neale, M. C., Nias, D. K. B., & Eysenck, H. J. (1986). Altruism and aggression: The heritability of individual differences. *Journal of Personality and Social Psychology, 50*(6), 1192–1198.

Ryle, G. (1949). *The concept of mind*. New York: Barnes & Noble.

Satterfield, J. H. (1987). Childhood diagnostic and neurophysiological predictors of teenage arrest rates: An eight-year prospective study. In S. A. Mednick, T. E Moffitt, & S. A. Stack (Eds.), *The causes of crime: New biological approaches* (pp. 146–167). Cambridge: Cambridge University Press.

Schlick, M. (1939). *Problems of ethics* (D. Rynin, Trans.). New York: Prentice-Hall.

Sellars, W. (1963). Empiricism and the philosophy of mind. In W. Sellars (Ed.), *Science, perception and reality* (pp. 127–196). London: Routledge & Kegan Paul. (Original essay published 1956)

Siddle, D. A. T. (1977). Electrodermal activity and psychopathy. In S. A. Mednick & K. O. Christiansen (Eds.), *Biosocial bases of criminal behavior* (pp. 199–211). New York: Gardner.

Skinner, B. F. (1953). *Science and human behavior*. New York: Macmillan.

Tarski, A. (1949). The semantic conception of truth and the foundations of semantics. In H. Feigl & W. Sellars (Eds.), *Readings in philosophical analysis* (pp. 52–84). New York: Appleton-Century-Crofts. (Original essay published 1944)

Thoman, E. B., Korner, A. F., & Benson-Williams, L. (1977). Modification of responsiveness to maternal vocalization in the neonate. *Child Development, 48,* 563–569.

Vendler, Z. (1984). Agency and causation. In P. A. French, T. E. Uehling, Jr., & H. K. Wettstein (Eds.), *Midwest Studies in Philosophy, Vol. 9. 1984* (pp. 371–384). Minneapolis: University of Minnesota Press.

von Wright, G. H. (1971). *Explanation and understanding.* Ithaca NY: Cornell University Press.

Wadsworth, M. E. J. (1976). Delinquency, pulse rates and early emotional deprivation. *British Journal of Criminology, 16*(3), 245–256.

Waismann, F. (1953). Language strata. In A. Flew (Ed.), *Logic and language* (2nd series, pp. 1–31). Oxford: Basil Blackwell.

Walker, N. (1977). *Behaviour and misbehaviour.* Oxford: Basil Blackwell.

Weiss, R. F., Boyer, J. L., Lombardo, J. P., & Stich, M. H. (1973). Altruistic drive and altruistic reinforcement. *Journal of Personality and Social Psychology, 25*(3), 390–400.

Wicklund, R. A. (1975). Objective self-awareness. In L. Berkowitz (Ed.), *Advances in experimental social psychology* (Vol. 8, pp. 233–275). New York: Academic Press.

Widom, C. S. (1989). Child abuse, neglect, and adult behavior: Research design and findings on criminality, violence, and child abuse. *American Journal of Orthopsychiatry, 59*(3), 355–367.

Winch, P. (1958). *The idea of a social science.* London: Routledge & Kegan Paul.

Wittgenstein, L. (1953). *Philosophical investigations* (G. E. M. Anscombe, Trans.). New York: Macmillan.

Yarrow, M. R., Scott, P. M., & Waxler, C. Z. (1973). Learning concern for others. *Developmental Psychology, 8*(2), 240–260.

Zahn-Waxler, C., & Radke-Yarrow, M. (1982). The development of altruism: Alternative research strategies. In N. Eisenberg (Ed.), *The development of prosocial behavior* (pp. 109–137). New York: Academic Press.

Zahn-Waxler, C., Radke-Yarrow, M., Wagner, E., & Pyle, C. (1988, April). *The early development of prosocial behavior.* Paper presented at the meetings of ICIS, Washington DC.

Heterogeneity of Antisocial Behavior: Causes, Continuities, and Consequences

Michael Rutter

MRC *Child Psychiatry Unit and Social, Genetic & Developmental Psychiatry Research Centre, Institute of Psychiatry, London*

Barbara Maughan
Joanne Meyer
Andrew Pickles
Judy Silberg
Emily Simonoff
Eric Taylor

Any consideration of the reasons why people engage in antisocial behavior must be based on a recognition of the heterogeneity of antisocial behavior (Rutter, in press-a). At one extreme, isolated acts that could have led to prosecution are committed at some time by the majority of young people. The extremely high base rate means that the great majority grow up to be ordinary, reasonably well func-

Particular thanks are due to Deborah Jones for her help in preparing this chapter and especially for her production of the figures used. The research reported here owes much to the contribution of many colleagues; we are particularly indebted to Lindon Eaves, Richard Harrington, John Hewitt, David Quinton, Lucinda Shillady, David Smith, and William Yule. Further details on the individual programs of research are given in the notes.

tioning adults. At the other extreme, some young people who show persistent and widespread antisocial behavior in childhood go on to exhibit antisocial personality disorders in adult life that are accompanied by pervasive and persistent social malfunction across a wide spread of life's domains. Such disorders are found in some 1 in 30 males in the general population (Robins, Tipp, & Przybeck, 1991). Between these two extremes are the third or more of boys living in cities who have an official court record (Rutter & Giller, 1983); about half of these have only one conviction, but the remainder have varying degrees of recidivism. In addition, a small proportion of criminal acts are associated with major mental disease or disorder.

Although there is a general recognition that antisocial behavior is heterogeneous, doubts and uncertainties remain on how best to subdivide this overall behavioral grouping. Indeed, there is not agreement as yet on whether the heterogeneity reflects qualitatively distinct subcategories or whether it is a consequence of varying admixtures of dimensional traits and risk factors. In this chapter, we focus on possible meaningful heterogeneity as reflected in the overlap between conduct disorder in childhood and three other broad groupings: emotional disorder (especially depression), hyperactivity, and reading difficulties. Data from studies over the last 30 years employing a range of epidemiological, longitudinal, clinical, and genetic research strategies are used to consider the possible implications for causal mechanisms, continuities and discontinuities between childhood and adult life, and consequences for adult functioning and psychopathology.

The questions to be addressed were laid out in the findings of the Isle of Wight surveys undertaken in the mid-1960s (Rutter, Tizard, & Whitmore, 1970). Findings for the children at age 10 emphasized the high frequency with which conduct disorders were accompanied by symptoms of overactivity, restlessness, fidgetiness, and inattention. The importance of the association was indicated by the results of the follow-up study at age 14–15 years (Schachar, Rutter, & Smith, 1981). The persistence of conduct disturbance across the time period extending from middle childhood into mid-adolescence was much higher in the children whose conduct disturbance was accompanied by hyperactivity, especially where this was evident both at home and at school. Follow-up findings were also informative in indicating the different course shown by emotional disorders and conduct disorders, with the latter more likely to persist (Graham & Rutter, 1973). But, the findings at both age periods emphasized the high frequency with which emotional and conduct disorders co-occurred. The epidemiological correlates suggested that, on the whole, these mixed disorders had more in common with "pure" conduct disorders than with "pure" emotional disorders, but the data on this point were necessarily limited. Severe reading difficulties were also extremely common in children showing conduct disorders. Over 40% of boys with conduct disorders showed severe reading difficulties, as did nearly a third of girls with conduct disorders. Co-occurrence of reading difficulties and emotional disorder was very much less frequent. The other finding from the Isle of Wight studies to which we draw attention is that reading difficulties were far more frequently found accompanying disorders that were already evident at age 10 than accompanying those disorders arising *de novo* at some point between 10 and 14 years. It appeared that age of onset might be an important source of meaningful heterogeneity. Persistence of disorder was also relevant; family risk factors were much more strongly associated with disorders that were evident at *both* age 10 and age 14 than with those manifest at only one of the two age periods.

Some Causal Considerations

Before considering how far research findings are informative on the meaning of this heterogeneity in antisocial behavior, we need to address the question of what is meant by *motivation*. The term is often used in the sense of the emotion or cognition that leads to a conscious choice or decision or will to behave in a particular way. That is to say, the focus is on what was in a person's mind that caused him or her to commit some act. Alternatively, the term *motivation* is used to refer to the underlying causes of a behavior, and that is the sense in which we primarily use it here. In order to understand why a person engages in some behavior, it is necessary to determine how genetic factors and prior experiences create a predisposition to act in that way—a predisposition that may operate through behavioral styles (e.g., impulsivity or sensation seeking), or patterns of attribution (e.g., assumptions of hostile intent), or thinking patterns (e.g., acting without thought for the future). The predisposition may, in addition, come about through the situations in which people find themselves. A teenager's decision to leave a hostile, rejecting home environment through the route of early marriage and pregnancy may involve no unusual motivational process, but, nevertheless, it is likely to place the teenager at an increased risk for a range of social outcomes involving risk circumstances. The factors involved in a decision to commit an antisocial act need to be considered as the end result of direct and indirect causal chains and not as a process that is independent of the past. Longitudinal research strategies are essential if there is to be an adequate understanding of how internal psychological processes serve to influence later environments, and vice versa. It is also necessary to appreciate that the motivational factors will include those that concern individual differences in liability to engage in antisocial behavior and the factors that concern the translation of that liability into the commission of antisocial acts. There can be no assumption that deliberate decisions are required. Clearly, conscious choices are involved, but they constitute only part of the story. This approach to motivation also differs from the former in its focus on both distal and proximal processes.

It is important to recognize that causal processes involve, not one causal question, but many (Rutter, in press-b; Rutter, 1994). With respect to antisocial behavior, there is the question of individual differences; why "X" is criminal whereas "Y" is not. There is also the quite different question of the causes of differences in level either over time or place (Rutter & Smith, 1995). Thus, one may ask why the crime rate has risen so greatly in most Western countries over the last 50 years or why the murder rate in the United States is 15 times that in Europe. A third causal question refers to differences in actualization. We need to consider why this person with a predisposition to antisocial behavior actually commits a crime now in this particular circumstance (Tonry & Farrington, 1995). This distinction is one that applies widely in psychopathology, and not just antisocial behavior. Whether someone attempts suicide will be influenced, not just by their suicidal tendencies, but by the availability of means of self-destruction and whether, at the relevant time, their inhibitions are reduced by drugs or alcohol. Similarly, severely stressful life events play a major role in the precipitation of onset of episodes of depression (Brown & Harris, 1978), but it is quite likely that such events are less important with respect to individual differences in the overall liability to depression when considered over time (Kendler, Neale, Kessler, Heath, & Eaves, 1993). A fourth question concerns changes over time within the individual. Thus, it is well documented that criminal behavior falls off markedly during early adult life (Farrington, 1986). The factors involved in desistance from crime may or may not be the same as those involved in the initiation of antisocial activities at a much earlier age (Sampson & Laub, 1993).

A rather different sort of distinction among causal explanations concerns the different levels to which they refer. To begin with, there are the features that concern neural structure and function. Thus, research has focused on the possible importance of serotonin levels and of neurotransmitter functions. Alternatively, research may focus on susceptibility traits such as novelty seeking (Cloninger, Adolfsson, & Svrakic, 1996). Recent research linking the D4 dopamine receptor gene with novelty seeking has indicated a potential bridge between these first two levels in causal explanation. However, susceptibility traits may involve not only temperamental characteristics but also styles of cognitive processing (Dodge, 1986; Dodge, Pettit, McClaskey, & Brown, 1986), and such traits are likely to be influenced, not only by genetic factors, but also by parenting and other experiences during the early years (Dodge, Pettit, Bates, & Valente, 1995). A third level of causal explanation might concern the route by which such susceptibility traits lead on in some individuals either to a disorder (for example, conduct disorder) or the manifestation of a tendency to engage in antisocial behavior. A fourth level of explanation might address the question of individual differences (among those with that disorder or propensity) with respect to the frequency and/or severity of their antisocial behavior. One might ask why this individual has only 1 criminal conviction whereas that one has 10. A fifth level concerns the factors involved in why an individual act is committed at the time and in the particular circumstances in which it took place. Thus, there is a sizeable literature on situational factors that influence delinquent and criminal activities (Tonry & Farrington, 1995).

Along with these approaches to causal explanation, it is necessary to adopt a developmental perspective (Loeber & Hay, 1994). That is, one also needs to consider how behavior may change in form over the course of lifespan development. For example, one may ask why and how hyperactivity in the preschool years leads to an oppositional/defiant disorder in early or middle childhood, why some cases of oppositional/defiant disorder become conduct disorders in adolescence, and why some cases of conduct disorder lead to personality disorders of various types in adult life.

Some Epidemiological Findings on Risk Factors

During the 1970s and early 1980s, epidemiological methods were used to examine quite a wide range of risk factors for antisocial behavior at individual, family, school, and community levels. In each of these studies, we sought to determine how the risk might be mediated. For example, following the Isle of Wight surveys (which concerned an area mainly made up of small towns), it was necessary to consider the extent to which the findings would be the same in the very different circumstances of socially disadvantaged inner London (Rutter, 1973; Rutter, Cox, Tupling, Berger, & Yule, 1975; Rutter, Yule, et al., 1975; Berger, Yule, & Rutter, 1975). A survey in London, using exactly the same methods as those employed in the Isle of Wight, was undertaken with a focus on 10-year-olds. The findings were clear-cut in showing that the rate of psychopathology in inner London was twice that on the Isle of Wight.[1] The difference was evident on both questionnaire and interview measures; moreover, it was found not to be an artifact of selective in- or out-migration. The twofold increase in disorder applied to children born and bred in the two areas.

The study included a detailed examination of a range of possible risk factors, and the findings showed that all these factors were considerably more prevalent in inner London than on the Isle of Wight (see Figure 1). About half the child population in inner London came from families exhibiting some form of psychosocial adversity, whereas this applied to only about 1 in 5 of the children living on the Isle of Wight (Rutter & Quinton, 1977). Multivariate analyses showed that almost the whole of the difference in rates of psychopathology between the two areas was explicable in terms of the area differences in family adversity. In other words, it seemed that the causal route was likely to involve some mechanism by which living in a socially disadvantaged inner-city area increased family adver-

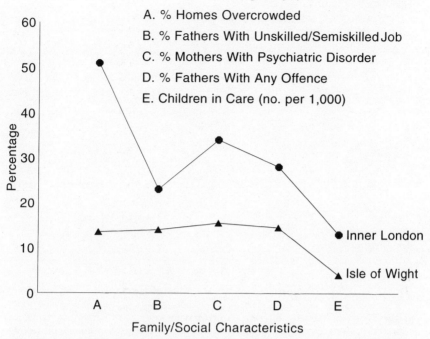

Figure 1. Psychosocial features in inner London and on the Isle of Wight (adapted from Rutter & Quinton, 1977).

sity rather than any direct effect on the child that was independent of the family. Follow-up data were informative, too, in showing that (at least as measured by teacher questionnaires) the main effect of the area in which children grow up applied to disorders that persisted to age 14–15 years but that were already manifest at age 10, and not to those developing *de novo* in adolescence without behavioral disturbance at age 10 (Rutter, 1980).

The Isle of Wight–London comparison also suggested that a contributory factor to the area difference was to be found in school adversity. Thus, indices such as high pupil turnover, high rates of absenteeism, and a high pupil-teacher ratio were more frequent in inner London than on the Island. These school characteristics were associated with disorder, with the main effect apparently being on children from nondisadvantaged families. This led to a more systematic study of possible school influences on children's behavior and scholastic attainments.[2] Our starting point lay in the epidemiological study of 10-year-olds in an inner London borough. We followed the children across their transfer into secondary school at age

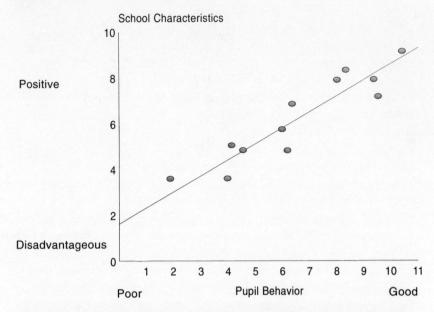

Figure 2. School characteristics and pupil behavior. From *Fifteen Thousand Hours: Secondary Schools and Their Effects on Children* (p. 142), by M. Rutter, B. Maughan, P. Mortimore, & J. Ouston, 1979, London: Paul Chapman Publishing Ltd. Copyright 1979 by Paul Chapman Publishing Ltd. Reprinted with permission.

11–12, focusing on the progress of those children who attended the 12 secondary schools taking the bulk of the children from the borough that we had studied (Rutter, Maughan, Mortimore, Ouston, & Smith, 1979). These children were followed throughout their secondary schooling and into their first year of employment (Gray, Smith, & Rutter, 1980). In parallel with studying the children's progress, we made a detailed study of the characteristics of the schools.

The findings were striking, not just in their demonstration of huge variations among the schools on all indices of pupil progress, but more particularly in showing that these variations were systematically associated with characteristics of the schools as social institutions. Because we had systematic longitudinal data extending from the period before the children entered secondary school, we were able to take account of variations among the schools in the characteristics of their pupil intake. The findings were clear-cut in showing major school effects on pupil behavior such as truancy, fighting, breaking school rules, and classroom disruption (see Figure 2). The causal inference that the associations represented effects of the school on the children, rather than the effects of the children on the school, was supported by the finding that the correlation between school characteristics and children's behavior during the later years of their secondary schooling (0.92) was considerably greater than the correlation between school characteristics and the children's behavior at the time of school entry (0.39). The school characteristics associated with better pupil behavior included good classroom management, appropriately high expectations of the pupils, good models of teacher behavior, positive feedback to the children, consistency of school values, pleasant working conditions and good teacher-child relationships, shared activities between staff and pupils, and opportunities for the children to exercise responsibility.

Although pupil misbehavior at school is associated with delinquency, the two are far from synonymous, and the role of the school was not quite the same for both. School effects on delinquency were quite strong, but the details differed from effects on misbehavior in that the composition of the school intake played a rather greater role than the characteristics of the school ethos. The implication was that peer group pressures might well be playing a larger role in relation to delinquency than with other aspects of the pupils' behavior. Causal inferences are, of course, always stronger when one can demonstrate effects following a change in the putative causal factor. We were able to use this strategy to a limited extent in a study of three schools that had been in considerable difficulties and that then experienced a change in school principal (Maughan, Pickles, Rutter, & Ouston, 1991; Ouston, Maughan, & Rutter, 1991). The results showed a dramatic effect on absenteeism and scholastic attainments in one of the schools and worthwhile benefits in a second school. The findings again support the inference that schools can and do influence children. Our findings on the importance of the school environment were initially greeted with some skepticism among academics, but subsequent studies by other research groups have broadly confirmed our findings and have shown that, if anything, we underestimated the importance of school effects (see Maughan, 1994; Mortimore, 1995).

Risk factors relating to the children's upbringing were examined in two main high-risk groups: those who were reared in residential Group Homes as a result of parenting breakdown (Quinton & Rutter, 1988) and those reared by mentally ill parents (Rutter & Quinton,

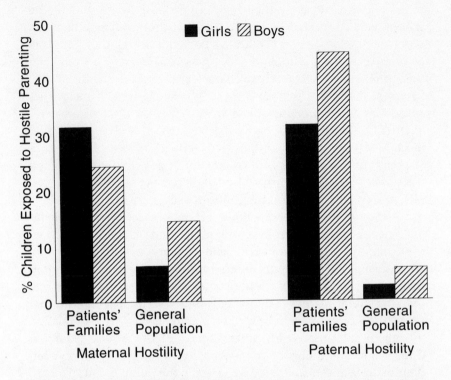

Figure 3. Frequency of hostile parenting in families with a mentally ill parent (high-risk group) and a general population community sample (adapted from Maughan et al., 1995).

1984). Both studies were based on epidemiological samples and both involved longitudinal study, as well as comparisons with the general population sample. The children taken into care by local authorities as a result of parenting breakdown showed a greatly increased rate of antisocial behavior, however measured, in both childhood and adult life. We consider the findings from that study in greater detail when looking at adult outcome later in this chapter.

The original focus on parental mental disorder, in the other study, derived from the expectation that this would constitute a major risk factor in its own right. Our comparison between the sample of families with a mentally ill parent and a general population community sample showed that the two groups differed greatly in marital discord and in adverse relationships between parents and children.[3] Children in families with a mentally ill parent (patients'

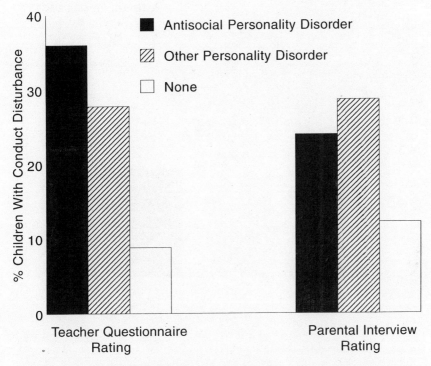

Figure 4. Parental personality disorder, parental hostility, and persistent child distur-bance on teacher questionnaires (adapted from Rutter & Quinton, 1984).

families) were much more likely to be exposed to hostile parenting than were those in the general population (see Figure 3).

This led us to look in greater detail at the relative contributions from parental mental disorder and from parent-child relationships. The parental diagnosis that was associated with the highest psycho-pathological risk for the children was antisocial personality disor-der, the main risk being for conduct disturbance in the offspring. Ac-cordingly, we examined the relative strength of effect of parental personality disorder and the child's exposure to hostile behavior by the parents (see Figure 4). The findings were striking in showing that the main effect derived from hostile parenting, rather than from parental personality disorder. In the absence of hostile parenting, there was no increase in risk associated with parental personality disorder. However, within the group of children exposed to hostile behavior, the risk was greater when this was combined with paren-

MOTIVATION AND DELINQUENCY

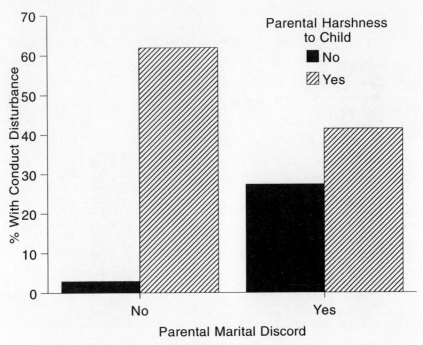

Figure 5. Parental harshness and marital discord in relation to conduct disorder in boys (adapted from Maughan et al., 1995).

tal personality disorder. These findings were evident in both questionnaire and detailed interview assessments.

At the time that this study was undertaken, the main focus in the research literature was on family-wide marital discord. Our research was unusual in measuring how the family environment impinged on each child at an individual level. Accordingly, we were able to determine the extent to which the risk for the children derived from child-specific risk experiences within the family rather than overall family circumstances. The analyses showed that, although both had some effect, the predominant impact came from individualized experiences of hostile parental behavior (see Figure 5). The finding is in line with comparable investigations by other research groups (see Reiss et al., 1995) and with the evidence from genetic research showing that child-specific environmental effects tend to be greater than family-wide shared environmental effects (Plomin & Daniels, 1987). In part, this difference is likely to stem from children's differential involvement in family-wide adverse experiences. For example, the same study showed that when mentally ill parents were feeling stressed and irritable, their hostility was not evenly distributed among the children in the family. The negative focus tended to be particularly on children with adverse temperamental characteristics (Rutter, 1978).

Time Trends in Crime

At the same time as these epidemiological/longitudinal studies were being undertaken, there was a growing awareness on both sides of the Atlantic that levels of crime were rising greatly. This led Academia Europaea to set up a study group to examine the phenomenon, not just in relation to crime, but with respect to a broader range of psychosocial disorders in young people (Rutter & Smith, 1995).[4] Detailed attention was paid to a range of methodological considerations that could have led to an artifactual impression of a rise in crime. The evidence from a wide range of European countries and from North America showed that during the period since World War II there had been a very considerable rise in crime (Smith, 1995). The trend was shown, not only by official crime statistics, but also by victim survey data and interview studies. Unfortunately, the available crime data refer to crimes, rather than individuals, and do not differentiate between isolated offences and recidivist crime. The interview data from the U.S. Epidemiological Catchment Area study, however, suggest that the rise does include antisocial behavior persisting from childhood into adult life (Robins et al., 1991). The implication is that there has probably been some increase in the proportion of the population with a liability to antisocial behavior, and not just in the actualization of that liability (i.e., the tendency of delinquency-prone individuals to engage in delinquent activities). Clearly, a rise as rapid and as marked as this had to be the result of some change in environmental circumstances, rather than the result of any change in the gene pool. The evidence on comparable rises in other psychosocial disorders was informative in bringing in the additional consideration that the rise applied to disorders in youths and young adults but not in older age groups. Accordingly, the explanation had to be found in terms of some environmental change

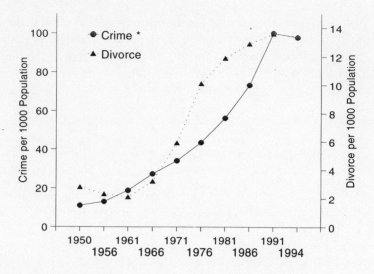

* Excluding offences of 'other criminal damage' value £20 & under

Figure 6. Changes in crime and divorce rates, 1950–1994 (data from Farrington, 1992; Home Office, 1994; OPCS, 1994).

that particularly impinged on younger age groups (Rutter, in press-b).

Social scientists have often been inclined to attribute changes in the level of crime to society-wide factors such as unemployment or income level. These probably are important at an individual level, but the evidence was clear that they could not be invoked as a main explanation for the rise in crime over time. The rise in antisocial activities began during the 1950s and accelerated during the 1960s and early 1970s at a time when unemployment rates were very low and when levels of affluence were increasing, together with an accompanying reduction in social inequalities. The parallel between the rise in crime and the rise in divorce was much closer; it is certainly possible that a rise in family breakdown has played a part in leading to a rise in crime (see Figure 6). However, quite a range of other possible explanations also need to be considered. In part, it may be that crimes have increased because opportunities for crime have risen. The rise in affluence has meant that there are more goods to steal, and changes in housing conditions (particularly the widespread introduction of high-rise housing) have meant that community surveillance is weaker. The growth of large self-service stores has meant that shopping has become less personalized; perhaps, too, this has made stealing less easy to control because the shopkeepers are less likely to know the customers and because there are far more customers milling around the shelves of goods on sale. In addition, it may be that levels of stress experienced by young people have gone up because of diminished job opportunities for unskilled workers, because of rising educational expectations, and because the extension of education has meant a prolonged period of dependence on parents. A third set of factors may involve a potentiation of antisocial activities through the greater availability and misuse of drugs and alcohol and perhaps by a focus on crime in the media, especially films and television. Public concerns about the adverse effects stemming from the media have often been in terms of people copying what they see on film. This may occasionally take place, but it is likely that the greater effect derives from creating an impression that "everyone does it" (solve problems by violence, take drugs, or steal things), and hence that such behavior is acceptable. As well as the increased liability to antisocial behavior that may have derived from the increasingly high rate of family breakdown, the parallel increase in mental disorders (such as depression, alcoholism, and drug problems) in young parents is likely to have had consequent risk effects on the children. Inevitably, there are difficulties in investigating causal factors for trends over time, and there are necessary uncertainties that apply to reliance on aggregated group data. Nevertheless, the phenomenon of change over time in rates of crime has been important in drawing attention to a range of possible causal influences that differ somewhat from those that are most striking in relation to the rather different causal question of individual differences in antisocial behavior.

Antisocial Behavior and Depression

We have already noted the evidence, from the Isle of Wight surveys onward, that there are many children who show an admixture of both emotional and conduct disturbance. Longitudinal data may help in sorting out the possible meaning of this comorbidity (see Caron & Rutter, 1991). One key question is whether conduct disturbance in childhood predisposes to emotional disturbance in adult

MOTIVATION AND DELINQUENCY

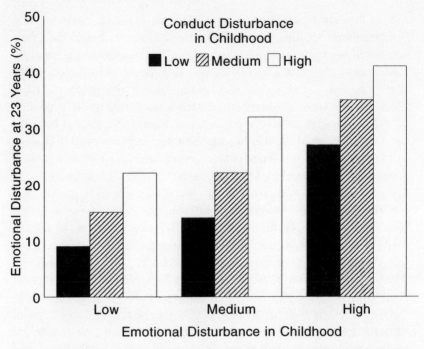

Figure 7. Emotional/Conduct disturbance in childhood and probability of high "malaise" score in females at 23 years (adapted from Rutter, 1991).

life among individuals who did *not* show emotional disturbance in childhood. The British National Child Development study of some 17,000 children followed from birth into adult life provided the necessary sample to examine this question. The childhood measures were derived from a combination of parent and teacher questionnaires given at 7, 11, and 16 years. The use of six data sources enables one to be reasonably sure that most important emotional difficulties will have been detected. As might be expected, emotional difficulties in childhood were associated with a two- to threefold increase in the rate of emotional disturbance at 23 years of age, as assessed on the Malaise Inventory (Rutter, 1991). However, what was very striking, and perhaps surprising, is that, within all levels of emotional disturbance in childhood, conduct disturbance was also associated with a doubling of the risk of emotional disturbance in adulthood. The report in 1991 provided the findings for males; Figure 7 gives the comparable data for females, which show exactly the same pattern. It is evident that conduct problems in childhood predict emotional disturbance in adult life even in the absence of emotional difficulties in childhood and adolescence. More detailed multivariate analyses, using logistic regression methods based on latent variables that account for measurement error and that focus on persistent emotional or conduct disturbance in childhood, confirmed this predictive relationship (Pickles & Clayton, 1996).

Leverage on the same issue was provided by a longitudinal study of child patients undertaken by Harrington and his colleagues (1991).[5] The main focus of that investigation was the adult outcome (at a mean age in the early 30s) for children who had shown a depressive disorder (as operationally defined on the basis of symptomatology) below 16 years of age. This depressive group was compared with a closely matched group of child patients showing some nondepressive form of psychopathology. In order to focus on the specific importance of depression, the two groups (both of which involved patients at the Maudsley Hospital) were matched on all symptoms other than that of depression itself. This design had the additional advantage of allowing us to examine the outcome for both depressive disorders and conduct disorders in childhood according to whether or not they co-occurred. The findings were surprisingly clear-cut. Conduct disturbances in childhood were powerfully predictive of a criminal conviction in adult life, and the presence or absence of depression in childhood made no difference to this adult outcome. The findings for the outcome of major depressive disorder in adult life were quite different. Depression in childhood proved to be a powerful, and diagnosis-specific, predictor, and to that extent, the findings were similar to those for conduct disorder. The key difference lay in the effect of comorbidity. Children with both depression and conduct disorder showed no increase in major depressive disorders in adult life. Together with other findings, the implication was that these comorbid depressive disorders were probably secondary to conduct disturbance and, hence, had a somewhat different meaning from "pure" depressive disorders in childhood (see also Harrington, Rutter, & Fombonne, 1996). On the other hand, the prognostic importance of conduct disturbances in childhood were completely unaffected by the co-occurrence of depression.

It is necessary to ask how this finding tallied with the earlier finding that conduct disturbances in childhood predicted emotional

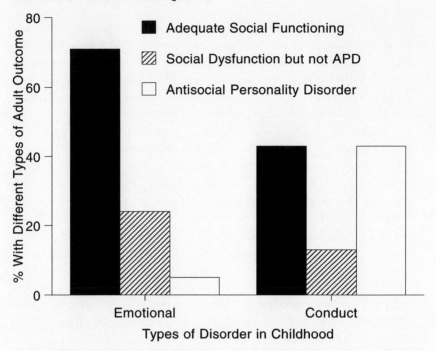

Figure 8. Type of child psychiatric disorder and personality dysfunction in adult life (adapted from Rutter et al., 1994).

disturbance in adult life. To answer that question, we focused on the difference in adult life between major and minor depressive disorders within the subgroup of child patients who showed pervasive social dysfunction of one sort or another in adult life (see Figure 8). The results showed that antisocial personality disorder was accompanied by minor depression in nearly a quarter of the individuals, but that major depressive disorders were strikingly uncommon, occurring in only 6% (Rutter, Harrington, Quinton, & Pickles, 1994). The implication was that although the co-occurrence of emotional difficulties did not seem to alter the course of antisocial behavior between childhood and adult life, nevertheless, antisocial behavior appeared to generate an increased tendency to minor depressive problems (minor, that is to say, in the pattern of symptomatology but often associated with substantial chronicity and social impairment). How might that come about?

To answer that question, we used our longitudinal study of school children in inner London followed from the age of 10 over the

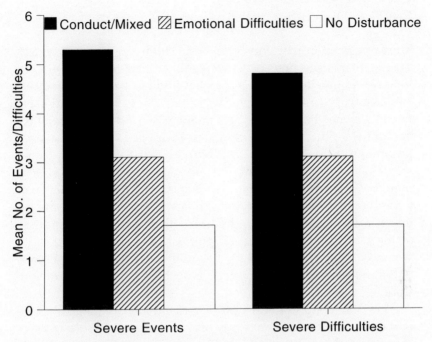

Figure 9. Severe events and difficulties in early adult life and type of disturbance at 10 years, in females (adapted from Champion et al., 1995).

next two decades (Champion, Goodall, & Rutter, 1995). The focus of this study was on whether children's behavior at age 10 predicted their environment as experienced during their late 20s (see Figure 9). The answer was that it did. Conduct disturbance as measured on a teacher questionnaire at age 10 was associated with a threefold increase in the mean number of severely negative acute life events (such as parental loss) and severely negative long-term difficulties (such as chronic family discord) experienced over a five-year period in the late 20s. There was also some increase in negative life experiences in adulthood for children who showed emotional disturbance in childhood, but the effect was much more marked in relation to conduct problems. It seems likely that part of the explanation for the association between antisocial behavior and minor depression is that people with conduct problems act in ways that predispose them to interpersonal tensions and other stressful situations. These stresses, in turn, then tend to provoke affective disturbance.

Reading Difficulties and Antisocial Behavior

The same longitudinal study of London children was used to examine the interconnections between reading difficulties and antisocial behavior in greater detail.[6] Our earlier findings had suggested that some kind of two-way interplay was likely. Thus, the association between a somewhat lower IQ and an increased risk of antisocial behavior held right across the IQ range and applied within social class groupings (Rutter, Tizard, & Whitmore, 1970). Data from other studies have been consistent in confirming this association (Goodman, 1995; Goodman, Simonoff, & Stevenson, 1995). Also there was a trend (albeit a statistically nonsignificant one) for developmental delays to be more frequent in children with antisocial problems than in the remainder of the general population—a mean score of 1.5 versus 0.9 (the scores reflecting the number of delays across a range of different developmental functions such as speech or motor control).

The follow-up into the adult life of the 10-year-old children as part of the epidemiological study of an inner London borough provided the opportunity to look at effects over time. First, the effect of disruptive behavior on progress in reading was examined. As might be expected, children with disruptive behavior (who had a much increased rate of truancy and unauthorized absenteeism from school) made slightly less progress in reading during secondary school (Maughan, Rutter, & Yule, 1996).

We then looked at the association the other way round, in terms of the effect of reading difficulties on the course of antisocial behavior over time (Maughan, Dunn, & Rutter, 1985; Maughan & Hagell, 1996; Maughan, Hagell, Rutter, & Yule, 1994; Maughan, Pickles, Hagell, Rutter, & Yule, 1996). As all studies have shown, there was quite a strong association between antisocial behavior and reading difficulties in childhood. Thus, even in a high delinquency area like inner London, the rate of delinquency was some 50% higher among boys who showed severe reading difficulties. The follow-up of the children who had shown severe reading difficulties had indicated a very high degree of persistence into adult life (Maughan et al., 1994), and it might be supposed that this would be accompanied by an equally persistent association with antisocial behavior. Thus, Moffitt (1993a) has argued that neuropsychological deficits may play a key

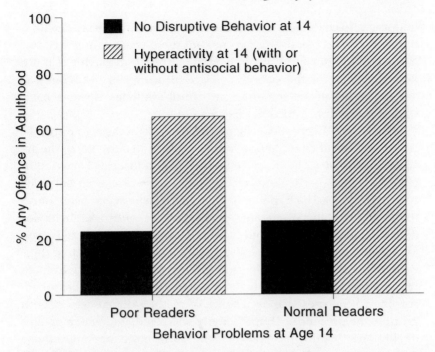

Figure 10. Hyperactivity and adult crime in individuals with and without severe reading difficulties at age 14 (adapted from Maughan et al., 1996).

role in the genesis of antisocial behavior. If that were the case, it might be supposed that this would be particularly true in relation to antisocial behavior persisting into adult life. In the event, the follow-up findings showed the opposite.

The rate of adult crime was actually slightly lower among the boys who had been poor readers than it was in the general population comparison group. Of course, this finding must be interpreted within the context of an inner London general population sample with a particularly high base rate of crime. Nevertheless, even when the adult outcome was considered in relation to broader aspects of psychopathology or social functioning, it was evident that the poor readers did *not* have any substantial increase in adult mental disorder. Multivariate analyses showed that reading difficulties were associated with disruptive behavior at age 10, that the latter predisposed children to poor school attendance at age 13, and that poor school attendance, in conjunction with some independent effect from disruptive behavior, led to juvenile delinquency. Juvenile delinquency, and conduct disturbances at 14, were associated with a much increased risk of adult crime, but there was no route to adult crime that did not come through earlier antisocial behavior. A more detailed study of the data showed that antisocial behavior was somewhat less likely to persist into adult life when it was accompanied by reading difficulties (see Figure 10).

There was one particularly puzzling aspect of these findings. In childhood, as other studies have also found (Hinshaw, 1992), the association between reading difficulties and antisocial behavior in childhood was particularly evident when the antisocial behavior was accompanied by hyperactivity. As hyperactivity has been found to be a predictor of greater persistence of antisocial behavior (Schachar et al., 1981), it would seem to follow that antisocial behavior would be particularly persistent when there were reading difficulties. To look at that matter more closely, we looked at the effect of hyperactivity at age 14 on the later course of antisocial behavior according to the presence or absence of reading difficulties. In both groups, the presence of hyperactivity was associated with a greater likelihood of adult crime, but this effect was more marked in those *without* reading difficulties (see Figure 10). The implication is that at least some forms of hyperactivity associated with reading difficulty may have a somewhat different meaning than that which applies in the absence of reading problems. It might also have been expected that hyperactivity as measured at age 10 would be particularly influential, as that had been found in the Isle of Wight sample (Schachar et al., 1981), but this was not the case. It is difficult to be sure exactly why there was no effect in this sample, but perhaps the reason lies in the high level of inattentive, restless behavior among children in socially disadvantaged inner-city schools, including overactivity that derives from sources quite different from those found in hyperkinetic disorders. Unfortunately, in this sample we did not have parental interview or questionnaire measures, as these might have resolved the issue.

Adult Experiences and Course of Antisocial Behavior

Attention has already been drawn to the association between behavior in childhood and adult experiences. One particularly important aspect of that effect concerns the choice of spouse or partner. Our follow-up of children who had spent much of their years of upbringing in group foster homes showed that, compared with the general population sample, they were much more likely to have a partner with deviant behavior involving antisocial activities, drug taking, or alcohol problems (Quinton & Rutter, 1988; Quinton, Pickles, Maughan, & Rutter, 1993; Zoccolillo, Pickles, Quinton, & Rutter, 1992).[7] This tendency was much stronger in females than males. Not surprisingly, these marriages, or cohabiting partnerships, with antisocial individuals were often characterized by marked marital discord and a high rate of marital breakdown. What was particularly striking, however, was the observation that when these women from high-risk backgrounds did happen to have a nondeviant supportive partner, their adult functioning was very much better.

The key question was whether those who married nondeviant men were less antisocial themselves in childhood. There was also the query whether this might represent some peculiarity of the circumstances of young people who had experienced an institutional rearing. To tackle both these questions, the institutional sample was combined with a general population sample also followed into adult life (already described above). Latent class methods, together with other statistical approaches, were used to ensure that the apparent protective effect of a supportive marital partner was not simply a consequence of measurement error (Pickles & Rutter, 1991; Quinton et al., 1993). The results were clear-cut in indicating that there was a true turning-point effect by which the presence of support from a nondeviant partner was associated with a much better adult outcome among girls who had shown conduct disturbance in childhood (see Figure 11). In the absence of such support, antisocial behavior showed a strong likelihood of leading to pervasive social malfunction in adult life. By sharp contrast, women who were equally antisocial as children (actually marginally more antisocial) tended to go on to show *adaptive* social functioning in adult life when they had support from a nondeviant partner. A closely comparable finding was evident in the re-analysis of the Gluecks' (1950) follow-up study data by Sampson and Laub (1993). The findings are important in indicating that adult experiences can play a crucial role in influencing the social outcome (including, but not confined to, criminal activities) of young people who have shown conduct problems

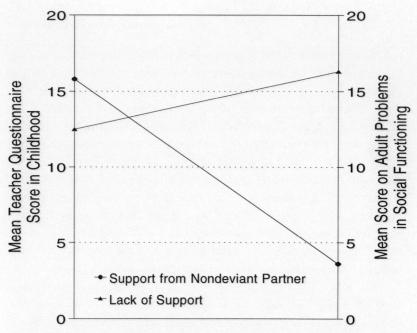

Figure 11. Turning-point effect of partner in females with antisocial behavior in child-hood (analysis by Pickles from data set reported in Quinton et al., 1993).

in childhood. This protective effect in our sample was substantially greater in females than males.

In order to understand how this protective effect came about, we needed to examine the intervening years in greater detail. The question was why some young people with antisocial behavior succeeded in making a harmonious marriage with a nondeviant partner whereas many did not. Both the age at which girls married and had their first child and (for any given age) the likelihood of the partner being antisocial were important (Pickles & Rutter, 1991). Girls showing antisocial behavior in childhood were much more likely to become a teenage parent and to have a deviant partner. A range of possible influences was examined. It was found that being part of a deviant peer group and having had an institutional rearing were associated with an increased risk of cohabitation with a deviant partner by age 20 and that a tendency to show planning (meaning the taking of deliberate decisions about key life choices) and the presence of a harmonious family environment were associated with a decreased risk. Early cohabitation with a deviant partner was associated with a markedly decreased likelihood of the individual being

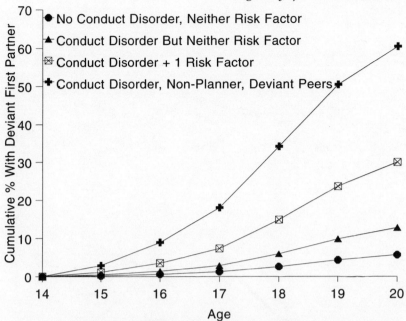

Figure 12. Childhood conduct disturbance, planning, and deviant peers, as risk factors for deviant first partners by age 20 years (analysis by Pickles from data set reported in Quinton et al., 1993).

with a current nondeviant supportive partner at the time of follow-up in the mid-20s.

The overall effect is most easily seen when the pathways are expressed in diagrammatic form. Thus, Figure 12 shows the cumulative probability over time of living with a deviant man according to the presence of conduct disorder, a lack of a tendency to plan, and participation in a deviant peer group. The probabilities concern estimated rates derived from a survival analysis using Cox regression; this assumes a multiplicative effect of risk factors on the hazard (although not on the probability itself). The proportion of women, without conduct disorder and without either of the two risk factors of nonplanning and deviant peers, who had a deviant first partner by the age of 20 years was very low (5.7%). The presence of conduct disorder, in the absence of the two risk factors, doubled the proportion, but the main effect came from the combination of conduct disturbance with the two risk factors. The proportion with a deviant partner at age 20 was 30% when there was one risk factor; when both

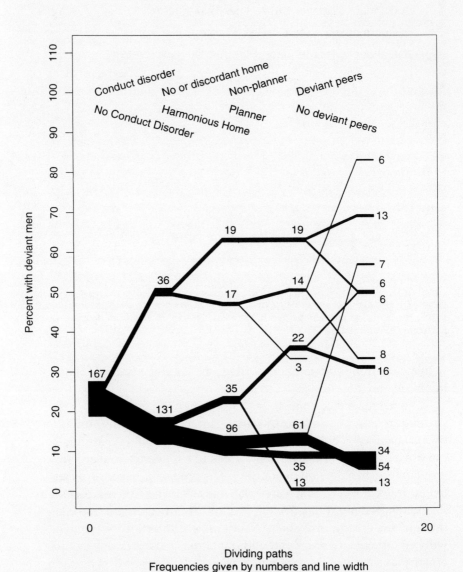

Figure 13. Paths of women to deviant men. From "Partners, Peers and Pathways: Assortative Pairing and Continuities in Conduct Disorder," by D. Quinton, A. Pickles, B. Maughan & M. Rutter, 1993, *Development and Psychopathology, 5*, p. 778. Copyright 1993 by Cambridge University Press. Reprinted with the permission of Cambridge University Press.

risk factors were present, the proportion rose to 60%—a more than tenfold increase in risk over the base rate.

Figure 13 (based on raw data rather than estimates) shows the overall indirect pathway by examining the routes to first cohabitation with a deviant man according to risk and protective factors laid out in time sequence. The overall tendency for partnership with a deviant man was greater for those showing conduct disorder in childhood, but the likelihood went up or down in a consistent way according to the presence or absence of the protective effect of a harmonious home in the teenage years, a tendency to plan, and a nondeviant peer group. At each point, the person's life situation made a substantial difference to the ultimate likelihood of partnership with a nondeviant spouse at follow-up. In each instance, of course, the prior risk factor made it less likely that the person would *have* the protective experience, but if they did, the beneficial effect was evident. The implication is that, although undoubtedly part of the persistence of antisocial behavior needs to be seen in terms of trait or disorder persistence, much of the continuity comes indirectly from the cumulative effect of life experiences. As Caspi and Moffitt (1993) have pointed out, stressful experiences on the whole accentuate, rather than change, prior psychological characteristics. On the other hand, major turning-point effects, with a redirection of life trajectory, can occur when individuals from a high-risk background encounter a very positive life experience that is out of synchrony with their previous chain of adversities and disadvantage (Pickles & Rutter, 1991; Quinton et al., 1993; Rutter, 1996d). These effects of positive life experiences in adulthood do not stand out as major influences in outcome when considered in population variance terms simply because it is unusual for high-risk individuals to have such protective experiences. Nevertheless, when they do, the benefits can be substantial with respect to their own functioning in adult life. We have studied this issue in relation to long-term effects, but the same considerations apply to shorter-term fluctuations in antisocial behavior (Horney, Osgood, & Marshall, 1995).

Studies of Hyperactivity and Hyperkinetic Disorder

The next set of studies to consider came from the program of research undertaken into hyperactivity and hyperkinetic disorders. In order to investigate the question of whether there was a meaningful distinction to be drawn between hyperkinetic and conduct disorders, Taylor and colleagues (Taylor, Sandberg, Thorley, & Giles, 1991) undertook a systematic epidemiological study of 7-year-olds living in inner London.[8] Initially, the groups were divided up on the basis of the screening questionnaire findings. Whereas the children with pure conduct disturbance did not differ from general population controls with respect to objectively measured activity (using actometers) or attentional performance (as measured by a range of tests) or IQ, the group with mixed hyperactivity and conduct disturbance did differ on all three counts. They were much more active, showed much worse attention, and had a mean IQ some 6 points below the mean for the general population. The next step in the research involved the more detailed, standardized, individual study and the redefinition of diagnostic groups defined in terms of this much more detailed information. Thus, for example, hyperactivity and inattention were measured on the basis of detailed descriptions of the children's behavior across a range of situations, using operationalized criteria, rather than in terms of questionnaire scores. The contrast between diagnostic groups became much sharper at this point. The hyperkinetic 7-year-olds in the disorder group had a mean IQ some 17 points below controls, their attentional performance was much worse, they were more likely to show neurodevelopmental impairment, and they were somewhat more likely to have experienced obstetric suboptimality (meaning an increase of minor complications during the pregnancy). The hyperkinetic disorder group was very much more likely to have shown language impairment and poor coordination, and the children were several times more likely to have shown early behavior problems. By contrast, the conduct disorder group was much more likely to have a family history of conduct problems, and the children were more likely to come from families exhibiting marked marital discord. It may be concluded that hyperkinetic disorder was particularly associated with cognitive impairment and neurodevelopmental difficulties, whereas conduct disturbance was not, but such disturbance *was* associated with family adversity and a family history of antisocial behavior. The findings were very much in line with those of other investigators (see Fergusson, Horwood, & Lloyd, 1991; Fergusson, Horwood, & Lynskey, 1993). The diagnosis of hyperkinetic disorder as used in this study was substantially narrower (and in some key respects different from) that associated with the North American concept of attention deficit disorder with hyperactivity (ADHD). Accordingly, the next step was to compare the findings for hyperkinetic disorder and ADHD. The results showed that, whereas hyperkinetic disorder contrasted sharply with both pure conduct disorder and general population controls, this contrast did not apply to ADHD. In some respects children with ADHD were intermediate, but on the whole they were closer to the conduct disorder group than to the hyperkinetic disorder group (particularly with respect to their IQ level).

These data all used clinical or epidemiological correlates to investigate possible heterogeneity, but response to treatment constitutes another, complementary, approach. A double-blind, crossover trial of stimulant medication was used to explore whether drug response (defined in terms of a benefit in relation to the active drug as compared with the placebo as used in the same child) helped with diagnostic distinctions (Taylor et al., 1987). It did not in any clear-cut way, although the overall hyperactivity level and degree of inattention did predict a positive drug response. A beneficial reaction to stimulant drugs was also more likely when the children showed low levels of anxiety and depression, and there was some tendency for neurodevelopmental impairment to predict a good drug response, although this effect disappeared when the other variables were taken into account. The degree of oppositional/conduct disturbance and the degree of family dysfunction had no effect on drug response.

A key issue in all studies examining relationships between family dysfunction and antisocial behavior of the children concerns the question of the direction of the causal arrow. To what extent has the family dysfunction predisposed children to antisocial behavior and to what extent did the antisocial behavior predispose the family to difficulties (Bell, 1968; Lytton, 1990)? The drug study provided one means of tackling this issue. The question was whether there was a change in parental behavior that accompanied the pharmacologically induced alteration in the child's behavior. Schachar and colleagues (Schachar, Taylor, Wieselberg, Thorley, & Rutter, 1987) found that, among drug responders, the use of methylphenidate was significantly associated with a rise in maternal warmth and

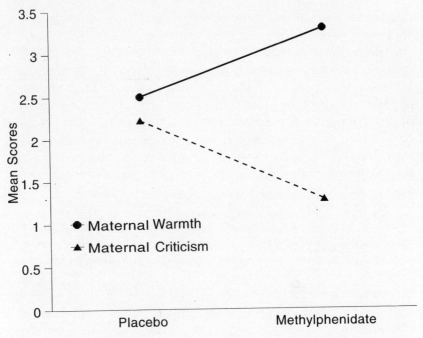

Figure 14. Effects of stimulants given to children on parental expressed emotions (adapted from Schachar et al., 1987).

a fall in maternal criticism (see Figure 14). The implication was that the child had an effect on parental behavior, although, of course, the finding did not rule out an additional effect the other way around. Indeed, other research has provided evidence of effects both ways (see Anderson, Lytton, & Romney, 1986).

Although our findings, like those of others, indicated the strength of differences between hyperkinetic disorder and conduct disorder, the fact remained that there was considerable overlap between these two patterns of psychopathology. We needed to address the question of how this came about and also what the implications were for the course of antisocial behavior over time. A follow-up study at the age of 17 years was undertaken for the groups first studied at age 7 (Taylor, Chadwick, Heptinstall, & Danckaerts, 1996) in order to tackle the question. Four main groups were compared: those showing hyperactivity (but not oppositional/conduct disturbance); those showing oppositional/conduct disturbance (but not hyperactivity); those with both types of psychopathology; and those

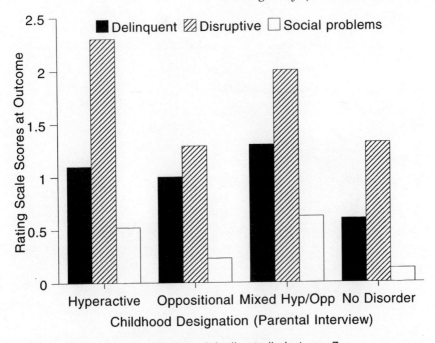

Figure 15. Hyperactivity and oppositional/conduct disturbance as predictors of outcome at 17 years for boys (adapted from Taylor et al., 1996).

with neither. All three psychopathological groups showed an increased level (relative to the general population) of antisocial behavior at age 17, the level being greatest in those with both hyperactivity and disruptive behavior at age 7. Hyperactivity at 7 predicted antisocial behavior at 17, but the reverse did not apply (i.e., antisocial behavior at 7 did not predict hyperactivity at 17). The effects of early hyperactivity were somewhat different, however, according to the type of outcome being considered. Hyperactivity was associated with some increase in delinquent behavior at outcome, but the main effect was most obvious with respect to other forms of disruptive behavior and social problems more generally (see Figure 15). The group with pure hyperactivity showed much the same level of antisocial behavior at age 17 as did the pure oppositional/conduct disorder group, and the outcome for both antisocial behavior and other forms of psychopathology was much worse in the group with the comorbid pattern. It seems that the presence of hyperactivity in

MOTIVATION AND DELINQUENCY

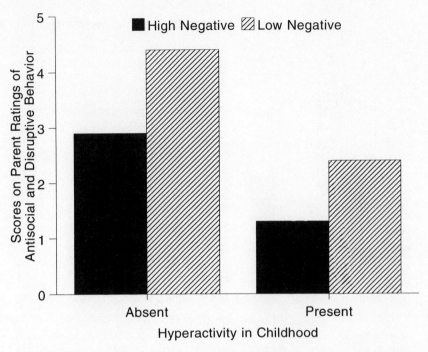

Figure 16. Negative expressed emotion with hyperactivity as predictors of outcome at 17 years for boys with antisocial problems at 7 years (adapted from Taylor et al., 1996).

early childhood is an important prognostic factor, that it does indeed predispose a child to antisocial behavior, but probably that the increased liability applies more to social malfunction that includes antisocial behavior rather than having any direct effect on delinquent activities as such.

We have already noted that hyperactivity is associated with negative parent-child relationships, so it is necessary to consider whether the effect on outcome derived from the hyperactivity in the child or rather from the negative parent-child relationships. The follow-up findings showed that both were important (see Figure 16). For children with both high- and low-negative expressed parental emotion, the outcome was worse for those with hyperactivity in childhood. Equally, however, for children who did and those who did not show hyperactivity in childhood, the outcome was worse for those experiencing parental criticism and hostility. In other words, the prognostic effect derived from *both* child characteristics and parent-child relationships. Research needs to focus on the interplay between risk factors in the child and risk factors in the environment (Rutter et al., in press).

Any research into individual risk factors has to contend with the fact that the putative individual risk factors for antisocial behavior cover quite a broad range, even when confined to those for which there is reasonably good empirical support (Farrington, 1995a, 1995b; Lahey, McBurnett, Loeber, & Hart, 1995). Thus, there are those factors that concern behavioral tendencies such as novelty seeking, impulsiveness, hyperactivity, aggressivity, and low autonomic reactivity. It is obvious that these concepts overlap to an important extent, and it is not as yet clear which concept incorporates the main risk effect. There is a second set of risk factors associated with cognitive limitation of one kind or another—including inattention, verbal impairment, and an executive planning deficit (Moffitt, 1993a). Thirdly, there are atypical thought processes as represented by a hostile attributional style (Dodge et al., 1995) or an internalized model of insecure attachment (Greenberg, Speltz, & DeKlyen, 1993). Although the behavioral tendencies, cognitive limitations, and atypical thought processes sound as if they refer to quite different risk factors, it is likely that they overlap; we do not know their relative importance or indeed what sort of underlying liability they reflect.

The issues are well illustrated by the behavioral phenomenon of impulsiveness. At a descriptive level, this is usually indexed by features such as children not being able to wait for their turn, or blurting out answers in class before they are asked, or interrupting other people's conversations. The problem here is that this could reflect a cognitive tendency, a behavioral characteristic associated with oppositional behavior, or both. The epidemiological findings from the study undertaken by Taylor et al. (1996) indicated that these behaviors increased in both the hyperactive group and the conduct disorder group. A program of experimental studies is being undertaken in order to determine more precisely what is involved in the apparently impulsive behavior that is specifically associated with hyperactivity. The study by Sonuga-Barke and his colleagues (Sonuga-Barke, Taylor, Sembi, & Smith, 1992) illustrates the approach. An experimental design was used in which children could choose either an immediate reward or a delayed reward and in which the experimental setup could be manipulated to ensure that the economic ben-

MOTIVATION AND DELINQUENCY

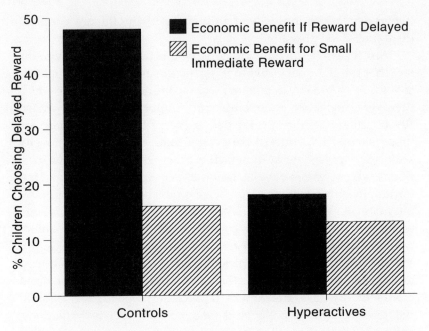

Figure 17. Reward-delay benefits and responses of hyperactive and control children (adapted from Sonuga-Barke at al., 1992).

efit to the child favored either a delayed reward or a smaller, but immediate, reward. Hyperactive children did not differ at all from controls in the experimental conditions in which the benefits were associated with a small immediate reward. By sharp contrast, however, the groups differed markedly when the economic benefit derived from a delayed reward (see Figure 17). This change in reward made virtually no difference in the hyperactive group, but in the control group, the children were much more likely to choose a delayed reward when it was beneficial for them to do so. On the other hand, when the experimental conditions were altered so that the children had to wait before they could proceed, regardless of which reward they chose, the hyperkinetic children tended to choose the delayed reward. It seemed that they had an aversion to delay that was not responsive to economic benefits, but they could wait if they had to. It may be concluded from the findings of Taylor's research program and the results of research undertaken by other investigators (Schachar, 1991; Schachar, Tannock & Logan, 1993) that the behavioral feature of impulsiveness in hyperkinetic children has several different bases when analysed at the level of neuropsychological process. First, the children show a lack of preparedness so that in circumstances when children can anticipate having to react in a particular way, hyperkinetic children show a prolonged reaction time. Second, they have difficulty suppressing or delaying a response (often called "inhibition") and hence tend to show unduly hasty responses when they would do better to take a little more time over their reactions. In different circumstances their reactions could therefore be either too quick or too slow. Third, there is a range of behavioral features for which further research is necessary to determine whether they can be explained in terms of these two processes. The tendency of hyperactive children to give inaccurate, careless responses could be due to hastiness; disorganized exploration of new situations could also be due to a premature and disinhibited response to most salient stimulus features. It remains to be seen whether these explanations will in fact hold.

Many of the earlier notions that a general deficit in attention constituted the basis of hyperactivity have had to be abandoned. Thus, children with a hyperkinetic disorder do not show impaired selective attention as was once thought to be the case. On the other hand, there is no doubt that cognitive limitations are a prominent part of what is involved in the hyperkinetic syndrome, and it remains quite possible that the key to the psychopathology will be found in some form of abnormality in cognitive processing. With respect to antisocial behavior, however, there is the additional question of whether the risk derives from some type of cognitive limitation or, rather, from the behavioral tendencies with which such cognitive features tend to be associated. The answer to that question will have to await further research.

Follow-up of Twins with Conduct Disorder

One possibly important aspect of heterogeneity in antisocial behavior concerns the persistence, or nonpersistence, from childhood into adult life. The pooled twin data from several studies of juvenile delinquency and adult crime showed that the genetic component in adult crime was substantially greater than that for juvenile delinquency (DiLalla & Gottesman, 1989). The finding is potentially important, but it is constrained by three pertinent limitations: the data were based on samples that were not entirely satisfactory; the results applied strictly to official crime records and not to antisocial behavior generally; the age difference derived from quite different samples, and there was uncertainty whether the difference was a consequence of the samples or the age. In order to examine possible age changes in heritability more directly, Simonoff and her colleagues undertook a systematic study of all twins with an IQ in the normal range who attended London's Maudsley Hospital when under the age of 16 years and who displayed an emotional or conduct disorder or some admixture of the two. Subjects with developmental disorders or psychoses were excluded.[9] The follow-up was confined to the twins who would be at least 25 years of age at the time of follow-up. All sets of twins were followed into adult life and were interviewed about their lifetime psychopathology and their life experiences, using systematic standardized investigator-based interview methods. At the time of writing, a few remaining twins have yet to be seen; the results are reported on the subsample of 15 monozygotic (MZ) pairs and 40 same-sex dizygotic (DZ) pairs, in both cases the sample being restricted to those where the designation of zygosity is definite. For present purposes, the 33 opposite-sexed dizygotic pairs are excluded, as are the pairs for whom complete data are available on only one member of the pair.

In keeping with the results from studies of singletons, conduct disorder in childhood proved to be a powerful predictor of antisocial personality disorder in adult life (the adult diagnosis being made without the requirement of childhood psychopathology). Nearly half of the individuals with conduct disorder in childhood showed antisocial personality disorder compared with only about 1 in 15 of those without conduct disorder. The within-pair correlations, treating antisocial behavior as a continuous dimension (rather than a present/absent category) at both age periods, showed a marked difference between childhood and adult life (see Figure 18). In childhood, the within-pair correlations for both MZ and DZ twins were moderately high, being just below the 0.5 level, but with no appreciable difference between the two types of twins. The implication is that shared environmental influences predominate. The finding is striking because the child patients with conduct disorder showed a good deal of psychopathology; by no stretch of the imagination did

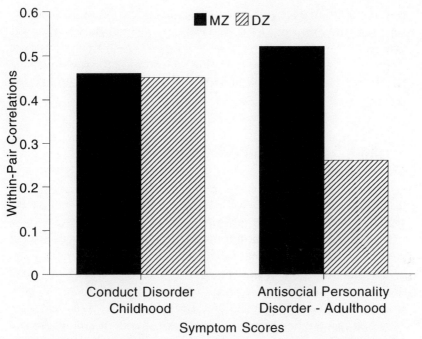

Figure 18. Within-pair correlations for MZ and DZ pairs on conduct problems in childhood and antisocial personality in adulthood (adapted from Simonoff et al., in press).

they fit the picture of relatively normal youngsters who happened to have committed a few delinquent acts. On the other hand, previous research had shown that family characteristics play a substantial role in children's referral to psychiatric clinics (Shepherd, Oppenheim, & Mitchell, 1971), and it was clear from both the contemporaneous case notes and the follow-up data that the majority of the young people came from extremely troubled families. Be that as it may, it was clear that environmental influences accounted for most of the variation and that a substantial proportion of the environmental effects were common to the two twins. The findings for adulthood were quite different. The within-pair MZ correlation was much the same, but slightly higher at just over 0.5, but the within-pair DZ correlation was just half the MZ correlation. The implication is that, within the same group of individuals, genetic factors play a greater role with respect to antisocial personality disorder in adulthood than with conduct disorder in childhood. Antisocial personality disorder, of course, applies to a much lower proportion of the general population than does conduct disorder in childhood. Further analyses to quantify findings more precisely will be undertaken when the sample is complete, but in the meanwhile it is clear that persistence or nonpersistence of antisocial behavior into adult life constitutes an important source of heterogeneity that needs to be taken into account.

Virginia Twin Study of Adolescent Behavioral Development

Genetic research strategies were applied to the study of antisocial behavior in the very much larger (some 1,400 twin pairs) general population sample of 8- to 16-year-olds in the Virginia Twin Study of Adolescent Behavioral Development (Eaves et al., in press; Hewitt et al., in press; Silberg, Meyer, et al., 1996; Silberg, Rutter, et al., 1996; Simonoff et al., in press).[10] This is a longitudinal study in which there will be at least three waves of data collection, but the present set of analyses is based on just the first wave. A wide range of both questionnaire and investigator-based standardized interviews were used.

So far, attention has focused mainly on the co-occurrence of hyperactivity and conduct disturbance. The first approach used maternal ratings exclusively and focused on the possible difference between the younger boys and the adolescents. In both age groups, the correlation between hyperactivity and conduct disturbance was substantial (a correlation of circa 0.4 to 0.5). However, the partitioning of the variance showed a contrast between the younger and older age groups. In the children, the overlap between hyperactivity and conduct disturbance was largely explicable in terms of the same genetic factors underlying both forms of psychopathology. By contrast, although that applied to a limited extent in the adolescent age period, the genetic components of hyperactivity and of conduct disturbance were largely separate and distinct (see Figure 19). Also, conduct disturbance differed from hyperactivity in showing a substantial effect from the shared environment in the adolescent age period.

A more detailed consideration of the possible mechanisms involved is provided by expansion of the data set to include both sexes and a wider range of measures from mothers, fathers, teachers, and

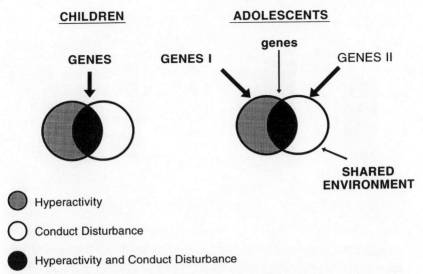

Figure 19. Genetic influences on the co-occurrence of hyperactivity and conduct disturbance in children and adolescents (adapted from Silberg et al., 1996).

the young people themselves. The first striking finding is the near-zero within-pair correlation for hyperactivity on maternal ratings for DZ pairs, as contrasted with within-pair correlations of 0.5 or above for maternal ratings of antisocial behavior in MZ pairs (Eaves et al., in press; Silberg, Rutter, et al., 1996). There are three main possible explanations for the near-zero within-pair correlations in DZ pairs for hyperactive behavior: the genetic component involves several interacting genes (i.e., epistasis); the interaction between the DZ twins serves to emphasize and exaggerate the difference between them; and when parents rate their twins they do so in ways that build on the contrast between them rather than in terms of comparison with children of the same age more generally. Both of the contrast explanations expect a greater variance in DZ pairs than MZ pairs whereas the gene-interaction hypothesis does not. The fact that, on the whole, we found greater variance in DZ pairs argues in favor of one or another of the contrast explanations.

Further light is shed by the introduction of data from the teacher questionnaires (see Figure 20). These showed a within-pair correlation for hyperactivity in DZ pairs of about 0.25—that is, substantially above zero. The difference from the maternal ratings strongly suggests a rating bias that derives from contrast effects. Statistical mod-

MOTIVATION AND DELINQUENCY

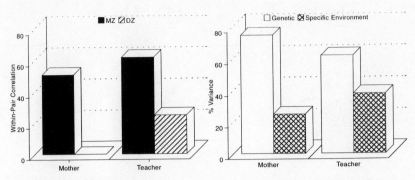

Figure 20. Within-pair correlations and genetic/environmental effects on hyperactivity as measured by mother and teacher questionnaires (adapted from Eaves et al., in press).

eling is in line with this inference and indicates that the genetic component for hyperactivity, once contrast effects have been taken into account, is somewhere in the region of 70% (Eaves et al., in press).

The findings for antisocial behavior, whether assessed by questionnaire or interview, were quite different. Both mother and child questionnaires for boys and girls showed a substantial environmental component that included both specific and shared elements. However, there was also a difference in findings that stemmed from whether the informant was the mother or the child and also whether the measurement was by questionnaire or standardized interview (see Simonoff et al., 1995). On the interview data, the environmental component was almost entirely child specific, whereas on the questionnaire measures there was also a substantial effect from the shared environment, especially in girls. The difference between mother and child reports (which applied to both interview and questionnaire measures) was that the genetic effect was at least twice as great on the mothers' reports as on the children's reports (see Figure 21 for findings on interview measures). Further analyses are required in order to determine exactly what these rater and instrument differences mean, although multivariate analyses indicate that rater bias is not likely to provide the main explanation (Simonoff et al., 1995). These differences have been found in other studies that have looked for them, so they clearly reflect nothing that is specific to the particular instruments that we used. The issue is not just that parents and children show relatively weak agreement in their reporting, but, rather, that the correlates of psychopathology differ ac-

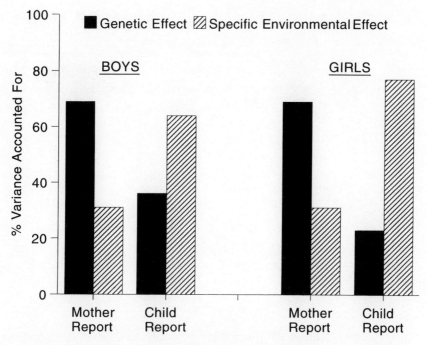

Figure 21. Genetic and environmental effects on conduct disturbance as assessed from interview with mothers and with children (adapted from Eaves et al., in press).

cording to who is reporting symptoms. A satisfactory solution to this problem has yet to be obtained because it is not known how this comes about.

Silberg, Meyer, et al. (1996) used latent class analyses in male adolescent twins, putting together data from all sources, in order to determine whether the findings could be used to infer different varieties of antisocial behavior. Using a conventional latent class analysis based on phenotypic data, four classes were derived: 1) a class of unaffected individuals with a generally low rate of psychopathology, with an estimated population prevalence of 72%; 2) a comorbid class with an estimated frequency of 14%, based upon moderately high endorsements of both hyperactivity and conduct disturbance from both mother and teacher questionnaires and, to a lesser extent, reading difficulties; 3) a class of children with conduct disturbance only, with an estimated prevalence of 8%, in which there were zero probabilities of endorsing hyperactivity items but a high probability of conduct problems, as shown on the modified version of the

Variations within Normal Range
(72% of population)

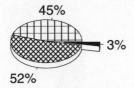

45%

3%

52%

Pure Conduct Disturbance
(8% of population)

97%

2% — 1%

Hyperactive - Conduct Disturbance
(14% of population)

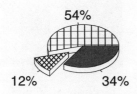

54%

12%   34%

Multisymptomatic Class
(6% of population)

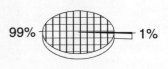

99%   1%

⊞ Additive Genes ⊠ Shared Environment ■ Unique Environment
■ Contrast Effect or Gene Interaction

Figure 22. Genetic evidence on heterogeneity of antisocial behavior (based on Silberg, Meyer et al., 1996).

Olweus scale, self-report ratings of oppositional and conduct problems from the child interview on the Child and Adolescent Psychiatric Assessment (CAPA) (Angold et al., 1995), reading difficulties, and, to a lesser extent, generalized anxiety; and 4) a multisymptomatic comorbid class consisting of individuals with a high probability of showing all the problem behaviors referred to above, with an estimated probability of about 6%.

As illustrated in the pie chart (Figure 22), these four classes differed dramatically in their partitioning of the variance within each class attributable to genetic and environmental effects. The multisymptomatic class showed variance that was almost entirely accounted for by genetic factors, whereas the pure conduct disturbance class showed variance that was almost entirely due to environmental factors of a shared kind. The hyperactive–conduct disturbance class was different yet again in that, although genetic factors predominated, rating contrast effects or dominant (interacting) genes were also important. The first class of relatively un-affected individuals showed additive genetic and shared environ-mental effects of roughly equal strength. For a variety of meth-odological reasons, it is likely that the true differences between these classes are not as great as these particular findings suggested (e.g., the differences between classes are as much a function of instru-ments as of types of psychopathology). But the genetic findings do suggest that there are both strongly genetic and strongly environ-mental varieties of antisocial behavior. The strongly genetic variety is one that involves a major admixture with hyperactive problems. The largely environmental variety is unassociated with hyperac-tivity; it particularly refers to antisocial behavior as reported by the adolescents themselves rather than their parents (and, therefore, is perhaps less likely to be accompanied by overt social malfunction) and probably is more likely to develop at a somewhat later age. Lon-gitudinal data will be needed to resolve some of these issues, but the genetic findings are at least consistent with the distinction drawn by Moffitt (1993b; Moffitt, Caspi, Dickson, Silva, & Stanton, 1996) be-tween the highly persistent, early-onset antisocial behavior and the transient adolescent-onset antisocial behavior.

All studies of antisocial behavior have noted the high frequency with which it is associated with mental disorder in parents. Probably the association is strongest with parental criminality, but it is also found with a wide range of other types of psychopathology (Far-rington, 1995a, 1995b; Rutter & Quinton, 1984). We sought to tackle this issue by using a latent class analysis, pooling the data for mothers and fathers, to derive composite classes of parental mental disorder (Shillady et al., 1996). The first class was made up of just over half the sample and included families in which neither parent had any appreciable psychopathology. The next two classes, pooled for present purposes and accounting for just over a third of the sam-ple, applied to families in which one or both parents had anxiety or depressive disorders. The last three classes, comprising some 13% of the overall sample, were made up of varied mixes of multiple paren-tal disorders including alcoholism and antisocial personality disor-der. The odds ratios for psychiatric disturbance in the children were determined for a range of disorders. For present purposes, the child diagnoses have been combined into broad groups of emotional dis-orders on the one hand and disruptive disorders on the other. There

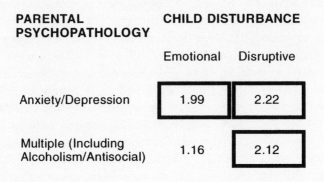

BOYS

PARENTAL PSYCHOPATHOLOGY	CHILD DISTURBANCE	
	Emotional	Disruptive
Anxiety/Depression	1.99	2.22
Multiple (Including Alcoholism/Antisocial)	1.16	2.12

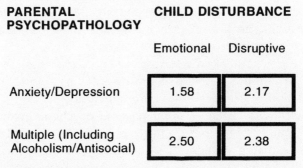

GIRLS

PARENTAL PSYCHOPATHOLOGY	CHILD DISTURBANCE	
	Emotional	Disruptive
Anxiety/Depression	1.58	2.17
Multiple (Including Alcoholism/Antisocial)	2.50	2.38

Figure 23. Odds ratios for psychiatric disturbance according to parental psychopathology (adapted from Meyer et al., 1996).

was little association between multiple parental disorders and emotional disturbance in the sons, but otherwise both the main classes of parental psychopathology were associated with an increased risk of both emotional disorders and disruptive disorders in both boys and girls (see Figure 23). With the possible exception of the association between parental affective disorder and persistent emotional disturbance in sons, the latter having a substantial genetic component (Shillady et al., 1996), this relative nonspecificity of risks for psychopathology in the children is similarly evident in other research (see Rutter, 1989). As already noted, mental disorder in parents is associated with a much increased risk of family dysfunction of various kinds and likely represents both a genetic risk factor and an environmental risk factor. Further analyses will be required to gain an understanding of how these different risk routes operate.

Finally, we have used the extended twin-family design provided by the Virginia Twin Study of Behavioral Development to test for environmentally mediated risks associated with measured environmental features and operating in a fashion that is shared across twin pairs. Although there is a vast literature on the associations between various forms of family dysfunction and antisocial behavior in the children, scarcely any of the research has utilized genetically sensitive designs. This is a crucial lack because of the consistent finding that parental criminality is one of the strongest predictors of antisocial behavior in the children and because parental criminality includes a substantial genetic component. The key consideration here, of course, is that parental criminality is itself associated with disorganized and discordant family functioning in many instances. Family dysfunction was assessed using maternal reports on Olsson's Family Adaptability and Togetherness Questionnaire (Olsson, Sprenkle, & Russel, 1979) and the Dyadic Adjustment Scale (Spanier, 1976), data on the childhood symptoms of conduct disorder shown by the parents were obtained using a standardized interview, and conduct disorder in the children was assessed using the CAPA interview (Angold et al., 1995). A path-analytic model was used to test hypotheses regarding the determinants of parent-offspring similarities for conduct disorder symptomatology (Eaves, Last, Young, & Martin, 1978). A series of submodels in which parameters were dropped from the full model, or constrained to equal other parameters, were also fitted to the data in order to determine which effects were significant.

As would be expected, there was substantial covariance between marital discord (as measured on the Spanier scale) and family dysfunction (as measured by the Olsson scale). However, the pattern of significant paths was somewhat different for these two putative environmental risk factors. Figure 24 provides a simplified model for the family origins of conduct disorder, concentrating on the paths that apply to family dysfunction. It should be noted, however, that the coefficients apply to the findings from the full model

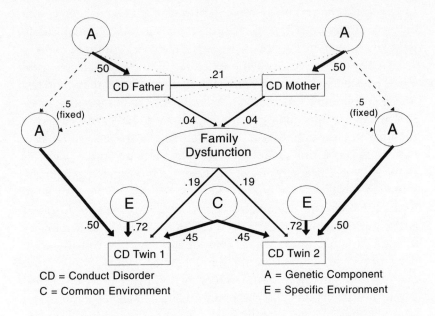

Figure 24. Simplified model for family origins of conduct disorder (adapted from Meyer et al., 1996).

Note: The figures in the body of the table all refer to path coefficients. Thus, .21 refers to the extent to which conduct disorder in the father is associated with the same feature in the mother. The coefficient of .50 on the path from A to CD Twin 1 and 2 refers to the genetic component; that of .72 to specific environmental effects; and that of .45 to shared environmental effects. The path coefficient of .19 from family dysfunction to CD Twin 1 and 2 refers to the shared environmental effect of this feature, after taking account of the other paths in the model.

and make mathematical sense only when the omitted coefficients are included. The main story, however, is evident in the figure shown. Having taken account of the rather weak association between the parental and child phenotypes, and the assortative mating between the parents, a significant environmentally mediated effect of family dysfunction was found. It accounts for only a rather small proportion of the shared environmental effect, and clearly other environmental factors will need to be examined. Nevertheless, these results provide a rigorously tested demonstration of the reality of an environmentally mediated risk for antisocial behavior that stems from family dysfunction.

Conclusions

Pulling together the findings from this program of research extending over the last 30 years demonstrates that the findings are as important in setting the agenda for the next 30 years as they are in showing what has been demonstrated in the past. Nevertheless, certain reasonably firm conclusions are possible.

When we initiated the research into antisocial behavior in the mid-1960s, little attention was being paid to the role of factors in the individual, and almost none to possible genetic factors. The main focus was on the supposed importance of broader social influences (such as poverty and social disadvantage) and of family breakdown and children's separations from their parents (see Rutter, 1972; Rutter & Madge, 1976; Rutter & Giller, 1983). School influences were regarded as unimportant, and there was a disregard of the extent to which children living in the same family differed in their experiences. There was also an almost complete neglect of the effects of children's behavior on their parents. All of that has changed as the result of research findings from many groups of investigators. Our own research has contributed to eight substantive conclusions on the causal factors involved in antisocial behavior.

First, it is clear that genetic factors play an important role in determining individual differences in at least some forms of antisocial behavior. The evidence indicates that this is most strikingly so in the case of antisocial behavior that is accompanied by hyperactivity. This subgroup tends to have an unusually early onset of antisocial behavior that also frequently leads to personality disorder in adult life. Perhaps it would not be much of a surprise if this finding of a strong genetic effect applied only to the severe, and uncommon, syndrome of hyperkinetic disorder, which affects perhaps some 2% of the population (Taylor, 1986; Taylor et al., 1991). After all, many clinicians have tended to view this disorder as representing some form of "organic" condition. But it is apparent that the genetic effect extends much more widely than that. The latent class analyses by Silberg, Meyer, et al. (1996) showed a predominant genetic effect in the two multisymptomatic classes that made up some 20% of the population. This also means that the findings cannot be restricted to the early-onset life course antisocial behavior that Moffitt (1993b) postulated to constitute a meaningful separate group (comprising some 5% of the general population) that differed from the much commoner transient adolescent-onset delinquent pattern. It seems likely, therefore, that the genetically influenced individual risk characteristics operate more widely (probably as a risk dimension) and that the degree to which these lead to persistent antisocial behavior that in turn leads to a personality disorder in adult life depends on the co-occurrence of other risk factors (see Moffitt et al., 1996).

Three main questions derive from this finding: What is the relationship between this common feature of hyperactivity and the rarer hyperkinetic disorder syndrome? What constitute the genetically influenced susceptibility traits for antisocial behavior? Does the risk for antisocial behavior that derives from hyperactivity require any kind of interplay with environmental risk factors? Taylor's research (1986; Taylor et al., 1991) has consistently shown very important differences between the hyperkinetic disorder and the other more common varieties of overactivity/inattention. In particular, the rarer syndrome includes a much stronger component of cognitive and neurodevelopmental impairment. The possibility that this syndrome is genetically, as well as clinically, distinct requires investigation (Eaves et al., 1993). Although the genetic component in antisocial behavior is particularly associated with hyperactivity, that does not necessarily mean that excess movement (or inattention) constitutes the key susceptibility trait. We have noted the heterogeneous range of behavioral and cognitive features that need to be considered.

The possibility of gene-environment interplay might, at first sight, seem a curious consideration to raise when the evidence suggests such a strong genetic effect for antisocial behavior associated with hyperactivity. It needs raising, nevertheless, for three different reasons: this broader class of hyperactivity–conduct disorder is associated with an increased rate of features thought to represent environmental risk factors; these risk factors have been shown to predict the longitudinal course of antisocial behavior; and the findings from adoptee studies suggest that gene-environment interactions apply with respect to antisocial behavior (Bohman, 1996; Cadoret, Yates, Troughton, Woodworth, & Stewart, 1995). Thus, Silberg, Meyer, et al. (1996) found that the multisymptomatic classes were associated with high rates of parental emotional disorder that, in turn, were accompanied by increased family discord and negative parent-child relationships, which predispose to a continuation of antisocial behavior (Rutter & Quinton, 1984). Also, the Taylor et al. (1996) follow-up study of children from 7 to 17 years of age showed that parental negatively experienced emotion predicted the persistence of psychopathology. Three possibilities need to be examined: the supposed environmental risk factors are epiphenomena that are genetically determined and unimportant in risk mediation; these factors stem from the effects of children's behavior on their families rather than the other way around (i.e., active or evocative person-environment correlations); and there is a crucial gene-environment interaction that is not detected in the usual twin analyses and that particularly concerns the *persistence* of antisocial behavior over the course of development (so requiring longitudinal data for their study). The specific study of the proximal processes involved in the interplay between nature and nurture in the genesis of antisocial behavior constitutes a major research priority (Rutter et al., in press).

The second conclusion concerns the role of environmental risk factors. Our genetic analyses demonstrate that they are very important in some forms of antisocial behavior—particularly variations within the normal range and antisocial behavior that is *not* accompanied by hyperactivity and that is reported by the adolescents themselves, rather than by their parents and teachers (Eaves et al., in press; Silberg, Meyer, et al., 1996). The question is what the environmental risk factors might be. The usual assumption is that family dysfunction and maladaptive parenting of one sort or another constitute the main causal factors. There is much evidence from other research that these are associated with early-onset antisocial behavior (Patterson, 1996). However, the epidemiological, longitudinal, and genetic findings all suggest that, on the whole, child-specific relationship features are more important than overall family characteristics. The crucial negative parenting features focused on individual children often derive from general family circumstances (such as discord), but the point is that they impinge differentially on individual children. It is these child-specific relationship problems (and other features such as surveillance, supervision, and effective feedback) that particularly require study.

However, our data, together with those of other researchers, emphasize that antisocial behavior tends to differ from other forms of psychopathology (and from most personality characteristics) in having a relatively strong shared environmental component. Because the "sharing" means that it affects all children in the same family to much the same degree, it is usually assumed that the risk stems from some family feature. Our findings suggest that this may not always be the case. The schools study findings point strongly to the importance of the school environment and of peer group influences. The time-trends data also suggest that population-wide factors (such as the changed meaning of adolescence and media influences) may be relevant. The crucial consideration is that because twins are of the same age, almost always attend the same school, and usually are in the same grade in school, they are much more likely than singleton siblings to share the same school and peer group influences. Insofar as they do, much of the school and peer group effects will appear as shared. The consequence is that a focus on subgroups of antisocial children in which shared environmental effects are strong may not be optimal for identifying family influences. The study of putative psychosocial causal factors needs to include school and peer group, as well as family, characteristics.

It is necessary, however, to go on to ask whether the pattern of environmental effects is likely to be the same in the more severe and pervasive forms of conduct disorder in the children who get referred to psychiatric clinics. Simonoff's twin study of this group (Simonoff, 1996), albeit based on a small sample, which calls for caution in generalizing findings, was striking in its evidence of a strong shared environmental effect. Because manifold chronic family problems were usual in this patient sample, it is most unlikely that they did not play some kind of key causal role. The results serve as a reminder that twin and adoptee studies both tend to include rather few severely disorganized families and, hence, may not be best placed to investigate the effects on children of those more extreme family environments. In general, epidemiologically based general population twin samples are to be preferred over clinic ones, but this is an instance in which a much enlarged clinic sample would be most informative.

The third conclusion concerns the important role of adult experiences in modifying the course of antisocial behavior. There are two features of our findings on this issue that stand out. First, there is the importance of investigating the course of antisocial behavior over long periods of time, with a recognition that major changes take place during the transition from adolescence to adult life, and that these changes are often systematically associated with current life circumstances in adulthood. This is an age period that particularly warrants further study for three main reasons. First, it is in the early and mid-20s that antisocial behavior decreases markedly in the general population. Second, this is a time when most young people leave school and have an increasingly wide range of activities outside the confines of the family. This means that there is a greater chance of *dis*continuity in environmental circumstances (and hence a greater opportunity for turning-point effects to occur). Third, early adult life is a time when people tend to have a much greater scope for selecting and shaping their environments. The last point leads to the second key feature of our findings; namely, that environments brought about as a result of the actions or behavior of the individuals themselves may nevertheless make a major impact on their subsequent functioning. The appreciation that the *origin* of a risk (or protective) factor has no necessary connection with its mode of risk (or protective) mediation has important research, as well as practical, implications (Rutter, Silberg, & Simonoff, 1993).

To date, there are no good longer-term published follow-up studies of individuals who have experienced an apparent change from a risk path to a more adaptive life trajectory (although we have such a data set that is now being analysed). The question to explore is whether the beneficial adult experiences bring out a lasting change in the liability to antisocial behavior or whether they are associated only with context-dependent changes in the actualization of a preexisting propensity.

The fourth conclusion is a development of the same point about adult experiences; namely, that the *course* of antisocial behavior is, to a considerable extent, dependent on indirect chain reactions. In the past, there has often been a tendency to assume that it was only *changes* in behavior that required explanation because trait persistence is the "norm." That represents a misunderstanding of what happens in development; growth (psychological and physical) involves both change and consistency (Rutter, 1996d; Rutter & Rutter, 1993). Our findings, together with those from other longitudinal studies (e.g., Caspi, Elder, & Bem, 1987, 1988), suggest a developmental process that reflects a series of interconnected probabilistic links in which continuity is influenced by the effects of people's behavior in selecting their environments and in shaping other people's responses to them.

The fifth conclusion is that it is highly likely that cognitive factors play two rather different roles in their influence on the origins and course of antisocial behavior. On the one hand, the findings on young children with the hyperkinetic disorder strongly point to fairly direct risk effects. Although long dismissed by criminologists, neuropsychological deficits may well be involved in the causal processes underlying that disorder and, therefore, in the antisocial behavior with which it is associated (Moffitt, 1993a). The follow-up data of Taylor et al. (1996) suggest that the antisocial consequences mainly come about as part of a pattern of more widespread social malfunction, rather than as an effect on lawbreaking as such. Nevertheless, the associations are quite strong, and there is a strong need for neuropsychological research (which will need to use experimental designs) to determine which cognitive processes are involved.

On the other hand, in a follow-up of children with severe reading difficulties, Maughan, Pickles, et al. (1996) suggested that the antisocial behavior shown by the children is likely to involve more indirect effects. The antisocial behavior was *less,* not more, likely to persist into adult life in young people with severe reading problems, and the predictive power of hyperactivity was less. The finding of the antisocial tendency was *not* a consequence of the individuals' acquiring good reading skills, because the reading difficulties were remarkably likely to persist into adult life (Maughan, Hagell, et al., 1994). Rather, the general improvement in social functioning and loss of psychopathology (in many, but not all, of the poor readers) seemed to stem from moving out of the educational environment in which they were failing and from gaining alternative sources of satisfaction and reward. It should be added, however, that this relatively good outcome applied to a group of young people who left school to seek jobs at a time of very low unemployment. Whether the same would apply in the much less favorable conditions operating today in the United Kingdom is another matter.

The sixth conclusion we draw is that any consideration of the course of antisocial behavior needs to examine its consequences, as well as its causes. Up to now, researchers have tended to pay most attention to alcohol abuse and drug use, which are quite strongly associated with antisocial behavior. That constitutes one focus of our own research (not reported here), but it is equally necessary to pay attention to the association with depression and other forms of emotional disturbance. Although little recognized in the past, the data indicate that conduct problems in childhood, even when they are *not* associated with emotional difficulties in that age period, constitute quite an important precursor of emotional disturbance in early adult life (as well as predisposing to suicidal behavior—Harrington et al., 1994). Our findings suggest that this important effect may derive, in part, from the tendency of antisocial individuals to act in ways that generate stressful interpersonal interactions and life circumstances for themselves. More generally, however, the results raise the crucial question of the role of personality disturbances in predisposition to depression. To what extent, for example, is poor parenting in early childhood a risk factor for depression (Harris, Brown, & Bifulco, 1990), not because it predisposes to depression as such, but because it predisposes to personality disorder? Similarly, does part of the genetic liability to depression reflect a liability to personality disturbance?

Although not a main focus in our own research, clearly the consequences of antisocial behavior include societal responses, the possible effects of labeling and the results of court decisions. As shown, for example, by the Sampson and Laub (1993) findings on the negative impact of incarceration (i.e., people who had been in prison found it more difficult to get jobs, and those out of work were more likely to return to crime), these consequences may well affect the likelihood that antisocial behavior persists.

A seventh conclusion from our research concerns the connections between distal and proximal risk processes. Thus, the comparative study of children in London and the Isle of Wight showed that child rearing in an inner-city area was associated with a doubling of the risk for conduct disorder—a geographical effect reflecting a distal risk. The finding that the effect was largely mediated through family discord, disorganization, and disadvantage indicated that the proximal process lay within the home and not in the children's interactions in the community. However, our more detailed studies of high-risk families went further in their demonstration that the main risk actually lay in child-specific adverse parent-child relationships rather than family-wide features. Thus, it was possible (indeed, necessary) to move from a very broad social risk indicator (i.e., child rearing in inner London) to a specific dyadic nonshared environmental risk process. The finding that the geographical area effect especially applied to early-onset chronic disorders strongly suggests that the risk processes apply to a basic liability to antisocial behavior. By contrast, this may well not be the case with either school influences or some of the societal factors that underlie the rise in crime over the last half-century. It has not been possible as yet, however, to determine the proximal processes involved.

An eighth conclusion is that study of the risk processes for antisocial behavior needs to include biological factors, but that the most profitable group to investigate in that connection is the small subgroup with hyperkinetic disorder. The particular need here is to focus on the cognitive processing abnormalities and to use functional imaging methods to determine their neural basis.

Finally, the whole body of research strongly underlines the need for both longitudinal data and genetically sensitive designs; for high-risk as well as general population samples; for a combination of dimensional and categorical measurement; for discriminating measures of environmental risk factors that operate in both a shared and nonshared fashion; and for a choice of well-designed measures and samples to test competing hypotheses on the varied range of causal questions that need to be tackled.

Model of Motivational Influences

Finally, we need to return to our starting point: the motivation of antisocial behavior. In doing so, we seek to integrate our findings with those of other research (see Cornish & Clarke, 1986; Farrington, 1995a; Felson & Tedeschi, 1993a, 1993b; Gottfredson & Hirschi, 1990; Heimer & Matsueda, 1994; Jessor, Donovan, & Costa, 1991; Loeber & Hay, 1994; Osgood, Wilson, O'Malley, Bachman, & Johnston, 1996; Patterson, 1982; Patterson, Reid, & Dishion, 1992; Rutter & Giller, 1983; Sampson & Laub, 1993; Tedeschi & Felson, 1994). The concepts and explanatory terms used by different commentators, reviewers, and theorists vary greatly, but there has been an increasing recognition that no single theory provides an adequate explanation. That is scarcely surprising because, as we noted at the outset, antisocial behavior includes a wide range of acts spanning status violations (such as truancy), illegal pleasures (e.g., drug use, joyriding, and other activities involving the thrills of risk taking and power assertion), acquisitive acts such as theft (with or without instrumental aggression), and hostile aggression both against property (e.g., vandalism) and persons (e.g., assault or homicide). The continuity between antisocial behavior in childhood and personality disorder in adult life also raises the query on the extent to which the defining criterion concerns *anti*social behavior or social *incompetence*.

Moreover, there is a growing body of evidence on the heterogeneity of antisocial patterns (Rutter, in press-a). Possibly the best validated (although even here the evidence is sparse) are the distinctions between conduct disorder associated with hyperactivity and "pure" conduct disorder (Taylor et al., 1991), and between early-onset, life-course-persistent antisocial behavior and late-onset, adolescence-limited delinquency (Moffitt, 1993b; Moffitt et al., 1996; Patterson, 1996). It appears that early-onset, life-course delinquency is associated with hyperactivity/inattention, poor social skills, varied and pervasive antisocial behaviors, associated family disorganization and coercive cycles of interpersonal interaction, and a strong genetic component. By contrast, adolescent-onset delinquency involves a lesser (but still increased) antisocial propensity accompanied by relative social competence and a lack of hyperactivity (see Patterson & Yoerger, this volume). It has to be added that, because oppositional/defiant disorders are so common in early childhood, there must also be an early-onset transient variety, about which we have fewer data. Equally, it is known that some late-onset varieties of delinquencies persist into adult life.

In addition, there may be a valid distinction between violent and nonviolent crime in adult life (see Bock & Goode, 1996); some antisocial behavior stems from mental illness; rare cases derive from medical conditions; and some cases represent highly principled moral acts (e.g., some aspects of the civil rights movement or the fight against apartheid). Is an entirely different motivational explanation needed for each of these varieties? We suggest not (at least for antisocial behavior not due to some overt illness). However, in putting forward a general model it is essential to note that very few data are available on antisocial behavior in females or in middle-class groups. Accordingly, although the explanations for these groups are

Figure 25. Schematic model of proximal motivational influences.

likely to include similar components, there may well be important differences. Nevertheless, the overall model of possibly operative causal factors is probably broadly similar across a range of antisocial behavior despite the critical fact that their relative importance, and the specifics of their operation, are likely to vary substantially both according to act (e.g., theft vs. violence vs. vandalism vs. sex offences) and person (male vs. female; white collar vs. blue collar; or differences among ethnic groups). That variation is crucially important, as we have emphasized here, but now we need to place the heterogeneity within a broader framework.

Figure 25 sets out the six broad groups of factors that may play a part in the causal processes leading to the commission of some antisocial act. That labeled *Antisocial Liability* recognizes the importance of individual differences in people's propensity to engage in antisocial behavior. That labeled *(Dis)inhibiting Features* reflects the fact that, despite individual differences, everyone has some potential for antisocial behavior; whether or not individuals engage in delinquent acts will be influenced by the strength of inhibitory controls. The other four factors serve as a reminder that a propensity to act antisocially is one thing, but the commission of a particular delinquent act is another. It will be dependent on available *Opportunities, Situational Presses* that foster antisocial activities, *Emotional Provocation*, and the individual's personal *Assessment of Cost-Benefits* of commit-

ANTISOCIAL LIABILITY	(DIS)INHIBITING FEATURES
Values	Values
Indirect Susceptibility Traits (e.g., impulsivity or novelty-seeking)	(Lack of) Anxiety
Learned Behavioral Patterns (e.g., aggression, self-seeking acquisition)	(Lack of) Empathy for Others
Cognitive Processing of Experiences (e.g., tendency to attribute hostile intent)	(Lack of) Internal Controls/Inhibitions
Reactivity to Environmental Adversities	
	(Lack of) Long-term Planning/Foresight
Lack of Status Attributes (e.g., high IQ, educational attainments social position, admired social qualities)	(Lack of) Surveillance/ External Controls
Previous Experiences	
"Permission" for Antisocial Behaviors (e.g., Cultural, contextual, media influences)	Alcohol / Drugs

Figure 26. Antisocial liability and (dis)inhibiting features.

ting the delinquent act (note the actual cost-benefits are not what matters; rather, it is the person's own assessment, however inaccurate and misguided, that will influence action).

The summary of some of the key aspects of an antisocial liability provided in Figure 26 emphasizes its multifaceted nature. Values favoring antisocial activities include an acceptance of the use of illegal drugs for their pleasurable effects as normal and desirable; the acceptability to many people of fiddling with income tax or expense returns or using a work telephone for private calls; and the perceived appropriateness in some groups of assaulting someone who insults you. The research findings on hyperactivity underline the importance of behavioral traits such as impulsivity or sensation seeking that do not in themselves concern antisocial features but that nevertheless, in some circumstances, create a susceptibility, or increased risk, for antisocial behavior. In addition, of course, there are learned antisocial behaviors (but subject to genetic influences) that lead more directly to delinquent activities (see Patterson, 1982, 1996; Patterson & Yoerger, this volume). The likelihood that someone will respond with violence to a negative interpersonal interaction will be influenced by their inference of the person's intent; the work of Dodge (1986; Dodge et al., 1986) has shown that aggressive boys show an increased liability to attribute hostile intent. All research into the effects of psychosocial stresses and adversities has indicated the importance of individual differences in vulnerability, and adoptee studies have suggested that part of the effects of genetic predisposition may lie in a greater susceptibility to environmental hazards (Bohman, 1996; Cadoret, Cain, & Crowe, 1983; Cadoret et al., 1995).

Our own research, like that of others, has shown that low educational attainment predisposes to antisocial behavior in childhood. The finding that it does not do so in adult life suggests that the connection is likely to be indirect, and perhaps reflects the many disadvantages experienced at school by children who fail educationally. As Tedeschi (this volume) notes, the social strain theory of delinquency has only rather modest empirical support, but it is likely that a lack of status attributes may predispose to antisocial behavior to some extent. Thus, unpopularity among peers is a risk factor (Parker & Asher, 1987), and a range of other personal qualities appear to have effects mediated through their impact on interpersonal interactions and attitudes (Engfer, Walper, & Rutter, 1994).

Labeling theorists have argued that judicial processing increases the likelihood that someone will continue his or her delinquent activities, and there is some evidence that this effect does operate to a limited extent on the first occasion, although probably not with subsequent offences (see Rutter & Giller, 1983). The precise mechanisms are ill-understood, but probably part of the explanation lies in the fact that, with most risky behaviors, there seems to be a diminishing resistance once there has been the first crossing of the prohibited threshold (whether the behavior is sexual activity, smoking, violence, or theft). Probably the process is enhanced by the person coming to accept, through public labeling, that he or she is someone who behaves in that way.

In addition, both at the individual and community-wide levels, a liability to engage in antisocial behavior will be influenced by the "permission" afforded by the impression that "everyone does it," especially admired role models, and that it brings rewards. There is evidence that portrayals of violence in the media operate in this way (Wartella, 1995), and, more arguably, it is possible that an awareness that some politicians get away with lying and cheating (over financial matters, arms deals, and other issues) and that some leaders of commerce can and do award themselves huge increases in salary while keeping down the wages of employees and making workers redundant creates an image that personal greed at the expense of others is both acceptable and rewarding.

Figure 26 summarizes some of the key facets of inhibiting or disinhibiting influences. Values are again influential in terms of an acceptance or lack of acceptance of qualities such as honesty, respect for others, and nonviolent solutions to problems. Empirical findings have shown that delinquents tend to have a diminished autonomic reactivity (Lahey et al., 1995; Raine, in press; Raine, Venables, & Williams, 1996), and it would seem that a low anxiety is likely to make it easier to engage in high-risk activities.

A lack of empathy for others has been one of the features most emphasized in writings on psychopathy and antisocial personality disorder (Hare, 1986), and possibly an awareness of the feelings of victims to some extent may inhibit person-directed criminal acts. Delinquents often define their crimes as ones that have no victim (because the theft is from an organization or because the person's loss will be covered by insurance). It is striking, however, that the population subgroups most likely to commit crimes are also the ones most likely to be victims (Rutter & Giller, 1983). Either delinquents do not feel a strong group identity, or if they do, they are not inhibited by a shared group identity with their victims.

Developmental studies have shown that the acquisition of sets of standards is a universal milestone in early childhood that probably derives from the growing cognitive capacity to appreciate other people's expectations and to recognize how things should be (Kagan, 1981). Although this acquisition is universal, the specifics of the standards that become internalized are more variable, are influenced by upbringing at home and at school, and are likely to create a greater or lesser tendency to inhibit antisocial inclinations.

Our studies, like those of others (Clausen, 1993) have shown the importance of a tendency to plan ahead with respect to key life choices and transitions. Planners tend to show better social functioning in adult life and are less likely to engage in antisocial activities. Probably, it is not so much that planning inhibits antisocial behavior directly, but rather that it enhances positive behavior and creates life situations that make crime a less necessary, and a less desirable, solution to life problems.

The control of delinquent activities brought about both by monitoring and supervision within the family (Patterson, 1982, 1996; Patterson & Yoerger, this volume) and by external surveillance in public places (Clarke, 1985, 1992) is well documented.

Finally the role of drugs and alcohol in reducing inhibitions is well established. There is some limited evidence that their use makes recourse to violence (to persons and property) more likely (Fergusson, Lynskey, & Horwood, 1996; Rutter, 1996a; Sumner & Parker, 1995), although there is probably less effect on theft.

This general model of antisocial liability and disinhibitory features is similar to that put forward by many other writers. What our own research has emphasized, however, is that community, school, and peer group characteristics, as well as family upbringing, are important; that hyperactivity constitutes an important individual risk factor; that genetic factors are more important for some forms of antisocial behavior than often appreciated; that both genetic and environmental influences operate through a variety of routes both direct and indirect; that the causal chains often involve multiple indirect links; that important changes can still take place in adult life; and that the influences on antisocial behavior that continues into adult life may not be the same as those that are concerned with the initiation of antisocial behavior in childhood.

Our own work has not, for the most part, focused on the specific circumstances that led someone to commit a delinquent act in a particular situation at a particular time, but those are a key feature of other chapters in this volume (see Heimer & Matsueda; McCord; Patterson & Yoerger; Tedeschi). It is necessary, however, to summarize here some of the operative mechanisms because many are the end product of the longer-term causal processes that we have studied. Thus, criminal activities are more likely to occur when there are good opportunities for them (see Figure 27 for a summary of some of the elements in opportunities, situational "presses," provoking features, and perceptions of cost-benefits). Although we lack sure knowledge on the causes of the major rise in crime over the last half-century, it is likely that the greater range of goods to steal brought about by increasing affluence may have played a role (Rutter & Smith, 1995). The much greater availability and acceptability of hand-

OPPORTUNITIES

Accessible Goods to Steal

Confrontational Situation

Unsupervised Time
(while playing truant, unemployed)

Available Means
(e.g., weapons)

SITUATIONAL 'PRESSES'

Group Activity
- Gangs
- Protest Situations
- Conflict Situations

Antisocial Models ———— Activities of
Other People

Previous Antisocial
Acts (broken windows,
graffiti, etc.)

PROVOKING FEATURES

Anger

Frustration

Lack of Alternative Rewards

Need for
- Material Resources
- Power
- Status

Resentment

PERCEPTION OF COST-BENEFITS

Material Rewards

Respect/Fear/Admiration by Others

Justice Justification

Achievement of Power Control

Figure 27. Opportunities, situational "presses," provoking features, perception of cost-benefits.

guns in the United States is almost certainly a major factor underlying its massively higher homicide rate compared with all European countries. It is not, of course, that having a gun makes people want to kill; rather, when someone feels under threat or wishes to be aggressive, death is more likely to result if the individual has a means of causing death ready to hand. Note, too, that the availability and acceptability of guns may constitute a prime explanation for the between-country differences in homicide rate without their playing much of a role in individual differences within a country (because variations in availability and acceptability within a country are so much smaller).

Doubtless, truancy and unemployment predispose to crime through various different routes, but one of the mechanisms is that both provide unsupervised time during which it is easier to engage in delinquent acts (Osgood et al., 1996).

Another sort of opportunity is provided by confrontational situations, either individual or group. Antisocial individuals tend to quarrel with other people, to challenge aggressively, and to provoke arguments (Robins, 1966). Not surprisingly, these provide increased opportunities for an escalation into assault that contravenes the law. The same applies to the tendency for such individuals to "hang out" with others in groups that seek confrontation in order to assert dominance.

These situations also often provide situational "presses" deriving both from group activities that seem to give "permission" to behave in ways that might not be acceptable in individual circumstances and from models of antisocial behavior. Thus, people acting as members of a gang often undertake acts of violence (including rape and killing) that they might find unacceptable when on their own. Protest marches, similarly, all too often seem to provide legitimacy for violence, looting, and other forms of antisocial behavior. The confrontational situations provided by some soccer matches in Europe, regrettably, seem to serve a similar purpose.

Models of antisocial behavior are also important in both interpersonal and situational terms. Thus, the group situations noted above all provide models of *other* people behaving in antisocial ways that seem to provide a "press" for the individual to do the same. But physical circumstances have been shown to have the same effect (Rutter & Giller, 1983). Thus, buildings that already have broken windows or graffiti are more likely to be vandalized than ones kept in good repair. Our schools research showed the same finding (Rutter et al., 1979).

Provoking features have probably been most investigated in relation to interpersonal aggression. Anger, frustration, and resentment all make violence more likely (Geen, 1995; Zillmann, 1979). One feature of our own research is the finding that a high proportion of antisocial individuals exhibit emotional disturbance and hence may be more vulnerable to these emotion-provoking features. But our results, like those of others, also underline the extent to which adults who were antisocial children frequently are in situations in which they lack alternative rewards (because they are unemployed or in low-paying jobs), they lack status (through work or other activities), and they have financial needs (because of a dependent family, a drug habit, or gambling). All create "incentives" for crime and a lack of incentives for prosocial and socially productive activities.

Finally, people's actions will be influenced by their assessment of the cost-benefits of antisocial behavior. The literature includes many debates on the extent to which antisocial behavior is rational and determined by people's analysis of the rewards to be obtained and the costs to be paid. There is no reason to regard antisocial behavior as different from other behavior in this connection. With the rare exceptions of criminal acts deriving directly from mental illness, antisocial acts are conscious, deliberate, and considered. Accordingly, they will be driven by the perception of material rewards, by the "justified" settling of scores stemming from other people's negative behavior, by the achievement of power and control, and by the earning of other people's fear, respect, or admiration. Research findings, however, put an important perspective on this decision making by their demonstration of the tendency to act for the moment rather than for the future (a lack of "planning"), to make decisions impulsively without a proper appraisal of the cost-benefits, to perceive hostile intent by others on the slightest provocation, and to arrive in situations where there is a limited range of alternative actions. The decision may be no less "rational" than those taken by others, but its outcome is likely to have been shaped to a major extent by both operative situations and by the person's decision-making style. What happens at the moment of deciding to commit an antisocial act is important, but our research emphasizes the crucial lifespan precursors that shape that decision.

Those precursors include genetically influenced individual characteristics. The notion that genes play a role in antisocial behavior has been violently rejected by some social scientists on the wholly mistaken assumption that it represents biological determinism leading to a search for "the gene for crime." Nothing could be further from the truth (Rutter, 1996b, 1996c). Genes play a role in motivation, *not* because there could be a genetic propensity for theft or homicide, but rather because motivation stems from the emotions and thought processes of an individual in a particular social context. Individual characteristics, resulting from the additive and interactive combination of genetic and environmental factors, are important because they influence a person's overall susceptibility to particular emotions and cognitions; because they affect the likelihood of reacting in particular ways as a consequence of social skills, behavioral habits, and social standing; and because individual characteristics also serve to shape and select the social contexts in which the individuals operate. The motivation to commit a certain act at a specific time and place is the end result of both developmental processes within the individual and of societal forces that are created by the individuals in that society and that, in turn, through social group processes, influence the actions of those individuals.

This overview of our multifaceted research program into antisocial behavior provides just a few frames from a film reel that still has a long way to run. The growth in understanding antisocial behavior from the research undertaken over the last three decades is considerable, but it has to be said that the answers to the questions with which we started have also provided us with a better indication of the many questions still to be tackled in the years to come.

NOTES

1. Research for the Isle of Wight–London comparison was supported by funding from the (U.S.) Foundation for Child Development and the (British) Social Science Research Council. The research workers who played a key role in the work included Michael Berger, Antony Cox, David Quinton, Olwen Rowlands, Michael Rutter, Celia Tupling, Bridget Yule, and William Yule.

2. This research on schools was supported by funding from the (British) Department of Education and Science and the Medical Research Council. The research workers who played a key role in the work included Barbara Maughan, Peter Mortimore, Janet Ouston, and Michael Rutter.

3. The study of families of mentally ill patients was supported by funding from the Invalid Children's Aid Association, the Medical Research Council, and the W. T. Grant Foundation. The research workers who played a key role in the work included Christine Liddle, David Quinton, and Michael Rutter.

4. The study of secular trends was supported by funding from the Johann Jacobs Foundation and the Medical Research Council. David Smith and Michael Rutter were the key workers responsible for the aspects of the study reported here.

5. Follow-up research on children with depressive disorders was supported by funding from the John D. and Catherine T. MacArthur Foundation and the Medical Research Council. The research workers who played a key role in the work included Diana Bredenkamp, Christine Groothues, Hazel Fudge, Richard Harrington, and Michael Rutter. Mayer Ghodsian and Andrew Pickles were responsible for the analyses of the National Child Development Study data.

6. This longitudinal research on London children was supported by funding from the Medical Research Council. The research workers who played a key role included Lorna Champion, Gillian Goodall, Ann Hagell, Barbara Maughan, Andrew Pickles, Michael Rutter, and William Yule.

7. This follow-up of children reared in group foster homes was supported by the Foundation for Child Development, Social Science Research Council, the W. T. Grant Foundation, and the Medical Research Council. The research workers who played a key role in the work included Barbara Maughan, Andrew Pickles, David Quinton, and Michael Rutter.

8. This research on hyperkinetic disorder was supported by the Medical Research Council and the John D. and Catherine T. MacArthur Foundation. The research workers who played a key role in the work included Oliver Chadwick, Susan Giles, Ellen Heptinstall, Michael Rutter, Seija Sandberg, Russell Schachar, Edmund Sonuga-Barke, Geoffrey Thorley, Eric Taylor, and Jody Warner-Rogers.

9. This follow-up research on twins with conduct disorder was funded by the Wellcome Trust and the Medical Research Council. The research workers who played a key role in the work included James Elander, Janet Holmshaw, Robin Murray, Andrew Pickles, Michael Rutter, and Emily Simonoff.

10. The Virginia Twin Study of Adolescent Behavioral Development was funded by NIMH grants, MH 45268 and MH, by the Medical Research Council, and by Junior Faculty Research Awards to Joanne Meyer and Judy Silberg, for the John D. and Catherine T. MacArthur Foundation. The research workers who played a key role in the work included Lindon Eaves, John Hewitt, Rolf Loeber, Hermine Maes, Joanne Meyer, Andrew Pickles, Michael Rutter, Lucinda Shillady, Judy Silberg, and Emily Simonoff.

REFERENCES

Anderson, K. E., Lytton, H., & Romney, D. M. (1986). Mothers' interactions with normal and conduct-disordered boys: Who affects whom? *Developmental Psychology, 22,* 604–609.

Angold, A., Prendergast, M., Cox, A., Harrington, R., Simonoff, E., & Rutter, M. (1995). The Child and Adolescent Psychiatric Assessment (CAPA). *Psychological Medicine, 25,* 739–753.

Bell, R. Q. (1968). A reinterpretation of the direction of effects in studies of socialization. *Psychological Review, 75,* 81–95.

Berger, M., Yule, W., & Rutter, M. (1975). Attainment and adjustment in two geographical areas: 2. The prevalence of specific reading retardation. *British Journal of Psychiatry, 126,* 510–519.

Bock, G. R., & Goode, J. A. (Eds.). (1996). *Genetics of criminal and antisocial behaviour.* Ciba Foundation Symposium No. 194. Chichester, England, & New York: Wiley.

Bohman, M. (1996). Predisposition to criminality: Swedish adoption studies in retrospect. In G. R. Bock & J. A. Goode (Eds.), *Genetics of criminal and antisocial behaviour. Ciba Foundation Symposium 194* (pp. 99–114). Chichester, England, & New York: Wiley.

Brown, G. W., & Harris, T. O. (1978). *Social origins of depression: A study of psychiatric disorder in women.* London: Tavistock.

Cadoret, R. J., Cain, C. A., & Crowe, R. R. (1983). Evidence for gene-environment interaction in the development of adolescent antisocial behavior. *Behavior Genetics, 13*, 301–310.

Cadoret, R. J., Yates, W. R., Troughton, E., Woodworth, G., & Stewart, M. A. (1995). Genetic-environmental interaction in the genesis of aggressivity and conduct disorders. *Archives of General Psychiatry, 52*, 916–924.

Caron, C., & Rutter, M. (1991). Comorbidity in child psychopathology: Concepts, issues and research strategies. *Journal of Child Psychology and Psychiatry, 32*, 1063–1080.

Caspi, A., Elder, G. H., Jr., & Bem, D. J. (1987). Moving against the world: Life course patterns of explosive children. *Developmental Psychology, 23*, 308–313.

———. (1988). Moving away from the world: Life course patterns of shy children. *Developmental Psychology, 24*, 824–831.

Caspi, A., & Moffitt, T. E. (1993). When do individual differences matter? A paradoxical theory of personality coherence. *Psychological Inquiry, 4*, 247–271.

Champion, L. A., Goodall, G. M., & Rutter, M. (1995). Behavioural problems in childhood and stressors in early adult life: A 20-year follow-up of London school children. *Psychological Medicine, 25*, 231–246.

Clarke, R. V. (1985). Jack Tizard memorial lecture: Delinquency, environment and intervention. *Journal of Child Psychology and Psychiatry, 26*, 505–523.

Clarke, R. V. (Ed.). (1992). *Situational crime prevention: Successful case studies.* New York: Harrow & Heston.

Clausen, J. A. (1993). *American lives: Looking back at the children of the Great Depression.* New York: Free Press.

Cloninger, C. R., Adolfsson, R., & Svrakic, N. M. (1996). Mapping genes for human personality. *Nature Genetics, 12*, 3–4.

Cornish, D. B., & Clarke, R. V. (Eds.). (1986). *The reasoning criminal.* New York: Springer-Verlag.

DiLalla, L. F., & Gottesman, I. I. (1989). Heterogeneity of causes for delinquency and criminality: Lifespan perspectives. *Development and Psychopathology, 1*, 339–349.

Dodge, K. A. (1986). A social information processing model of social competence in children. In M. Perlmutter (Ed.), *Eighteenth Annual Minnesota Symposium of Child Psychology* (pp. 77–125). Hillsdale NJ: Lawrence Erlbaum.

Dodge, K. A., Pettit, G. S., Bates, J. E., & Valente, E. (1995). Social information-processing patterns partially mediate the effects of early physical abuse on later conduct problems. *Journal of Abnormal Psychology, 104*, 632–643.

Dodge, K. A., Pettit, G. S., McClaskey, C. L., & Brown, M. (1986). Social competence in children. *Monographs of the Society for Research in Child Development, 51*(2, Serial No. 213).

Eaves, L. J., Last, K. A., Young, P. A., & Martin, N. G. (1978). Model-fitting approaches to the analysis of human behavior. *Heredity, 41*, 249–320.

Eaves, L. J., Silberg, J., Hewitt, J. K., Meyer, J., Rutter, M., Simonoff, E., Neale, M., & Pickles, A. (1993). Genes, personality, and psychopathology: A latent class analysis of liability to symptoms of attention-deficit hyperactivity disorder in twins. In R. Plomin & G. E. McClearn (Eds.), *Nature, nurture, and psychology* (pp. 285–303). Washington DC: American Psychological Association.

Eaves, L. J., Silberg, J. L., Meyer, J. M., Maes, H. H., Simonoff, E., Pickles, A., Rutter, M., Neale, M. C., Reynolds, C. A., Erikson, M. T., Heath, A. C., Loeber, R., Truett, K. R., & Hewitt, J. K. (in press). Genetics and developmental psychopathology: 2. The main effects of genes and environment on behavioral problems in the Virginia Twin Study of Adolescent Behavioral Development. *Journal of Child Psychology and Psychiatry.*

Engfer, A., Walper, S., & Rutter, M. (1994). Individual characteristics as a force in development. In M. Rutter & D. F. Hay (Eds.), *Development through life: A handbook for clinicians* (pp. 79–111). Oxford: Blackwell Scientific.

Farrington, D. P. (1986). Age and crime. In M. Tonry & N. Morris (Eds.), *Crime and justice.* Chicago: University of Chicago Press.

———. (1992). Trends in English juvenile delinquency and their explanation. *International Journal of Comparative and Applied Criminal Justice, 16,* 151–163.

———. (1995a). The challenge of teenage antisocial behavior. In M. Rutter (Ed.), *Psychosocial disturbances in young people: Challenges for prevention* (pp. 83–130). New York: Cambridge University Press.

———. (1995b). The development of offending and antisocial behaviour from childhood: Key findings from the Cambridge Study in Delinquent Development. The Twelfth Jack Tizard Memorial Lecture. *Journal of Child Psychology and Psychiatry, 36,* 929–964.

Felson, R. B., & Tedeschi, J. T. (Ed.). (1993a). *Aggression and violence: Social interactionist perspectives.* Washington DC: American Psychological Association.

———. (1993b). A social interactionist approach to violence: Cross-cultural applications. *Violence and Victims, 8,* 295–310.

Fergusson, D. M., Horwood, L. J., & Lloyd, M. T. (1991). Confirmatory factor models of attention deficit and conduct disorder. *Journal of Child Psychology and Psychiatry, 32,* 257–274.

Fergusson, D. M., Horwood, L. J., & Lynskey, M. T. (1993). The effects of conduct disorder and attention deficit in middle childhood on offending and scholastic ability at age 13. *Journal of Child Psychology and Psychiatry, 34,* 899–916.

Fergusson, D. M., Lynskey, M. T., & Horwood, L. J. (1996). Alcohol misuse and juvenile offending in adolescence. *Addiction, 91,* 483–494.

Geen, R. G. (1995). Human aggression. In A. Tessler (Ed.), *Advanced social psychology* (pp. 383–417). New York: McGraw-Hill.

Glueck, S., & Glueck, E. (1950). *Unraveling juvenile delinquency.* New York: Commonwealth Fund.

Goodman, R. (1995). The relationship between normal variation in IQ and common childhood psychopathology: A clinical study. *European Child and Adolescent Psychiatry, 4,* 187–196.

Goodman, R., Simonoff, E., & Stevenson, J. (1995). The impact of child IQ, parent IQ and sibling IQ on child behavioural deviance scores. *Journal of Child Psychology and Psychiatry, 36,* 409–425.

Gottfredson, M. R., & Hirschi, T. (1990). *A general theory of crime.* Stanford: Stanford University Press.

Graham, P., & Rutter, M. (1973). Psychiatric disorder in the young adolescent: A follow-up study. *Proceedings of the Royal Society of Medicine, 66,* 1226–1229 (Section of Psychiatry, pp. 58–61).

Gray, G., Smith, A., & Rutter, M. (1980). School attendance and the first year of employment. In L. Hersov & I. Berg (Eds.), *Out of school: Modern perspectives in truancy and school refusal* (pp. 343–370). Chichester, England: Wiley.

Greenberg, M. T., Speltz, M. L., & DeKlyen, M. (1993). The role of attachment in the early development of disruptive behavior problems. *Development and Psychopathology, 5,* 191–213.

Hare, R. D. (1986). Twenty years of experience with the Cleckley psychopath. In W. H. Reid, D. Dorr, J. Walker, & J. W. Bonner (Eds.), *Unmasking the psychopath: Antisocial personality and related syndromes.* New York: Norton.

Harrington, R., Bredenkamp, D., Groothues, C., Rutter, M., Fudge, H., & Pickles, A. (1994). Adult outcomes of childhood and adolescent depression: 3. Links with suicidal behaviours. *Journal of Child Psychology and Psychiatry, 35,* 1309–1319.

Harrington, R., Fudge, H., Rutter, M., Pickles, A., & Hill, J. (1991). Adult outcomes of childhood and adolescent depression: 2. Links with antisocial disorder. *Journal of the American Academy of Child and Adolescent Psychiatry, 30,* 434–439.

Harrington, R., Rutter, M., & Fombonne, E. (1996). Developmental pathways in depression: Multiple meanings, antecedents and endpoints. *Development and Psychopathology, 8,* 601–616.

Harris, T., Brown, G. W., & Bifulco, A. (1990). Loss of parent in childhood and adult psychiatric disorder: A tentative overall model. *Development and Psychopathology, 2,* 311–327.

Heimer, K., & Matsueda, R. L. (1994). Role-taking, role-commitment, and delinquency: A theory of differential social control. *American Sociological Review, 59,* 365–390.

Hewitt, J. K., Silberg, J. L., Rutter, M., Simonoff, E., Meyer, J. M., Maes, H., Pickles, A., Neale, M. C., Loeber, R., Erickson, M., Kendler, K. S., Heath, A. C., Truett, K. R., Reynolds, C., & Eaves, L. J. (in press). Genetics and developmental psychopathology: 1. Phenotypic assessment in the Virginia Twin Study of Adolescent Behavioral Development. *Journal of Child Psychology and Psychiatry.*

Hinshaw, S. P. (1992). Externalizing behavior problems and academic underachievement in childhood and adolescence: Causal relationships and underlying mechanisms. *Psychological Bulletin, 111,* 127–155.

Home Office. (1994). *Criminal statistics England and Wales.* London: Author.

Horney, J., Osgood, D. W., & Marshall, I. H. (1995). Criminal careers in the short-term: Intra-individual variability in crime and its relation to local life circumstances. *American Sociological Review, 60,* 665–673.

Jessor, R., Donovan, J. E., & Costa, F. M. (1991). *Beyond adolescence: Problem behavior and young adult development.* Cambridge: Cambridge University Press.

Kagan, J. (1981). *The second year: The emergence of self-awareness.* Cambridge: Harvard University Press.

Kendler, K. S., Neale, M. C., Kessler, R. C., Heath, A. C., & Eaves, L. J. (1993). A longitudinal twin study of 1-year prevalence of major depression in women. *Archives of General Psychiatry, 50,* 843–852.

Lahey, B. B., McBurnett, K., Loeber, R., & Hart, E. L. (1995). Psychobiology of conduct disorders. In G. P. Scholevar (Ed.), *Conduct disorders in children and adolescents: Assessments and intervention* (pp. 27–44). Washington DC: American Psychiatric Press.

Loeber, R., & Hay, D. F. (1994). Developmental approaches to aggression and conduct problems. In M. Rutter & D. F. Hay (Eds.), *Development through life: A handbook for clinicians* (pp. 488–516). Oxford: Blackwell Scientific.

Lytton, H. (1990). Child and parent effects in boys' conduct disorder: A reinterpretation. *Developmental Psychology, 26,* 683–697.

Maughan, B. (1994). School influences. In M. Rutter & D. F. Hay (Eds.), *Development through life: A handbook for clinicians* (pp. 134–158). Oxford, England: Blackwell Scientific.

Maughan, B., Dunn, G., & Rutter, M. (1985). Black pupils' progress in secondary school: 1. Reading attainment between 10 and 14. *British Journal of Developmental Psychology, 3,* 113–121.

Maughan, B., & Hagell, A. (1996). Poor readers in adulthood: Psychosocial functioning. *Development and Psychopathology, 8,* 457–476.

Maughan, B., Hagell, A., Rutter, M., & Yule, W. (1994). Poor readers in secondary schools. *Reading and Writing: An Interdisciplinary Journal, 6,* 125–150.

Maughan, B., Pickles, A., Hagell, A., Rutter, M., & Yule, W. (1996). Reading problems and antisocial behaviour: Developmental trends in comorbidity. *Journal of Child Psychology and Psychiatry, 37,* 405–418.

Maughan, B., Pickles, A., & Quinton, D. (1995). Parental hostility, childhood behavior and adult social functioning. In J. McCord (Ed.), *Coercion and punishment in long term perspectives* (pp. 34–58). New York: Cambridge University Press.

Maughan, B., Pickles, A., Rutter, M., & Ouston, J. (1991). Can schools change? 1. Outcomes at six London secondary schools. *School Effectiveness and School Improvement, 1,* 188–210.

Maughan, B., Rutter, M., & Yule, W. (1996). *Reading problems and emotional well-being: The Isle of Wight revisited.* Manuscript submitted for publication.

Meyer, J. M., Rutter, M., Simonoff, E., Shillady, C. L., Silberg, J. L., Pickles, A., Hewitt, J. K., Maes, H. H., & Eaves, L. J. (1996). *Familial aggregation for conduct disorder symptomatology: The role of genes, marital discord and family adaptability.* Manuscript in preparation.

Moffitt, T. E. (1993a). The neuropsychology of conduct disorder. *Development and Psychopathology, 5,* 135–152.

———. (1993b). Adolescence-limited and life-course-persistent antisocial behavior: A developmental taxonomy. *Psychological Review, 100,* 674–701.

Moffitt, T. E., Caspi, A., Dickson, N., Silva, P., & Stanton, W. (1996). Childhood-onset versus adolescent-onset antisocial conduct problems in males: Natural history from ages 3 to 18 years. *Development and Psychopathology, 8,* 399–424.

Mortimore, P. (1995). The positive effects of schooling. In M. Rutter (Ed.), *Psychosocial disturbance in young people: Challenges for prevention* (pp. 333–363). New York: Cambridge University Press.

Office of Population Censuses & Surveys. (1994). *Marriage and Divorce Statistics.* London: Author.

Olsson, D. H., Sprenkle, D. H., & Russel, C. S. (1979). Circumplex model of marital and family systems: 1. Cohesion and adaptability dimensions, family types, and clinical applications. *Family Processes, 18,* 3–28.

Osgood, D. W., Wilson, J. K., O'Malley, P. M., Bachman, J. G., & Johnston, L. D. (1996). Routine activities and individual deviant behavior. *American Sociological Review, 61,* 635–655.

Ouston, J., Maughan, B., & Rutter, M. (1991). Can schools change? 2. Practice at six London secondary schools. *School Effectiveness and School Improvement, 2,* 3–13.

Parker, J. G., & Asher, S. R. (1987). Peer relations and later personal adjustment: Are low-accepted children at risk? *Psychological Bulletin, 102,* 357–389.

Patterson, G. R. (1982). *Coercive family process.* Eugene OR: Castalia.

———. (1996). Some characteristics of a developmental theory for early onset delinquency. In M. F. Lenzenweger & J. J. Haugaard (Eds.), *Frontiers of developmental psychopathology* (pp. 81–124). New York: Oxford University Press.

Patterson, G. R., Reid, J. B., & Dishion, T. J. (1992). *Antisocial boys: A social interactional approach.* Eugene OR: Castalia.

Pickles, A., & Clayton, D. (1996, June). *Logistic regression with mismeasured risk exposures: A latent variable approach.* Paper presented at the meeting of the Danish Society for Theoretical Statistics, Copenhagen, Denmark.

Pickles, A., & Rutter, M. (1991). Statistical and conceptual models of "turning points" in developmental processes. In D. Magnusson, L. R. Bergman, G. Rudinger, & B. Törestad (Eds.), *Problems and methods in longitudinal research: Stability and change* (pp. 133–165). Cambridge: Cambridge University Press.

Plomin, R., & Daniels, D. (1987). Why are children in the same family so different from one another? *Behavioral and Brain Sciences, 10,* 1–15.

Quinton, D., Pickles, A., Maughan, B., & Rutter, M. (1993). Partners, peers, and pathways: Assortative pairing and continuities in conduct disorder. *Development and Psychopathology, 5,* 763–783.

Quinton, D., & Rutter, M. (1988). *Parenting breakdown: The making and breaking of inter-generational links.* Aldershot, England: Avebury.

Raine, A. (in press). Antisocial behavior and psychophysiology: A biosocial perspective and a prefrontal dysfunction hypothesis. In D. Stoff, J. Breiling, & J. D. Maser (Eds.), *Handbook of antisocial behavior.* New York: Wiley.

Raine, A., Venables, P. H., & Williams, M. (1996). Better autonomic conditioning and faster electrodermal half-recovery time at age 15 years as possible protective factors against crime at age 29 years. *Developmental Psychology, 32,* 624–630.

Reiss, D., Hetherington, M., Plomin, R., Howe, G. W., Simmens, S. J., Henderson, S. H., O'Connor, T. J., Bussell, D. A., Anderson, E. R., & Law, T. (1995). Genetic questions for environmental studies: Differential parenting and psychopathology in adolescence. *Archives of General Psychiatry, 52,* 925–936.

Robins, L. N. (1966). *Deviant children grown up.* Baltimore: Williams & Wilkins.

Robins, L. N., Tipp, J., & Przybeck, T. (1991). Antisocial personality. In L. Robins & D. A. Regier (Eds.), *Psychiatric disorders in America: The epidemiologic catchment area study* (pp. 258–290). New York: Free Press.

Rutter, M. (1972). *Maternal deprivation reassessed.* Harmondsworth, England: Penguin Books.

———. (1973). Why are London children so disturbed? *Proceedings of the Royal Society of Medicine, 66,* 1221–1226.

———. (1978). Family, area and school influences in the genesis of conduct disorders. In L. Hersov, M. Berger, & D. Shaffer (Eds.), *Aggression and antisocial behaviour in childhood and adolescence* (pp. 95–113). Oxford: Pergamon.

———. (1980). *Changing youth in a changing society: Patterns of adolescent development and disorder.* Cambridge: Harvard University Press. (Original work published 1979)

———. (1989). Psychiatric disorder in parents as a risk factor for children. In D. Shaffer, I. Philips, & N. B. Enzer (Eds.), *Prevention of mental disorders, alcohol and other drug use in children and adolescents* (pp. 157–189). Rockville MD: Office for Substance Abuse Prevention, U.S. Department of Health and Human Services.

———. (1991). Childhood experiences and adult psychosocial functioning. In G. R. Bock & J. A. Whelan (Eds.), *The childhood environment and adult disease* (pp. 189–200). Chichester, England: Wiley.

———. (1994). Beyond longitudinal data: Causes, consequences, changes and continuity. *Journal of Consulting and Clinical Psychology, 62,* 928–940.

———. (1996a). Commentary: Testing causal hypotheses about mechanisms in comorbidity. *Addiction, 91,* 495–498.

———. (1996b). Concluding remarks. In G. R. Bock & J. A. Goode (Eds.), *Genetics of criminal and antisocial behaviour* (pp. 265–271). Chichester, England, & New York: Wiley.

———. (1996c). Introduction: Concepts of antisocial behaviour, of cause, and of genetic influences. In G. R. Bock & J. A. Goode (Eds.), *Genetics of criminal and antisocial behaviour* (pp. 1–15). Chichester, England, & New York: Wiley.

———. (1996d). Transitions and turning points in developmental psychopathology: As applied to the age span between childhood and mid-adulthood. *International Journal of Behavioral Development, 19*, 603–626.

———. (in press-a). Antisocial behavior: Developmental psychopathology perspectives. In D. Stoff, J. Breiling, & J. D. Maser (Eds.), *Handbook of antisocial behavior*. New York: Wiley.

———. (in press-b). Individual differences and levels of antisocial behavior. In A. Raine, D. Farrington, P. Brennan, & S. A. Mednick (Eds.), *Biosocial bases of violence*. New York: Plenum Press.

Rutter, M., Cox, A., Tupling, C., Berger, M., & Yule, W. (1975). Attainment and adjustment in two geographical areas: 1. The prevalence of psychiatric disorder. *British Journal of Psychiatry, 126*, 493–509.

Rutter, M., Dunn, J., Plomin, R., Simonoff, E., Pickles, A., Maughan, B., Ormel, J. H., Meyer, J., & Eaves, L. (in press). Integrating nature and nurture: Implications of person-environment correlations and interactions for developmental psychopathology. *Development and Psychopathology*.

Rutter, M., & Giller, H. (1983). *Juvenile delinquency: Trends and perspectives*. Harmondsworth, England: Penguin Books.

Rutter, M., Harrington, R., Quinton, D., & Pickles, A. (1994). Adult outcome of conduct disorder in childhood: Implications for concepts and definitions of patterns of psychopathology. In R. D. Ketterlinus & M. Lamb (Eds.), *Adolescent problem behaviors: Issues and research* (pp. 57–80). Hillsdale NJ: Lawrence Erlbaum.

Rutter, M., & Madge, N. (1976). *Cycles of disadvantage: A review of research*. London: Heinemann Educational Books.

Rutter, M., Maughan, B., Mortimore, P., Ouston, J., & Smith, A. (1979). *Fifteen thousand hours: Secondary schools and their effects on children*. London: Open Books.

Rutter, M., & Quinton, D. (1977). Psychiatric disorder—Ecological factors and concepts of causation. In H. McGurk (Ed.), *Ecological factors in human development* (pp. 173–187). Amsterdam: North-Holland.

———. (1984). Parental psychiatric disorder: Effects on children. *Psychological Medicine, 14*, 853–880.

Rutter, M., & Rutter, M. (1993). *Developing minds: Challenge and continuity across the lifespan*. Harmondworth, England: Penguin; New York: Basic Books.

Rutter, M., Silberg, J., & Simonoff, E. (1993). Whither behavior genetics? A developmental psychopathology perspective. In R. Plomin & G. E. Mc-

Clearn (Eds.), *Nature, nurture, and psychology* (pp. 433–456). Washington DC: American Psychological Association.

Rutter, M., & Smith, D. J. (Ed.). (1995). *Psychosocial disorders in young people: Time trends and their causes.* Chichester, England: Wiley.

Rutter, M., Tizard, J., & Whitmore, K. (Eds.). (1970). *Education, health and behaviour.* London: Longmans.

Rutter, M., Yule, B., Quinton, D., Rowlands, O., Yule, W., & Berger, M. (1975). Attainment and adjustment in two geographical areas: 3. Some factors accounting for area differences. *British Journal of Psychiatry, 126,* 520–533.

Sampson, R. J., & Laub, J. H. (1993). *Crime in the making: Pathways and turning points through life.* Cambridge: Harvard University Press.

Schachar, R. J. (1991). Childhood hyperactivity. *Journal of Child Psychology and Psychiatry, 32,* 155–191.

Schachar, R. J., Rutter, M., & Smith, A. (1981). The characteristics of situationally and pervasively hyperactive children: Implications for syndrome definition. *Journal of Child Psychology and Psychiatry, 22,* 375–392.

Schachar, R. J., Tannock, R., & Logan, G. (1993). Inhibitory control, impulsiveness and attention deficit hyperactivity disorder. *Clinical Psychology Review, 13,* 721–739.

Schachar, R. J., Taylor, E., Wieselberg, M., Thorley, G., & Rutter, M. (1987). Changes in family function and relationships in children who respond to methylphenidate. *Journal of the American Academy of Child and Adolescent Psychiatry, 26,* 728–732.

Shepherd, M., Oppenheim, B., & Mitchell, S. (1971). *Childhood behaviour and mental health.* London: University of London Press.

Shillady, L. L., Silberg, J. L., Simonoff, E., Pickles, A., Maes, H. M., Rutter, M. L., Hewitt, J. K., Eaves, L. J., & Meyer, J. M. (1996). *Parental psychopathology as a risk factor for childhood disorder: a latent class analysis of 1,408 families.* Manuscript in preparation.

Silberg, J. L., Meyer, J., Pickles, A., Simonoff, E., Eaves, L., Hewitt, J., Maes, H., & Rutter, M. (1996). Heterogeneity among juvenile antisocial behaviors: Findings from the Virginia Twin Study of Adolescent Behavioural Development. In G. R. Bock & J. A. Goode (Eds.), *Genetics of criminal and antisocial behaviour* (pp. 76–86). Chichester, England, & New York: Wiley.

Silberg, J. L., Rutter, M. L., Meyer, J., Maes, H., Simonoff, E., Pickles, A., Hewitt, J., & Eaves, L. (1996). Genetic and environmental influences on the covariation between hyperactivity and conduct disturbance in juvenile twins. *Journal of Child Psychology and Psychiatry, 37,* 803–816.

Simonoff, E. (1996). Personal communication.

Simonoff, E., Pickles, A., Hewitt, J., Silberg, J., Rutter, M., Loeber, R., Meyer, J., Neale, M., & Eaves, L. (1995). Multiple raters of disruptive child behavior: Using a genetic strategy to examine shared views and bias. *Behavior Genetics, 25,* 311–326.

Simonoff, E., Pickles, A., Meyer, J. M., Silberg, J. L., Maes, H. H., Loeber,

R., Rutter, M., Hewitt, J. K., & Eaves, L. J. (in press). The Virginia Twin Study of Adolescent Behavioral Development: Influences of age, gender and impairment on rates of disorder. *Archives of General Psychiatry*.

Smith, D. J. (1995). Youth crime and conduct disorders: Trends, patterns and causal explanations. In M. Rutter & D. J. Smith (Eds.), *Psychosocial disturbances in young people: Time trends and their causes* (pp. 389–489). Chichester, England: Wiley.

Sonuga-Barke, E. J. S., Taylor, E., Sembi, S., & Smith, J. (1992). Hyperactivity and delay aversion: 1. The effect of delay on choice. *Journal of Child Psychology and Psychiatry, 33*, 387–398.

Spanier, G. B. (1976). Measuring dyadic adjustment: New scales for assessing the quality of marriage and other dyads. *Journal of Marriage and Family, 38*, 15–28.

Sumner, M., & Parker, H. (1995). *Low in alcohol*. Manchester, England: Department of Social Policy and Social Work, University of Manchester.

Taylor, E. (Ed.). (1986). *The overactive child: Clinics in developmental medicine no. 97*. London: MacKeith Press; Oxford, England: Blackwell Scientific.

Taylor, E., Chadwick, O., Heptinstall, E., & Danckaerts, M. (1996). Hyperactivity and conduct problems as risk factors for adolescent development. *Journal of the American Academy of Child and Adolescent Psychiatry, 35*, 1213–1226.

Taylor, E., Sandberg, S., Thorley, G., & Giles, S. (1991). *The epidemiology of childhood hyperactivity*. Oxford: Oxford University Press.

Taylor, E., Schacher, R., Thorley, G., Wieselberg, H. M., Everitt, B., & Rutter, M. (1987). Which boys respond to stimulant medication? A controlled trial of methylphenidate in boys with disruptive behaviour. *Psychological Medicine, 17*, 121–143.

Tedeschi, J. T., & Felson, R. B. (1994). *Aggression and coercive actions: An interactionist perspective*. Washington DC: American Psychological Association.

Tonry, M., & Farrington, D. P. (Eds.). (1995). *Building a safer society: Strategic approaches to crime prevention*. Chicago: University of Chicago Press.

Wartella, E. (1995). Media and problem behaviours in young people. In M. Rutter & D. J. Smith (Eds.), *Psychosocial disorders in young people: Time trends and their causes* (pp. 296–323). Chichester, England: Wiley.

Zillmann, D. (1979). *Hostility and aggression*. Hillsdale NJ: Lawrence Erlbaum.

Zoccolillo, M., Pickles, A., Quinton, D., & Rutter, M. (1992). The outcome of childhood conduct disorder: Implications for defining adult personality disorder and conduct disorder. *Psychological Medicine, 22*, 971–986.

A Developmental Model for Late-Onset Delinquency

Gerald R. Patterson
Karen Yoerger

*Oregon Social Learning Center,
Eugene, Oregon*

It is apparent that current theories about delinquency have failed in two crucial respects. First, none of these theories can account for significant variance in societal rates of juvenile offending. By itself, this constitutes a major failure for the social sciences. Second, although longitudinal studies identify many variables that predict later delinquency (Loeber & Dishion, 1983), the level of prediction is abysmally low. For example, a review of one major study showed a false positive error of 85% (Utting, Bright, & Henricson, 1993). These failures are the outcomes of both inadequate theory and inadequate measurement. This chapter addresses both issues.

This report is based on the earlier presentations by Patterson (1994) and Patterson and Yoerger (1993c). An earlier version was presented at the conference panel "Early- and Late-Onset Delinquency" at the American Society of Criminology, Miami, November 1994.

Dr. Patterson gratefully acknowledges the financial support provided by Grant Nos. R37 MH 37940, Center for Studies of Violent Behavior and Traumatic Stress, National Institute of Mental Health (NIMH), U.S. Public Health Service (PHS), and R01 MH 38318 Prevention Research Branch, Division of Epidemiology and Services Research, NIMH U.S. PHS, in collecting the data sets used in this report. The analyses of the findings were supported by Grants Nos. R37 MH 37940 and P 50 MH 46690, Prevention Research Branch, NIMH, U.S. PHS, and by R01 DA 07031, National Institute on Drug Abuse, U.S. PHS.

If you have questions or would like to obtain a copy of this manuscript, please write: G. R. Patterson, Ph.D., Oregon Social Learning Center, 207 East Fifth Avenue, Suite 202, Eugene OR 97401.

We believed the theory could be improved by examining the assumption that delinquents represent a homogeneous class. We took the position that there are two, or perhaps more, very different paths to delinquency. The general formulation has been cast as an early-onset and late-onset theory of juvenile delinquency (Farrington & Hawkins, 1991; Patterson, Capaldi, & Bank, 1991; Patterson, Crosby, & Vuchinich, 1992; Patterson, DeBaryshe, & Ramsey, 1989; Patterson, & Yoerger, 1993b; Simons, Wu, Conger, & Lorenz, 1994). Alternatively, other investigators have examined the difference between transient and persistent offenders as being the crucial trajectories (Moffitt, 1993; Pulkkinen, 1986).

In keeping with the long history of research findings, we assumed that as compared to the late-onset group, the early-onset group was at significantly greater risk of adult criminal careers. We hypothesized that boys arrested early—before the age of 14.0 years—represent a very different kind of delinquent as compared to those who are first arrested later in adolescence. We hypothesized that the two groups differ significantly in terms of the context in which the family is embedded, the level of parental skill in family management practices, and the levels of child deviancy and social skills. The two groups can be differentiated by their growth patterns for both antisocial and delinquent behavior. The timing and the level achieved in growth clearly differentiate the two groups. Examination of the data relating to these hypotheses constitutes the primary focus for this chapter.

All of the constructs in both the early- and late-onset models are defined by multiple (agent-method) indicators (Bank, Dishion, Skinner, & Patterson, 1990; Patterson & Bank, 1986, 1987). This approach to measurement is thought to be a considerable improvement over the monoagent (adolescent or parent) or monomethod (self-report, interview) assessments that defined most of the child and family variables used in earlier longitudinal prediction studies (Loeber & Dishion, 1983).

A Social Interactional Perspective

The general formulation for the two paths to delinquency reflects a social interactional perspective (Patterson & Reid, 1984; Patterson,

Reid, & Dishion, 1992; Reid, Taplin, & Lorber, 1981). From this point of view, all social behaviors—including antisocial and delinquent behaviors—exist because they serve a recognizable function. The general strategy is similar to Harris's (1979, p. 381) functional analyses of cultural practices. In this context as applied to the study of child-adolescents, function is defined in part by the fact that social behaviors produce predictable reactions from the social environment. The predictability of some reactions by others to certain social behaviors is well documented in sequential lag analyses of both childhood and adult behaviors (Dishion, Patterson, & Griesler, 1994; Gottman & Roy, 1990, p. 273; Patterson, 1973; Patterson & Cobb, 1971; Patterson & Moore, 1979).

Patterned reactions of others lead the child-adolescent to overselect some behaviors and to underselect others. One particularly interesting aspect of this process is that in certain situations the predictable reactions from the social environment actually lead the child to select deviant behaviors rather than prosocial ones (Patterson, 1982; Patterson, Littman, & Bricker, 1967; Sanson-Fisher, Poole, & Thompson, 1979). In some documented instances the selection process can become so extreme as to expose both the child and the reacting member of the social environment to extreme physical injury (Carr, Taylor, & Robinson, 1991; Horner & Day, 1991; Snyder, Edwards, McGraw, Kilgore, & Holton, 1994).

EARLY-ONSET PATH

We assumed that the training for boys arrested before the age of 14 actually begins very early, and it begins in the home. The proximal cause for antisocial behavior would be found in the immediate reactions provided by parents, siblings, and peers (Snyder & Patterson, 1995). The best predictors of antisocial behavior would, therefore, consist of measures of the reactions that lead simultaneously to an overselection of antisocial behaviors and an underselection of prosocial acts. This perspective contrasts with the positions taken by Moffitt (1993), Tedeschi (this volume), Heimer and Matsueda (this volume), and McCord (this volume). These investigators assumed that the effects of experience on child adjustment are entirely mediated by any one of a variety of cognitive mechanisms (e.g., internal control, negative attributions, decision processes) based on cost-utilities analyses, evaluative attitudes toward delinquency, intentions, or anticipated punishments. In contrast, we assumed that much antisocial and delinquent behavior is overlearned and performed more or less automatically and is not the outcome of controlled cognitive processing (Patterson, Reid, & Dishion, 1992). Driving a car is very much like most coercive and antisocial behavior (Howard, 1983); neither activity requires much access to working memory or extensive attentional capacity. As pointed out by Langer (1984), Howard (1983), and Kanfer (1987), much social interaction consists of automatic processing, where one may use all sorts of heuristics to compensate for the fact that each person has very limited channel capacity (Tversky & Kahneman, 1974). The idea of the perfectly rational person carefully processing the myriad complexity of ongoing social interaction (McCord, this volume) is appealing but constrained by the fact that the biological computers people employ have very limited capacities. Incidentally, as pointed out by Dawes (1988) in his brilliant review of findings from the cognitive revolution, even under ideal conditions humans are capable of only a very limited rationality. In a later section we discuss the comparison of behavioral and internal mechanisms for antisocial outcomes.

The behavioral model begins with observations of families in which the reactions of both parents and siblings establish the child's coercive behaviors, such as whining, temper tantrums, and hitting, as having real functional value. In these families coercive behaviors are functional in the sense that they are the only effective means for terminating conflict. Later, the child learns that antisocial acts such as stealing and lying are also functional. With practice, the child learns when and in what settings these skills can be practiced. We suspect that the process begins as early as 18 months in some families. It may seem counterintuitive that in these families the parents and siblings inadvertently provided the reactions that in the long run will increase their own misery (Patterson, 1979, 1982; Snyder, 1995b). Data are presented in a later section that examine this key assumption as it relates to the performance of antisocial behaviors. In the elementary grades, the "problem" child selects deviant peers to form his or her support group and in so doing receives further training. Under the group's tutelage, the child selects new forms of antisocial behavior that are identifiable delinquent acts. The high frequency of these acts leads to an early arrest and then to chronic and violent offending.

LATE-ONSET PATH

Training for the second path to juvenile offending is thought to begin in early to middle adolescence. This path described 54.9% of all those in the Oregon Youth Study (OYS) who were arrested by the age of 18. We assumed that this path also begins with disruptions in parenting practices, particularly in the monitoring process. In late-onset families, antisocial and coercive child behaviors are not permitted to work quite so well as they do in early-onset families; but, presumably, the relative payoffs for deviancy are higher in late-onset families than they are in families of nondelinquent boys. In late-onset families, the relative payoffs for prosocial skills (e.g., school work, chores, good relationships, keeping your word) are much better than payoffs found in the early-onset families but are not as high as in families that will produce nondelinquent boys. Both the early and late paths are characterized by rapid growth in antisocial behavior, but they differ markedly in when that growth occurs and in the kind of antisocial behavior that is growing.

Early-onset families allow coercive and antisocial acts to become functional as early as preschool years. However, late-onset families do not permit these behaviors to pay off until early adolescence. Although early-onset families provide low payoffs for prosocial skills, the child's antisocial behavior further exacerbates the problem of training for prosocial skills; the effect is to produce a child who is both deviant and socially unskilled. However, the late-onset families tend to be relatively more supportive of prosocial skills. When the growth in antisocial behavior occurs in early adolescence, the youth already has a array of moderately developed prosocial skills.

For many early-onset boys, deviancy training begins during the preschool years. It is provided first by family and then in later stages by deviant peers. As the process continues for the early-onset group, disruptions in the parenting process make indirect contributions even during late adolescence. For the late-onset group, the training is primarily by deviant peers and secondarily by family members. In either case, we hypothesized that deviancy training—

regardless of when it occurs—is associated with a breakdown in parenting practices, such as monitoring, discipline, family problem solving, and positive reinforcement. More specifically, we assumed that changes in rates of deviancy are significantly related to changes in disrupted parenting (e.g., Patterson & Forgatch, 1995). Although the relation between parenting skills and child adjustment is thought to be bidirectional, in experimental studies the magnitude of improvement in parenting skills correlates significantly with the magnitude of reduction in deviancy. In effect, the level of parenting skill is a major determinant of whether a child's deviant or prosocial behavior becomes functional in a given family. This point is elaborated later in the chapter.

Finally, we hypothesized that both paths may reflect a mix of biological and environmental variables. For example, we suspected that early-onset boys may emerge from the combination of a difficult-to-train (temperament) toddler with parents who are relatively inexperienced. The review of results from twin design studies by Goldsmith (1983) and Goldsmith and Campos (1986) suggests a genetic presence for at least some of the variance in temperament measures. Data from three adoption study designs examined by Cadoret, Cain, and Crowe (1983) showed significant environment-gene interaction terms predicting adolescent antisocial behavior. However, we do not know whether the mechanism that explains the gene-environment interaction is temperament. There are at least a half dozen equally plausible mechanisms. It is interesting to note that twin designs show no contribution of genetics to official records of delinquency (Gottesman & Goldsmith, 1994). Given the well-known flaws in twin design studies (Hoffman, 1985; Patterson & Leve, 1996; Wahlsten, 1990), it is difficult to know how to interpret these findings. The fact that twin and adoption designs produce different outcomes suggests that tracing these contributions will not be an easy task.

The coercive model implies that if we can measure the relative rates of payoff or the parenting practices that control those rates, then we should be able to account for the majority of the variance in measures of antisocial or delinquent behavior. We examine these findings in a later section. Alternatively, theories, such as Moffitt's (1993) formulation about transient and persistent offenders or those by Tedeschi (this volume), McCord (this volume), or Heimer and

Matsueda (this volume), make compelling arguments for the utility of internalized mechanisms as explanations for delinquent outcomes. For example, Moffitt's persistent offender may have biological as well as neurological limitations that in turn impact the social environment in such a way that the child fails to internalize effective self-controls. In spite of the popularity of such "internal mechanism" models, we believed that they have seldom if ever been adequately tested. One such test might, for example, include measures of internalized mechanisms and measures of parenting or reinforcing contingencies in the same multivariate design. Do both sets of variables make significant and unique contributions? Or is it, as we suspect, that existing measures of internalized mechanisms make only indirect contributions to explaining antisocial outcomes (Patterson, in press)? In our first efforts to carry out a study of this kind, we demonstrated that at a univariate level both the parenting and the cognitive variables (measures of antisocial attitudes) correlated significantly with predictions of early arrest and school dropout (Patterson, in press; Patterson & Yoerger, 1996). The cognitive variables included the child's verbal IQ as a measure of Moffitt's impaired executive function (Patterson & Yoerger, 1995). In the other study (Patterson, in press), the internal mechanism was specified by measures of antisocial attitudes based on Elliott, Huizinga, and Ageton's (1985) effort to test social control theory. In both studies, when measures of parenting were introduced, the contributions of the internal variables became nonsignificant. In other words, the measures of internal mechanisms made significant but redundant contributions to predicting both early arrest and school dropout. At this very preliminary stage, it remains to be demonstrated that we can effectively measure internal variables. Of even more importance, it remains to be shown that the measures account for unique variance when compared to alternative candidates for causal status.

In summary, a social interactional perspective makes the assumption that in some special social environments, child-adolescent social behaviors—including antisocial and delinquent acts—become functional. In this instance, the term *functional* implies that parents, siblings, or peers provide payoffs that enhance the likelihood that these behaviors will be selected in the future. Whether future growth is higher for prosocial or for deviant behaviors depends upon what the social environment provides for these behaviors. To understand deviancy we must study not only the payoffs for deviancy but also the relative payoffs for prosocial behavior. The formulation reveals what must be done if an effective intervention or prevention is to occur. This topic is discussed in a later section.

Improved Measurement

Classic measurement theory has considered unreliability as the primary source of measurement error (Cronbach, 1949; Wiggins 1973). Contemporary interest in modeling, with its emphasis on the use of multiple indicators, has led to an expanded list of concerns. Modern measurement theory is focused additionally on the effects of errors of specification (the omission of relevant measures) and on the necessity for disentangling correlated residuals (Hayduk, 1987; Bollen, 1989). Additionally, even in a well-specified model, each indicator may reflect a systematic bias. In studies of family process, systematic bias may be a major source of measurement error. The implicit assumption was that all agents (e.g., mother, father, teacher, peer, or observer) may be selectively biased in reports of their own behavior and the behavior of others. Our preliminary studies suggested that the source of bias may be quite different for each agent. For example, our data showed that teachers tend to underestimate the magnitude of deviancy for children whom they do not know well. But mothers, as compared to fathers or teachers, seem to select higher rates of relatively trivial exemplars of deviant child behavior and consequently have lower predictive validity for their scores (Bank, Duncan, Patterson, & Reid, 1993).

BIAS IN MATERNAL RATINGS

Typically, studies show that maternal reports have both internal consistency and adequate test-retest reliabilities (Achenbach, Howell, Quay, & Conners, 1991). There is growing evidence, however, that maternal ratings may vary from sample to sample. For example, ratings by socially disadvantaged mothers may have lower validity. West and Farrington (1973) noted that the correlations between parents' and teachers' ratings were appreciably lower for socially disadvantaged families than for families who were not disadvantaged. They cited a similar set of findings from a study by Glidewell, Gildea, Domke, and Kantor (1959). Tulkin (1977) showed that the convergence between mothers' reports of beliefs about child rearing and observed maternal behavior was lower for socially disadvantaged mothers than for middle-class mothers. In an effort to replicate these findings, data from the oys were used to calculate the convergent correlations between teachers' and mothers' Child Behavior Checklist (cbc-l) ratings of boys' antisocial behavior. For the high-social-status families (i.e., above the median), the correlation was .58 ($p < .001$); for low-social-status families, the correlation was .29 ($p < .01$). We cannot be sure, of course, but we suspected that the reduced convergence reflects the unreliability of ratings by the socially disadvantaged mothers rather than the unreliability of the teacher ratings. In any event, the findings emphasized the necessity for using more than a single method or agent for defining either family process or child adjustment variables.

We assumed that maternal depression may be another source of maternal bias in ratings of both child adjustment and family process variables. For example, Greist, Wells, and Forehand (1979) showed that maternal ratings of child adjustment correlated more highly with maternal self-reported depressed mood than it did with observed child behavior. Similar effects have been shown by Dumas and Wekerle (1995) and Middlebrook and Forehand (1985). The findings suggest that extraneous variables, such as maternal depression, may further inflate shared method variance when estimating the correlation between family process and child adjustment variables (i.e., mother's depression influences her ratings of family process and child adjustment in similar ways).

The findings for the contribution of maternal depression to maternal ratings of family process and child adjustment exemplify the need to use multiple indicators to define key concepts. For these reasons, each component of the early- and late-onset model was defined by multiple indicators. This permitted the use of structural equation modeling (sem) procedures such as those described in Hoyle (1995), Hayduk (1987), and Bollen (1989). These procedures made it possible to examine the relationship between latent constructs (e.g., family problem solving and childhood antisocial behaviors) after accounting for the contributions of shared method variance. We assumed that predictions from child adjustment to later delinquency would be improved by reliance upon multiple indicators. Presumably these predictions will be even further enhanced if separate predictions are made for early- and late-onset groups.

Early-Onset Model

The relation of age to crime has been well understood for years. The Gluecks took the position that early onset was a key variable in predicting long-term negative outcomes. The earlier the onset, the worse the outcome (Glueck & Glueck, 1940). Sampson and Laub's (1993) reanalyses of the Glueck data set strongly supported this position. However, there was little or no understanding of how these differences in outcome came about. Farrington and Hawkins's (1991) empirical evaluation of a set of over 40 variables from the London cohort identified 12 that differentiated early- from late-onset offenders. Four of the variables identified high-risk contexts, and others described poor parenting and child dispositions that placed the child at increasing risk. In the multiple regression analysis, two variables (troublesomeness, low leisure time with father) produced unique and significant contributions to the multiple R value .46. We suspect that a replication study would not be able to produce these same two variables, but the real problem lies in the fact that the variables do very little to explicate the process that produces early onset.

This chapter provides a detailed examination of differences between early and late onset in contextual, family process, and child adjustment variables. The discussion is theory driven in that a single model specifies how context, family process, and adjustment outcomes fit together (Patterson, 1996; Patterson, Reid, & Dishion, 1992). Although this section emphasizes the processes that uniquely define the early-onset group, the larger body of this chapter expands on these differences as they relate to the late-onset group.

A basic premise in social interactional theory is that given repeated transactions, both members of a dyad are altered in some measurable fashion. The pattern describing how the two persons change over time might be thought of as a dyadic trait; it is quite stable over time (Patterson, 1984). In formulating such a pattern for parent and child, we chose to proceed simultaneously at two different levels: we endeavored to explain why the child's deviant and social behaviors changed over time, and because parents were also changing over time, we wanted to explore whether some of these changes were brought about by what the child or adolescent was doing. However, it seemed to us that some of the changes in the dyad also reflected intrusions by forces from outside the dyad or even from contextual forces outside the family itself, such as changes in economic conditions, parental depression, or successful efforts to intervene (Patterson, Reid, & Dishion, 1992). We assumed that the effect of such contextual variables on child adjustment was mediated by changes in parenting practices, such as discipline, monitoring, or family problem solving (Patterson, 1983). For example, in recently divorced families, the impact of the massive changes in context on child adjustment would be minimal in those families where the now single parent maintained effective discipline, monitoring, and problem-solving practices. The data collected in the longitudinal study of divorced families support this assumption (Forgatch, Patterson, & Ray, 1996; Patterson & Forgatch, 1990).

We hypothesized that parenting practices controlled the payoffs provided by family members for coercive and prosocial behaviors. In a very real sense, parenting behaviors serve as mediators between contextual variables and the contingencies that control child-adolescent behaviors. It became apparent that we had not one but rather two parallel theories. One is concerned with why the child does what he or she does, and the other theory explains why parents do what they do (Patterson, 1996).

In the discussions that follow, both early- and late-onset models are evaluated as performance theories (Patterson, Reid, & Dishion, 1992). Given outcome measures based on assessment of child outcomes collected in the child's natural environment, how much of the variance is accounted for by the variables that purport to explain why children change? In the present model, this requires that the measures of parenting practices must account for the majority of the variance. Presumably the contribution of contextual variables, such as socioeconomic status (SES), poverty, divorce, or parental depression, to child adjustment would be mediated by measures of parenting practices.

WHY ARE SOME BOYS ANTISOCIAL?

Several decades of studies demonstrate that children's coercive anti-social behaviors are more functional in some environments than in others. It is only in the last decade that we have been able to resolve some of the difficulties in studying the nature of these functions. To date, most of the relevant studies of function are based on observation data and are focused on conflict episodes (Snyder & Patterson, 1995). We have known for some time now that conflict episodes occur two to three times more frequently in families with antisocial boys than with nonantisocial boys (Patterson, 1982; Patterson, Reid, & Dishion, 1992; Snyder et al., 1994). These conflicts could, of course, produce negative emotion, such as anger, that in turn causes the antisocial behavior. However, our modeling studies suggest that negative emotion does not play a direct role in causing antisocial behavior (Forgatch & Stoolmiller, 1994). Alternatively, the modeling studies strongly suggest that emotions play an indirect rather than direct role (Capaldi, Forgatch, & Crosby, 1994; Patterson, 1996).

Although conflicts certainly generate negative emotion, their prime function in our model is to define the setting in which training for deviancy and prosocial skills can occur. Children learn the details about what works and does not work in their family, but what children learn in normal families is quite different from what they learn in distressed families (Patterson, 1982, 1995). Given a conflict in a normal family, the child learns that certain prosocial behaviors, such as talking, laughing, or negotiating, are followed by a termination of the conflict (i.e., the child's behavior served a function; it "worked"). In such families, the child finds that coercive behaviors also work on occasion. The process for selecting what works and what does not is analogous to escape conditioning. The individual is presented with an aversive stimulus (the conflict behavior of the family member) and tries out different behaviors until he find one that works. This particular behavior is followed very quickly by a termination of the conflict (i.e., he escapes from the aversive stimulus. In escape conditioning parlance, the response that leads to termination of the aversive stimulus is strengthened or more likely to be selected on future occasions. Some of the relevant laboratory studies are discussed in (Epling and Pierce 1995). The applications of these ideas to family interaction are discussed in greater detail in Patterson, Reid, and Dishion (1992), Snyder (1995a), and Snyder and Patterson (1995).

The analysis was carried out at the intra-individual level and required examination of the usefulness (in terminating conflict) of every behavior the child tried. A statement about the usefulness of deviant behaviors for a given child must be compared with how useful nondeviant behaviors are in the same situation (Snyder & Patterson, 1995). Modern learning theory emphasizes the utility of such an application of the matching law to the study of social behavior (Davison & McCarthy, 1988). What this means is that in a given situation there should be a match between the relative frequencies of child behaviors and the relative payoffs provided for these behaviors. If the highest payoff is for whining or arguing, then that is the behavior that is most likely to occur in that setting. In laboratory situations where only two or three responses are available and all extraneous stimuli are controlled, correlations of .9 or above are expected. However, even in the highly complex give-and-take of family interaction, the match between relative payoffs and relative frequency of behavior is quite good. For example, in the observation study by Snyder and Patterson (1995), the average correlation was .65 for normal families and .81 for distressed families. It seems clear that the child matches his or her behavior to environmental payoffs.

Further examination of dyadic exchanges in family settings reveals an extremely interesting finding. Snyder and Patterson (1995) found that in families with problem boys, prosocial behaviors were, by and large, simply not effective in terminating family conflict. In these families, the only thing that seemed to work was coercive behaviors. Given these findings, we were not surprised then to find that antisocial boys are significantly retarded in a variety of prosocial skills, as noted in the reviews by Patterson (1982) and Patterson, Reid, and Dishion (1992). We expect that when these studies are extended to examine the relative payoffs based on positive reinforcement in nonconflict settings that the relative payoffs will be in short supply. We believe that, in general, these families simply do not support the development of prosocial skills. It could be that these parents are put off by the high density of aversive behaviors that accompany the problem child as suggested in the correlational studies by Patterson (1986) and Patterson and Dishion (1988). We suspect, however, that these parents tend to be noninvolved, even with their infants. Many of their reactions are not contingent upon what the infant is doing but directed more by their own mood. The fact that the parent does not reinforce the infant's prosocial overtures may create a situation where the infant must rely upon coercive behavior to have any impact on the social environment. Is this how coercion begins? We simply do not know the answer to this fundamental question.

According to this formulation, an aggressive child is actively matching his or her behavior to family reactions. But if one just looks at the intra-individual scores for prosocial and deviant behaviors, they will not, by themselves, account for individual differences in aggression. For example, it is possible to have two boys with the same relative rates of payoffs for deviant behaviors. Let us say that in both cases child deviant behaviors are effective in terminating conflict about 40% of the time. What is missing here is information about the number of trials where this training occurs. Some families may have only 10 conflicts during the observation sessions whereas another family may have 100. Snyder and Patterson (1995) assumed that if we know how often the training occurs and how high the relative payoffs are during training, then we should be able to account for individual differences in antisocial behavior. Assuming the model is correct, we should be able to observe mother-child interactions in the home and use the two variables (relative payoffs and frequency of conflict) to account for much of the variance in antisocial outcomes.

So far we have carried out two different studies that test this hypothesis. In the first study, observation data was collected in a laboratory setting for mothers and preschool children. Five hours of data served as the base for calculating the relative payoff and the conflict density scores. These data were used to predict child aggressiveness in interacting with the mother in the same setting a week later. The density and relative payoff variables accounted for 76% of the variance in the observed deviancy rates for the children.

The results are, of course, promising. But the samples were small, and there is a possible confounding of results based on the shared method (observation) for both the independent and dependent variables. It is, therefore, reassuring to note that Snyder (1995a) used comparable observation data from a larger clinical sample of boys to replicate the findings. Observation data collected prior to treatment formed the basis for calculating the matching law variables. The criteria consisted of objective measures of outcome collected 2 years after parent training intervention (arrest, out-of-home placement, and school discipline contacts). In examining each of the criterion variables separately, Snyder and his colleagues accounted for from 35% to 47% of the variance. Both studies are examples of how the child matches his or her relative rates of deviant behavior to the relative payoffs provided by the social environment. Davison and McCarthy (1988) provide a good overview of recent work on applications of the matching law.

This seems to be a reasonable beginning. The variables seem to explain at a microlevel what families do that causes coercive and antisocial behavior. The combination of conflict density and relative payoffs consistently accounts for sufficient variance in a range of criterion variables to suggest that the procedures are appropriate to the model. Obviously, we are only beginning to develop a complete account of this process. We need to expand the studies to include the analyses of siblings and peers and to include relative payoffs for prosocial and deviant behaviors in nonconflict episodes. These studies together with an examination of genetic variables constitute the agenda for the next decade of work in this area.

A more detailed presentation of the coercion mechanism can be found in Patterson (1982, 1995) and Snyder (1995a). These studies also included analyses of some of the mechanisms associated with escalation in amplitude of coercive behavior as well as some speculation about the application of avoidance conditioning to account for a child's movement from coercive behavior to antisocial acts, such as stealing and truancy. More than a decade of correlational analyses and experimental manipulations in special education classrooms provides dramatic and convincing support for the ubiquitous role of escape conditioning (or negative reinforcement) as a major determinant for deviant and prosocial behavior (Carr, 1988; Carr, Newsom, & Binkoff, 1980). It is interesting to note that in conflict settings where this kind of training occurs, the behavior of both the child and the adult show that they are responsive to these contingencies (Carr et al., 1991; Horner & Day, 1991). In these exchanges teachers are controlled in much the same manner as are the children. It is worth noting that the perspective is very optimistic, as the aegis for change and prevention trials are a salient part of the model. For example,

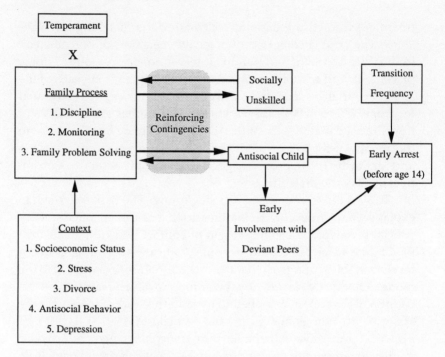

Figure 1. Early-onset parenting model.

the problem is not "in" the child; if you wish to change the child, you must change the way the environment reacts to him or her.

PARENTING MODELS

As shown in Figure 1, the effect of contextual variables, such as divorce, unemployment, or depression, on child adjustment is thought to be mediated by the impact on parenting practices (Patterson, 1983). Rutter (this volume) gives a perfect example in demonstrating that the effects of parental pathology on childhood outcome were mediated by whether or not this became hostile parenting. If hostile parenting was not present, then parental pathology had no significant effect on adjustment outcomes.

In our own work, when the criterion variable is childhood antisocial behavior, we have consistently found that the mediational model holds. In an earlier section we cited the studies for divorced families that supported this assumption. Bank, Forgatch, Patterson, and Fetrow (1993) demonstrated a similar effect for antisocial parent as a contextual variable; Larzelere and Patterson (1990) also demonstrated that the effect of SES on delinquency was mediated by parenting practices. In another study, a SEM showed a similar effect for the impact of stress (including unemployment) upon child adjustment for a sample of intact but at-risk families in the OYS. This model was replicated in the Iowa Youth Study of farm families undergoing severe economic stresses (Conger, Patterson, & Gé, 1995).

It is important to note that the term *context* may have very different referents. Some contextual variables, such as unemployment, divorce, or depression, refer to changes in status that may alter family interaction patterns. However, other contextual variables seem to serve as marker variables that identify subgroups that are at risk of having disrupted parenting practices. For example, both antisocial and socially disadvantaged parents are significantly at risk of disrupted parenting (Bank, Forgatch, et al., 1993; Patterson & Capaldi, 1991; Patterson & Dishion, 1988). We assume that status in this second contextual group does not tend to shift much over time. In contrast, who is divorced or unemployed may shift a great deal, and presumably it is the shifts that may be disrupting, as indicated in Forgatch et al. (1996) and Patterson and Capaldi (1991).

As shown in Figure 1, changes in discipline, monitoring, and family problem solving will produce changes in the contingencies provided by family members and peers for both prosocial and deviant behaviors. For example, an increase in parental monitoring might result in the child spending less time with deviant peers and more time in activities supervised by adults. Similarly, the use of more effective family problem solving could result in more clearly defined rules and the use of more effective negative sanctions for deviant behavior. The details of these and other relevant parenting practices are presented in Patterson (1982), Patterson, Reid, and Dishion (1992), and Snyder (1995a). The multiple indicators used to define parenting practices and child adjustment are detailed in Patterson, Reid, and Dishion (1992), and the psychometric studies are found in Capaldi and Patterson (1989).

Can a parenting model be replicated across samples, and how much variance in criterion measures of antisocial behavior are accounted for by such models? The findings from three different SEM studies are summarized in Figure 2. Each of the studies used similar

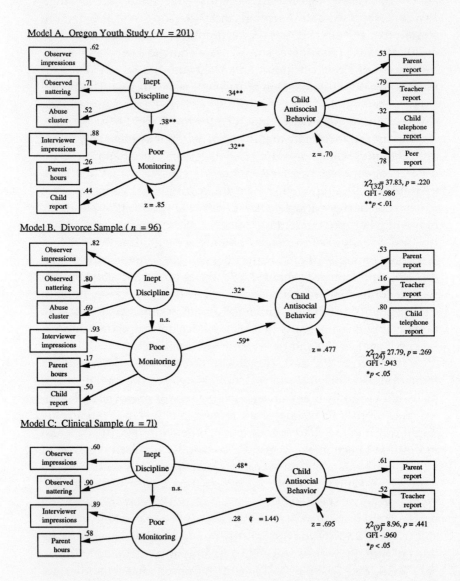

Model A. Oregon Youth Study (N = 201)

Model B. Divorce Sample (n = 96)

Model C: Clinical Sample (n = 71)

Figure 2. Two replications of the parenting model. From M. S. Forgatch, "The Clinical Science Vortex: A Developing Theory of Antisocial Behavior." In *The Development and Treatment of Childhood Aggression* (pp. 291–315), ed. D. J. Pepler and K. H. Rubin, 1991, Hillsdale NJ: Lawrence Erlbaum Associates. Copyright 1991 by Lawrence Erlbaum Associates, Inc. Reprinted with permission.

indicators to define three major constructs in the parenting model. For each sample, the chi-square test showed an acceptable fit between the a priori model and the data sets. The fact that the models accounted for a range of 30% to 52% of the variance in antisocial behavior attests to the robustness of the model. Metzler and Dishion (1992) replicated the general model based on a large sample of normal adolescents. Eddy and Fagot (1991) extended the parenting model down to families of normal preschool boys and girls. The model was replicated, and in all cases it accounted for a minimum of 30% of the variance in criterion measures of out-of-control behavior. The model meets the requirements for status as a performance model.

Antisocial children are doubly handicapped. Not only have they trained to be deviant, but their families have failed to train them in the prosocial skills required for survival with normal peers and in the classroom. When these antisocial children enter school, the effect of the dual nature of their problems is to produce a cascade of qualitatively new problems. Patterson and Yoerger (1993b) summarize a series of SEM that demonstrate that antisocial children's deviant behaviors and omitted social-skill training lead to rejection by normal peers, academic failure, and depressed moods.

We assumed that parenting practices make important contributions to the lack of prosocial skills and to presence of the antisocial behaviors. However, once children have acquired high rates of antisocial behavior, it becomes even more difficult to teach prosocial skills. In effect, their deviant behaviors further accelerate the negative growth curves for prosocial behaviors. In modeling studies, when the contribution of antisocial behavior is included, the path coefficients from antisocial to prosocial skills range from .4 to .5 (Patterson, Reid, & Dishion, 1992). We concluded from these studies that parenting practices are indirect determinants of some prosocial outcomes and antisocial behaviors make direct contributions.

The key hypothesis for the early-onset parenting model was that a composite of antisocial behavior measured in childhood could be used to predict early first arrest (prior to 14.0 years of age). Patterson, Crosby, and Vuchinich (1992) examined the contribution of three covariates to the distribution of hazard rates for first arrest. The OYS was an at-risk sample living in the higher crime areas of a medium-sized metropolitan community. Police arrest data were collected on a yearly basis on boys from 10 to 14.0 years of age. A continuous time–regression analysis showed that the composite scores for both parental discipline and parental SES made significant contributions to the distribution of hazard rates for arrest. Poor parenting skills and lower status contributed to increased risk for early arrest. As predicted, when the composite measure of childhood antisocial behavior was included, the parenting contribution became nonsignificant. Antisocial boys from low-status families made significant contributions to increased risk during this early-start interval. An SEM analysis of the data from the same OYS sample showed that the effect held even when a latent construct for early-onset delinquency was defined by both self-report and official records as indicators (Patterson et al., 1991). In that study the latent construct for antisocial behavior assessed during childhood accounted for 44% of the variance in the latent construct for early juvenile offending. This is in contrast to 21% of the variance for early convictions in the multiple regression analyses of the London cohort by Farrington and Hawkins (1991). In making this comparison, keep in mind that the SEM analysis assumes perfect specification (in a sense, it corrects for attenuation); the effect is to increase the variance claimed as accounted for.

It was stated earlier in this chapter that prediction of juvenile offending required improvements in both theory and in measurement. We hypothesized that it would be possible to predict early onset of juvenile offending more effectively than to predict juvenile offending in general. The reason for this is that the predictors that are effective for early-onset delinquency are thought to be different from those that are most effective in predicting late-onset delinquency. Improving the measurement for the predictors should result in further improvements in predictive efficiency.

In the OYS, the data for the antisocial indicators were assessed for children at about 10 years of age, whereas the police arrest data were collected each year on children through age 17.9 years. As shown in Figure 3a, by simply taking a median split for the composite measure of antisocial behavior assessed during childhood, it successfully identified 47 of the 53 boys arrested by age 14.0. The very low false negative error of 5.8% means that the predictor missed only 6 of the 53 boys arrested early. The hit rate was 69.9%. Probably the best means for estimating the overall efficiency of the 2 x 2

a. Early Arrest: Median Cut

Early Arrest

		Yes	No	Hits 69.9%
Above Median on Child Antisocial Behavior	Yes	47 (38)[a]	56	False positive 54.4%
				False negative 5.8%
	No	6 (5)	97	RIOC 77.4%

b. Ever Arrested during Adolescence

Ever Arrested by Age 17.9 Years

		Yes	No	Hits 65.1%
Above Median on Child Antisocial Behavior	Yes	72 (63)	31	False positive 30.1%
				False negative 39.8%
	No	41 (40)	62	RIOC 33.3%

[a] 10 cases of children being arrested prior to initiation of the Oregon Youth Study were deleted.

Figure 3. Predicting early arrests.

table is to calculate the relative improvement over chance (RIOC). Farrington and Loeber (1988) provided a lucid discussion of the pros and cons related to the use of this index. In Figure 3a, the RIOC value of 77.4% is considerably higher than comparable values for other longitudinal prediction studies reviewed in the Loeber and Dishion (1983) report.

The high RIOC value may reflect primarily the nature of the OYS at-risk sample; or it may reflect the improvements brought about by the multiple indicator measurement of the antisocial trait. To examine the latter possibility further, the data for early-onset delinquency were reanalyzed using only the teacher ratings of antisocial behavior (Achenbach & Edelbrock, 1986) as the independent variable. The median split for teacher ratings collected produced a false positive error of 60.2% and a false negative error of 11.7%. The RIOC was 54.7%. It seems that our success rests, in part, on our improvements in measurement.

We hypothesized that we would be able to predict early arrest more efficiently than we would be able to predict arrest at any time in adolescence. The data summarized in Figure 3b are consistent with this idea. The findings showed that for the OYS sample, 54.9% of the children had been arrested by the end of adolescence. The RIOC of 33.3% corresponded closely with the average value noted in the Loeber and Dishion (1983) review of prediction studies. The findings are consistent with the hypothesis that early-onset arrest can be more reliability predicted than can juvenile offending in general.

It has been known for decades that early onset of arrest is related to negative outcomes including a high risk for a criminal career. However, it has been less well understood that the progression from childhood antisocial behaviors to early arrest and chronic and violent offending can be accounted for by a single model. Forgatch, Patterson, and Stoolmiller (1994) examined this idea using the longitudinal data from two at-risk samples. The data showed, as expected, highly significant relations between each stage in the progression. At each juncture in the progression, there were significant differences in incidence between the early and late offenders. More recent analyses showed that the same set of context and measures of parenting practices related significantly to each stage in the sequence (Patterson, Forgatch, Yoerger, & Stoolmiller, 1997). The findings are consistent with the idea that if you understand the determinants for childhood antisocial behavior, you also understand some of the maintaining mechanisms that lead to early arrest and chronic and violent offending. The data also show each point in the trajectory is related to increased risk of adult arrest.

Late-Onset Model

BRIEF OVERVIEW

A general formulation for the late-onset model was outlined by Patterson (1994) and Patterson and Yoerger (1993a, 1993b). To some degree, many of the late-onset boys are identifiable during childhood and can be differentiated with modest success from both nondelinquent and early-onset boys. However, as we shall see, a very interesting subgroup of boys forms an exception because they cannot be delineated in childhood.

The late-onset families live in contexts that place them at moderate risk, as do their somewhat limited parenting skills. As children, these boys tend to show about average levels of antisocial behavior; they also tend to be at least marginally socially skilled. We assumed that, in the long run, the availability of payoffs for these skills compared to the relative payoffs for deviancy predicts their desistence from crime. In all aspects assessed, the late-onset boys seem to be marginally adjusted and, conversely, marginally deviant. In a sense, they are much better off than are the early-onset boys but not so well off as nondelinquent boys.

We hypothesized that the members of the deviant peer group play a major role in training the late-onset boys in their movement from childhood forms of coercive and antisocial acts into juvenile offenses. The deviant peer group also plays a key role in the metamorphosis from antisocial behavior to juvenile offending for the early-onset boys (Patterson, 1993). It is the level of antisocial behavior that determines when the child breaks down parental efforts to monitor behavior. An early-onset child may end up unsupervised and on the street as early as age 6 or 7. In the late-onset boys, the disruption of adult efforts to supervise takes place much later—during early to middle adolescence. Notice that the timing for the deviant peer-based metamorphosis is different for the two groups. What the boys bring to the process is also very different. The early-onset boys are both extremely deviant and extremely unskilled, whereas the late-onset boys are both moderately deviant and moderately skilled. The difference in starting points almost guarantees differences in growth patterns.

We hypothesized that involvement with deviant peers leads to the rapid development of covert but not overt antisocial acts for both groups. For the present, we assume that training for overt acts, such as temper tantrums and physical hitting, takes place only in interactions with siblings and parents (Patterson, 1984). If this is true, then both early and late groups should evidence growth in covert antisocial acts (substance use, stealing, truancy, etc). However, the growth will occur at different times, starting in childhood for the early-onset group and in middle adolescence for the late-onset group.

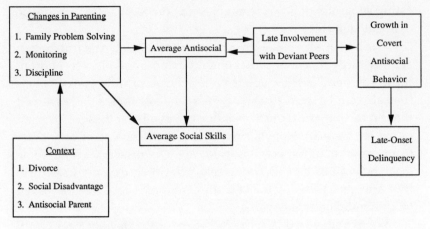

Figure 4. Late-onset model.

Eventually the results of the training of late-onset boys in covert antisocial acts are noticed by parents and teachers. The increase in covert acts is followed by increasing risk of late-onset police arrest. This general model is outlined in Figure 4. Again, the contribution of contextual factors to the development of the marginal prosocial and antisocial skills is thought to be mediated by parenting practices.

A SOCIAL INTERACTIONAL PROCESS FOR LATE-ONSET DELINQUENCY

We have not yet collected extensive observation data in the homes of late-onset boys and their families. For this reason the hypotheses about the social interactional processes that characterize these families are entirely speculative. We hypothesize, however, that when these studies are carried out, they will demonstrate that during conflict situations the relative payoffs for prosocial solutions will be much higher than were the payoffs for the early-onset group. This would mean that prosocial solutions work sometimes, but coercive solutions work somewhat better. When positive reinforcers for prosocial behaviors are eventually studied, we assumed again that the relative payoffs for prosocial behaviors would be significantly better for the late-onset boys than for the early-onset boys.

We assumed that these differences in relative payoffs for prosocial and coercive behaviors determine the individual differences in the development of prosocial skills and deviant behavior. The data for relative payoffs are presumably the key to our understanding of why late-onset boys are more socially skilled but less deviant than early-onset boys.

MARGINALITY HYPOTHESES

In many respects, an appropriate metaphor for the late-onset youth might well be "marginal man." The majority of the different comparisons examined in this section seem to be defined as a point in space, a kind of never-never land halfway between the early-onset and the nondelinquent boys. Our findings are quite similar to those obtained in the large-scale study by DiLalla and Gottesman (1989). They contrasted persistent and transitory offenders and found that the latter were better adjusted; however, transitory offenders were not so well adjusted as nonoffenders.

The Social-Skill Hypothesis. The first test of the marginality hypothesis was based on the measures of social-survival skill (i.e., those skills that have to do with relationships that endure and with work). Four measures from the oys battery used at grade 4 were selected as indicators. The social-skill construct was based on 11 items from the cbc-l for parents (Achenbach & Edelbrock, 1983) and for teachers (Achenbach & Edelbrock, 1986). Another indicator was based on four items from the peer nomination (e.g., "Kids who act as leaders in school"). A peer relations construct was defined by four items from the cbc-l filled out by parents, three items from the cbc-l filled out by teachers, and six items from the peer nomination task (e.g., "Kids whom I like as friends"). The self-esteem construct was based on two self-report measures filled out by the child (child perception, child skill). The achievement construct was based on parent and teacher ratings on four cbc-l items and scores from two achievement tests. Details of the psychometric studies of the peer relations, self-esteem, and achievement constructs are presented in Capaldi and Patterson (1989).

The three groups (early, late, and nondelinquent) were compared on their mean values for each of the social-skill measures. The findings are summarized in Table 1. There were 12 outcomes pre-

Table 1. *Social Skills as Tests for the Marginality Hypothesis*

Variable	Mean			Scheffe		
	Early onset (N = 53)	Late onset (N = 60)	Not delinquent (N = 93)	Early vs. not	Late vs. not	Late vs. early
Child social skill	−.61	.07	.30	X[a]		X
Poor peer relations	.58	−.01	−.32	X	X	X
Academic achievement	−.30	−.10	.24	X	X	
Self-esteem	−.30	.12	.09	X		X

[a]Tests were significant at .05 level or better.

dicted by the marginality hypothesis as it applied to late-onset boys. Of these, 11 outcomes were consistent with the hypothesis; 9 were significant. Late-onset boys were significantly more socially skilled, had better peer-relational skills, and had higher self-esteem than did early-onset boys. But in keeping with the marginality hypothesis, late-onset boys were also less skilled in peer relations and school achievement than were nondelinquent youth.

The social-skill variables defining work and heterosexual relationships are thought to play a key role in determining who drops out of the crime process and who does not. In keeping with the findings from the longitudinal study by Caspi and Elder (1988), we assumed that as young adults, the offenders who possessed even marginal levels of work- and relationship-enhancing skills would be more likely to desist in their offending. In keeping with Conger and Simons's (1997) formulation of the matching law, it would be assumed that late-onset boys would find the payoffs for prosocial activities relatively higher than the payoffs for continued offending. We predicted that when the late-onset boys of the OYS sample became young adults, they would be more likely than early-onset boys to drop out of the deviancy process.

Contextual and Parent-Practice Variables. We hypothesized that the marginality hypothesis could be extended to include contextual and parenting-skill variables as well. Presumably the late-onset group would emerge from contexts that were midway between the nondelinquent and early-onset groups. In a similar vein, we hypothesized that the families of late-onset youth would be characterized by marginally skilled discipline practices.

A comparison study of contexts for early- and late-onset groups by Capaldi and Patterson (1994) was based on the data from the OYS. Nine variables were entered that defined the key contextual and family-process variables. A discriminate function analysis showed that five variables loaded significantly on a single function, differentiating early- from late-onset boys. The canonical correlation for that function was .48.

The marginality hypothesis requires a comparison of early, late, and uninvolved groups; and the findings from the ANOVA are summarized in Table 2. All seven of the differences among the three groups were significant. However, the marginality hypothesis also requires paired comparisons among the three groups. Of 14 such comparisons, 9 were significant and consistent with the marginality hypothesis. The data showed that, as compared to late-onset families, the early-onset families were embedded in more negative contexts. They had significantly more transitions (from intact to single-parent families, etc.), higher parental antisocial behavior, lower likelihood of parent employment, and lower socioeconomic status. The two groups did not significantly differ on income. Incidentally, these findings provide a reasonably good fit with the contextual variables found in Farrington and Hawkins's (1991) analysis of the data from the London cohort that differentiated early from late onset. In the OYS, parents of early-onset boys were also significantly less effective in their discipline practices than were parents of late-onset boys.

As compared to the families of nondelinquent boys, late-onset families showed significantly higher parental antisocial behavior and lower income. The two groups did not significantly differ on transitions, parent employment, socioeconomic status, or discipline. Finally, the findings for levels of childhood antisocial behaviors were also consistent with the marginality hypothesis. The early-onset boys were significantly more antisocial than were late-onset boys, who in turn were significantly more antisocial than were uninvolved boys.

CONTRIBUTION OF DISRUPTED MONITORING

It was hypothesized by Patterson and Yoerger (1993b) that for the late-onset boys, the role played by parenting skills varies from one developmental phase to another. During childhood, parental disci-

Table 2. *Multivariate Analysis of Variance of Age of Arrest by Contextual Risk Factors at Grade 4*

$N =$	(Early) first arrest prior to age 14.0 (43) Mean	(Late) first arrest at age 14 + (52) Mean	Early vs. Late	No arrest (89) Mean	Late vs. None	Comparison Mean p level
Context						
Parental antisocial behavior	0.49	0.08	†	−0.28		<.001
Parental transitions	1.79	1.17	*	0.82		<.001
One or both parents employed	0.67	0.90	*	0.84		<.05
Socioeconomic status	−0.43	0.02	†	0.20		<.01
Income	−0.37	−0.13		0.25	†	<.01
Family Process						
Poor discipline	0.53	−0.21	**	−0.13		<.001
Child Behavior						
Boys' antisocial behavior	0.82	−0.05	**	−0.37	†	<.001

Note: Variables were standardized except for number of parental transitions since the boy's birth (scored 0, 1, 2, or 3+) and parental employment (0 = no employed parent, 1 = one or two employed parents).

†$p < .05$, *$p < .01$, **$p < .001$.

pline played important roles in determining the marginal levels of deviancy and prosocial skills. However, in early to middle adolescence, it was disruptions in parental monitoring that contributed indirectly to juvenile offending. The assumption was that parents can and do control the amount of time the adolescent invests in deviant peers. In the next section, it becomes clear that almost all adolescents have some contact with deviant peers; but presumably the adolescent who has extensive contact over a prolonged period is most likely to receive intensive training in delinquency skills. This hypothesis is discussed further in a later section.

Studies by Paikoff and Brooks-Gunn (1990) and Montemayor and Flannery (1989) had shown that during adolescence there is increasing conflict between adolescents and their parents. We hypothesized that these conflicts would be associated with disrupted parental monitoring (Patterson & Yoerger 1993b). We also assumed that outside disrupters might also be associated with ineffective parental supervision. To test this idea, a disrupter risk score was formed where each variable was scored as 0 or +1. The list of disrupters included unemployment or recent financial loss, a severe illness or death, family transition (divorce, etc.), change of residence, or pubescence. An event was scored only if it had occurred during the interval when the boys were 11 to 12 years of age.

Although the pilot test of the model supported the general formulation, the sample was too small to provide an adequate test (Patterson & Yoerger, 1993b). The present analyses included all boys scoring below the median on the antisocial construct at grade 4. Eighty subjects remained after listwise deletion. The nonsignificant chi-square ($p = .50$) showed an acceptable fit between the data set and the a priori model. As shown in Figure 5, all of the path coefficients were significant. As expected, the disrupter variables are related to less effective parental monitoring; parental monitoring in turn is related (path .61) to increasing involvement with deviant peers. This effect for nonantisocial boys was replicated in the findings from the Iowa Youth and Family Project (Simons, Wu, Conger, & Lorenz, 1994). The sample consisted of 76 adolescent boys who had not previously been identified as early starters. In the late-onset model, the path coefficient from ineffective parenting contributing directly to involvement with deviant peers was $-.323^*$ ($p < .05$).

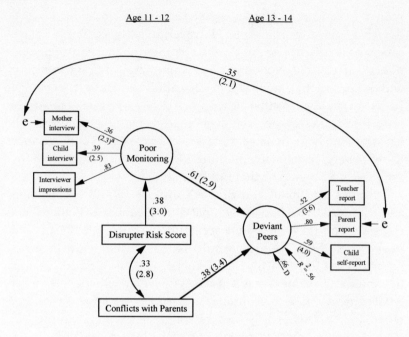

$N = 80$ (of 103 cases below mean of Wave 1 Antisocial construct score)

$\chi^2_{(16)} = 15.36$, $p = .50$; values within parentheses are t-test scores; BBN = .893; BBNN = 1.010; CFI = 1.000.

Figure 5. Parenting and late-onset delinquency.

In Figure 5, increasing disruption was correlated with increasing conflict between parent and adolescent. This conflict in turn contributes to further involvement with deviant peers, which offers nice support for Elder's (1980) hypothesis that parent-adolescent conflict fuels a "flight to the peer group." The findings are consistent with the idea that training parents to be more vigorous in their efforts to supervise and monitor their adolescent may be an important deterrent for juvenile offending.

INVOLVEMENT WITH DEVIANT PEERS

As noted earlier, involvement with deviant peers plays a primary role in the early-onset model's metamorphosis of childhood antisocial acts to delinquent activities (Dishion et al., 1994; Patterson, 1993, 1996). Deviant peers play a comparable role in the late-onset model, where they both model and shape the performance of antisocial attitudes and covert antisocial acts, such as substance use and truancy. Eventually the modeling and support include behaviors that would be classified as juvenile offenses, and this in turn is related to increasing risk of police arrest. Although both Moffitt (1993) and the present writers emphasize the direct contribution of deviant peers to offending, this point of view differs markedly from Hirschi's (1969) social control theory. In the latter, deviant peers are viewed as a product of the deviancy process rather than as prime determinants for juvenile offending. Our position is that deviant peer involvement is both a product and a determinant.

Availability of Deviant Peers. Societies and individual families differ in their approaches to granting autonomy to adolescents. In many primitive societies, the onset of pubescence was a convenient marker variable. It was signified by a ritual such as moving from the family dwelling to bachelor quarters, where the novice was under the control of adult males. However, the comparable rite of passage for the Western industrialized society is beset with ambiguity. Much of the uncertainty revolves around the issue of unsupervised time (i.e., when, where, with whom, and doing what?). The question is when and in what ways should parental supervision be relaxed. If the controls are relaxed too soon, the child may be at risk of hanging out with deviant peers. Alternatively, if the controls remain in place too long, the adolescent is at risk of never becoming autonomous.

The ambiguity of the parental monitoring role increases with the age of the adolescent; this is further exacerbated by the increasing availability of deviant peers. Our public schools may maximize contacts with deviant peers. In the Dishion, Patterson, and Kavanagh (1992) report, over half the boys that the target boys hang out with were met in the school setting. It is the ideal setting for contacts with members of the deviant peer group. During early and middle adolescence, most of the peer group reports to this setting 5 days a week. During that time there are substantial periods of time when the interaction cannot be closely supervised by adults, and there are some settings where there is no adult supervision at all. In many ways, this setting is ideal for shopping among members of the peer group for a wide range of partners, from crime to marriage.

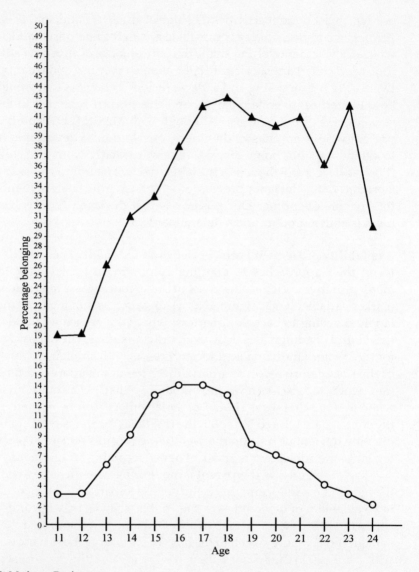

▲ Moderate Deviancy

O High Deviancy

Figure 6. Contacts with deviant peers by age. From D. S. Elliott and S. Menard, "De-linquent Friends and Delinquent Behavior: Temporal and Developmental Patterns." In *Delinquency and Crime: Current Theories* (pp. 28–67), ed. J. D. Hawkins, 1996, Cam-bridge: Cambridge University Press. Copyright 1996 by Cambridge University Press. Reprinted with the permission of Cambridge University Press.

Studies by Cairns and Cairns (1991) speak to the fact that, by and large, antisocial children and adolescents are not social isolates. They belong to extensive and rapidly changing social networks. It seems that deviant peers may be a ubiquitous presence in many of these social groups. The extensive self-report survey by Elliott and Menard (1996) provides a detailed portrayal of just how common-place contacts with deviant peers might be. Their data describe the contacts with deviant peers for youth between the ages of 11 and 24 years. The findings are summarized in Figure 6.

During childhood, less than a quarter of the boys reported con-tacts with groups that contain moderate to high densities of deviant peers. From early to middle adolescence, there is rapid growth in such contacts, which peaks between the ages of 16 and 18 years. For example, by age 14, about 40% of the boys report contact with groups that contain moderate to high densities of deviant members. By age 17, this applies to slightly over half of the boys.

The school setting is rich in possibilities for contacts with devi-ant peers. We assumed that the parents can and do have an impact on the frequency and duration of these contacts that occur in the evenings and on weekends. We assumed that it is at such times that the intensive training for antisocial attitudes and for covert acts actu-ally take place.

Selective Seekers. We hypothesized that each individual actively shops among settings, activities, and peers in such a manner as to maximize the relative payoff available (Patterson, 1996; Patterson, Reid, & Dishion, 1992). There is a cluster of three hypotheses re-quired for the selective seeker formulation. The first hypothesis is the well-known "likes tend to select likes." Presumably this is a gen-eral principle that applies to the selection of friends, lovers, mar-riage partners, and perhaps business associates as well. For exam-ple, Kandel, Davies, and Baydar (1990) made a good case in support of homophily in their studies of adolescents. Eight different studies showed that bright people tend to self-select bright people to inter-marry (Buss, 1984). Patterson and Dishion (1988) found a correlation of .39 ($p = .001$) between latent constructs for antisocial fathers and antisocial mothers. Even more to the point, Dishion, Andrews, and Crosby (1995) showed that antisocial boys tend to select one another to "hang out with." As noted earlier, a corollary hypothesis is that the more antisocial the child, the earlier he or she will become a member of a deviant peer group. In keeping with Moffitt's (1993) hypothesis, we suspected that these young antisocial children form the core of the deviant peer group particularly in its early stages of development.

Deviancy Shaping. The second assumption contained in the selective seeker model is that children select friends with whom to hang out who maximize the individual's payoffs (Dishion et al., 1994; Patterson, 1996). There are numerous ways that this idea might be tested. One would be to calculate a cost-benefit ratio describing each dyad's observed playground interactions with peers (Snyder, 1995a; Snyder, West, Stockemer, Gibbons, & Almquist-Parks, 1996). "Maximize payoffs" was defined by calculating the ratio of positive to negative exchanges. In this study of preschool children, the data in fact showed correlations in the .6 to .7 range between friendship preferences and observed cost-benefit ratios. Children preferred as friends those peers who provided a higher ratio of positive to negative exchanges. Note in passing that the data also showed this cost-benefit ratio was lower for aggressive children than for nonaggressive children. The data from the Snyder studies are consistent with the hypothesis that likes are more mutually reinforcing.

The third assumption for the selective seeker formulation is that deviant individuals are more likely to reinforce each other for deviancy. This raises the question, for what do deviant individuals reinforce each other? Clinical work with groups of deviant adolescents suggests that they use rich schedules of positive reinforcement for antisocial talk and behaviors. This clinical impression was strongly supported by an observation study in a corrections institution (Buehler, Patterson, & Furniss, 1966). They found that within the institutional setting, both deviant peers and staff were more likely to provide positive reinforcement for deviant behavior than for prosocial behavior. The effect was replicated by Sanson-Fisher et al. (1979).

These findings were replicated and considerably extended in the programmatic studies carried out by Dishion and his colleagues. They arranged for each boy in the oys to bring along a boy with whom he generally spent a good deal of time hanging out (Dishion et al., 1994). Analyses of the videotaped interaction showed a significant match between the relative rate of rule-breaking talk for the interchange and the relative rate of payoff by the peer for rule-breaking talk. In normal dyads the same reinforcement was available, but it was contingent upon prosocial talk. Incidentally, the relative rates of rule-breaking talk correlated significantly with later delinquency. Deviant dyads mutually reinforce each other for deviant talk. Even a casual viewing of these tapes leaves one with the strong impression that one is observing a process that leads to the formation of antisocial attitudes and in turn is an analogue for what would occur in a natural setting where rule-breaking talk can quickly change to rule-breaking behavior. One implication of this assumption is that over time members of deviant groups should become increasingly similar to each other, at least on a dimension of deviancy. In keeping with this assumption, Kandel et al. (1990) also showed that the dyads tended to become more similar over time.

Early investigators estimated that as many as 8 of 10 boys committed their offenses in the company of others. A half century later, the situation remains very similar and implicates the deviant peers in the role of instigator and coparticipant as well as a reinforcing support group and as a model for delinquent acts. Given such a setting with much of the interaction consisting of overlearned responses, one might wonder about the extent to which each of the members of the group is governed by the social-cognitive seven-step process as outlined by Dodge, Petit, Bates, and Valente (1995). Is the delinquent act the outcome of a subjective calculus of cost and benefit? Or in the context of group interaction is the event a variation on an overlearned jazz riff that has been practiced many times before? The strongest empirical case made to date for the cognitive alternative was presented in the report by Dodge, Bates, and Petit (1990), where the measures of social cognition carried less than 10% of the criterion variance.

These findings suggest that deviant peers play a significant role in shaping antisocial attitudes and behaviors. However, these findings are only indirectly related to the problem of growth. Although we assumed that the more time spent with deviant peers, the greater the acceleration in the growth of new forms of antisocial behavior, changes over time in the kinds of antisocial acts performed could reflect what the adolescent observes on television or in his in-

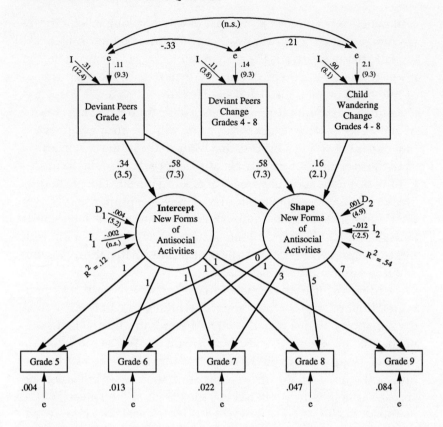

Figure 7. A growth model for changes in form. From "Orderly Change in a Stable World: The Antisocial Trait as a Chimera," by G. R. Patterson, 1993, *Journal of Consulting and Clinical Psychology, 61,* pp. 911–919. Also in *The Analysis of Change,* ed. J. Gottman, (1995), Mahwauk NJ: Lawrence Erlbaum Associates. Copyright 1993 Lawrence Erlbaum Associates, Inc. Reprinted with permission.

teractions. The changes might also reflect changes in the child's own physical and cognitive development.

Longitudinal data from the OYS were used to examine growth in two forms of covert behavior. Most children do not engage in these activities, but many adolescents do. One of them might be thought of as a juvenile offense but not the other. Teacher and parent ratings of truancy and substance use served as the dependent variables and were assessed each year at grades 5 through 9 (Patterson, 1993). As Figure 7 indicates, at grade 4 the path coefficient of .34 from deviant peers to the intercept for the new forms of antisocial behavior shows that the boys who were the first to practice the new forms were already heavily involved with deviant peers. Notice, too, that the boys who showed the most growth (shape score) were also boys who were first to be involved with deviant peers. As shown by the path coefficient of .58, early involvement with deviant peers is a major determinant for accelerated growth in the new forms, whereas boys who showed marked increases in deviant peer involvement between grades 4 and 8 also contributed heavily to the growth in the new forms as shown by a path coefficient of .58. Boys who showed marked increases in wandering during the same interval also made small but significant contributions to growth. Combing the information from all of the covariates showed that the model accounted for 54% of the growth in new forms of antisocial behavior. It is interesting to note that the deviant peer construct contributed significantly to where the growth started and also to the magnitude of growth.

The interactions with deviant peers has several salient characteristics. For example, the longitudinal study of adolescents and their peers showed that the friendships for antisocial boys were of significantly shorter duration than those for nonantisocial boys (e.g., many friendships lasted for less than a year; Dishion et al., 1994). Dyads, where one or both members were antisocial, were characterized by significantly higher rates of directives and noxious behavior and of a lower order of social skills as compared to nonantisocial members of dyads. Both of these effects have been replicated in the programmatic studies by Cairns and Cairns (1994).

LATE-ONSET BOYS WHO ARE LATE BLOOMERS

The simplest form of the late-onset model would have it that those children who are most antisocial become involved with deviant peers first and also get arrested first. Presumably those with less extreme antisocial scores will be arrested next, and those with only slightly above average scores will be arrested during late adolescence. To test this overly simplistic idea, we used the sample of all individuals arrested before the age of 18 years ($N = 113$). In keeping with the hypothesis, the correlation of the childhood (grade 4) measure of antisocial behavior and age of first juvenile arrest was $-.43$ ($p < .001$). Inspection of the scatter plot showed it to be essentially linear. There were six outliers, but their contributions seemed equally distributed in working for and against the hypothesis. The correlation was consistent with the hypothesis that boys who were only moderately antisocial tended to be among the last to be arrested.

These findings are in keeping with a hypothesized single-deviancy dimension as put forth by Gottfredson and Hirschi (1990). Of the 103 children scoring above the median at grade 4 on the antisocial composite score, 9 were arrested prior to the study, 38 were first arrested before the age of 14.0 years, and another 25 were first arrested during the late-onset interval. By the end of adolescence, 72 of the 103 boys scoring above the median on antisocial behavior had been arrested at least once. On the face of it, the single-dimension hypothesis seems to work very well in predicting early and late onset of arrest.

There is, however, good reason to believe that a simple extension of the early-onset model is insufficient for the task at hand. The problem lies in the fact that some individuals who were not antisocial as children became antisocial between the ages of 11 and 18 years. The timing for these late bloomers creates a problem for theorists such as Gottfredson and Hirshi (1990). The subgroup of late-blooming antisocial boys first emerged as we examined the intra-individual growth patterns for the two-factor latent growth model for antisocial behavior (Patterson, 1993). As a result of that study, we began to suspect that there was a small group of boys who were systematically increasing in antisocial acts. At grade 4 it was the familiar covariates, parental discipline and monitoring, that accounted for the intercept for general antisocial behavior. However, the boys who were growing in antisocial acts were those who were showing increasing amounts of time invested in deviant peers. At this point we knew two things about deviant peer involvement. On the one hand, it was related to the metamorphosis to new forms of antisocial acts; but on the other hand, their involvement was also related to a small group of boys systematically becoming more antisocial. We did not know whether the changes included overt or covert acts.

Table 3. *Prevalence of Late Bloomers*

Variable	Prevalence by School Grade								
	4	5	6	7	8	9	10	11	Total
When involvement with deviant peers first identified	100	29	19	13	3	5	2	1	172
When antisocial trait first identified	98	21	18	6	6	7	6	1	163

When did increases in antisocial acts for late bloomers become noticeable to adults? To determine at what age this happened, we relied upon the fact that childhood antisocial behavior for the OYS was assessed yearly. Based on items from the CBC-l (Achenbach & Edelbrock, 1983), parents and teachers filled out the 18- and 16-item questionnaires that were used to build our own internally consistent scales to measure both antisocial behavior and involvement with deviant peers. The mean of the parent and teacher scores defined the distribution of score for both the deviant peer involvement and the antisocial scales. The first row of Table 3 enumerates by age the number of boys not previously identified as being involved with deviant peers but now clearly identified by one or more adults as "hanging out with them." As shown, 100 boys at grade 4 were identified as involved with deviant peers, and 98 were classified as above the median on antisocial behavior. Notice that the bulk of the late bloomers first emerged at grades 5, 6, and 7. By the end of adolescence, 172 of the boys had been identified at some time or another as above the median in their involvement with deviant peers, and 163 had been identified at one time or another as being antisocial.

GROWTH IN ANTISOCIAL BEHAVIOR

We hypothesized that involvement with deviant peers causes the growth, first in antisocial behaviors and then in the increasing risk of police arrest. However, it is not clear whether the growth includes the entire spectrum of antisocial acts or only a limited set of these behaviors.

A study of growth in antisocial behavior during adolescence

poses an extremely important paradox. Cairns and Cairns (1991) showed that when boys and girls between the ages of 10 and 15 years self-report antisocial behaviors, the data showed only a slight decrease over time. Patterson and Yoerger (1993b) showed that teacher ratings of antisocial behavior increased significantly from grade 4 to 5 and then showed stable mean levels through grade 8. The two studies agree in saying that there is little if any "growth" in antisocial behavior during this interval. These findings are obviously discrepant with the findings from the age and crime-frequency data. These sociological studies invariably show dramatic growth in both self-reported and official records of crime between the ages of 10 and 17.

There is a most curious discrepancy between sociology's view of juvenile offending and psychology's view of antisocial behavior. We hypothesized a resolution to this seeming paradox. Psychology's emphasis upon zero growth in mean level for antisocial acts through adolescence reflects two different patterns that, when combined, seem to reflect zero growth. We hypothesized that during this interval, covert antisocial behaviors are increasing at the same time as overt antisocial acts are decreasing. It is the growth in covert antisocial behaviors that covaries with growth in crime.

Parents' ratings of antisocial behavior were obtained annually in the oys longitudinal study. After listwise deletion, there were 158 complete data sets. Based on our previous studies (Patterson, Reid, & Dishion, 1992) and those of Loeber and Schmaling (1985), 28 items were selected that assessed both covert and overt behaviors. Given our interest in describing growth of covert and overt antisocial acts, we decided to form the two scales based on items that showed comparable growth patterns over time. For each of the seven items thought to form a covert scale, we examined both the linear and quadratic components describing their pattern of change over time. A principal axis factor analysis was carried out first for the linear change scores and then separately for the quadratic scores. Items that loaded less than .3 on either the linear or quadratic factors were to be dropped, which actually resulted in only two items being deleted. A similar analysis was carried out for the 21 items of the overt scale. All items met the loading criteria. The details of the analyses are summarized in the Appendix. We were pleasantly surprised by the consistency with which the a priori selected items also formed scales that were reasonably homogeneous in their definition of growth.

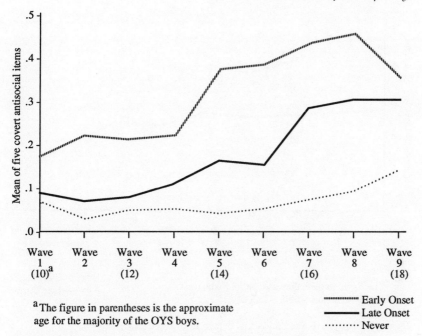

[a]The figure in parentheses is the approximate age for the majority of the OYS boys.

.... Early Onset
————— Late Onset
·········· Never

Figure 8. Changes in covert antisocial behavior for three groups.

We were also satisfied that the resulting scales constitute sensitive indicators of change, or the lack of it, for the early, late, and non-delinquent groups.

We hypothesized that positive growth for covert antisocial acts would be greater for the early-onset group but would also occur for the late-onset group. We had no basis for guessing what would happen with the nonarrested group but suspected they would show little if any growth. The findings for changes in mean level of covert antisocial behavior are summarized in Figure 8. Clearly, the perceptions of parents and teachers reflect increasing frequencies of covert antisocial behaviors for adolescents in all three groups. The ANOVA for repeated measures showed a highly significant main effect for trials, $F = 8.36$ ($p = .000$), and between groups as well, $F = 34.08$ ($p = .000$). Inspection of growth curves for individual items suggested that the most consistent growth was in hanging out with deviant peers, alcohol use, and truancy.

In order for the mean slope of antisocial behavior to be zero during the adolescent interval, it would follow that there must be a gen-

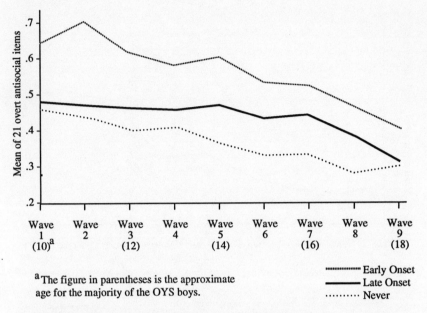

a The figure in parentheses is the approximate
age for the majority of the OYS boys.

········ Early Onset
——— Late Onset
·········· Never

Figure 9. Changes in overt antisocial behavior for three groups.

eral decrease in frequency for overt forms of the problem behaviors. Figure 9 summarizes the negative growth for overt antisocial behaviors. Consistent with the hypothesis, the trend for the three groups is for these behaviors to show a general decrease. The ANOVA showed the main effect for trials to be highly significant, $F = 8.18$ ($p = .000$). The differences between groups were significant as well, $F = 4.38$ ($p = .014$).

Observation studies of family interaction discussed earlier suggested that conflict episodes played a critical role in training for coercive behaviors in both the preschool and elementary grades. We do not yet know whether escape-conditioning arrangements (aversive-overt antisocial behavior that leads to termination of conflict) are the only way of training for overt antisocial behaviors. For the sake of discussion, let us assume that they are. One may ask if the interaction in deviant peer groups might not complement the training provided in the family setting. For example, overt antisocial behavior (threatening, temper tantrums) might well be a frequent and successful means for handling conflict in the deviant peer setting. If this is accurate, then there should be an increase in overt antisocial behavior during periods of maximum involvement with deviant peers.

Table 4. *Late-Onset Life History Tables*

| | Given antisocial emerges at: | | | | | | |
| | Grade 4 (Early) | | | Grades 5–11 (Late) | | | |
Age at First Arrest	Number at Risk	Frequency First Arrests	Hazard Rate	Number at Risk	Frequency Arrest	Hazard Rate	Never at Risk
14.0–14.9	61	7	.115	59	4	.068	
15.0–15.9	54	8	.148	55	5	.091	
16.0–16.9	46	8	.174	50	6	.120	
17.0–17.9	38	9	.237	44	5	.114	
		Total 32			Total 20		Total 8
							Grand Total 60

The data in Figure 9 indicate that is not the case. It seems reasonable to conclude that escape conditioning during conflict episodes may not be a central component of deviant peer training for deviancy. By the same token, the findings in Figure 8 suggest that the training by deviant peers may be critical for covert antisocial behavior. Inspection of the growth curves for individual items suggested that the high growth behaviors are truancy, drug and alcohol use, and stealing inside and outside the house.

GROWTH IN CRIME

In the Oregon sample, 10 boys were arrested before the study began and 53 were arrested when the boys were between the ages of 10 and 14.0. Sixty boys were first arrested during the late-onset interval. We were particularly interested in examining the 60 late-onset boys to determine whether they were a homogeneous group. As shown in Table 4, there seemed to be two main contributions to status as late onset. Thirty-two boys could be identified at grade 4 because they had scored at least at a marginal level on the childhood measure of antisocial behavior. The distribution of their hazard rates suggested that ages 16 and 17 were peak risk periods for them.

There is a second group that is a major contributor to late onset. It consisted of 20 boys from the 59 late bloomers for covert antisocial behavior discussed earlier. These 20 cases accounted for 33% of all boys arrested in the late-onset interval. Their hazard rates tended to peak at about 16 and 17 years of age. A theoretical model that as-

Table 5. *Multivariate Model Using Only Initial Childhood Measures as Covariates*

Variable	B	SE B	Significant (1df)	R	Ex(B)
Time	.88	.23	.000	.14	2.40
Antisocial	1.87	.39	.000	.18	6.50
Deviant Peer	.58	.25	.021	.07	1.79
Constant	−3.92	.27	.000		

sumes delinquency is the outcome of a single deviancy dimension identifiable in childhood will oversimplify the situation by precisely these 20 cases. Whether this is a minor or a major anomaly depends upon one's point of view.

Our general strategy was to strive for as complete an explanation as possible. Given this perspective, we would like to understand where the 20 late bloomers come from and to determine whether adding this information to the general model really makes a significant contribution. The means for doing this seems relatively straightforward. In a multivariate model, we would begin by introducing the two variables assessed during childhood that would account for all 53 early-onset boys and for 32 of the late-onset boys. According to the model, this would be the composite measures of antisocial behavior and deviant peer involvement. The outcome variable would be time elapsed to first arrest. The question now is, would adding information about later involvement with deviant peers make a significant contribution in accounting for hazard rates of arrest? More to the point, would the contribution be unique in that it tells us something that was not inherent in the childhood measures?

A discrete-time event history analysis was used to examine these questions further. The model included a control for the differences in risk as a function of age of child. The findings for the first model are summarized in Table 5. Only the childhood measures of "fixed variables" for antisocial and deviant peer composites are included to keep the analyses as conservative as possible. The 10 cases arrested prior to the study were deleted. Time was coded as 0 for early and +1 for late interval.

The data showed that age made a difference. The odds for being arrested were 2.4 times greater during the late interval than during the early interval. As expected, high fixed values assessed during

Table 6. *Discrete-Time Event History Analyses of Combined Fixed-Time and Time-Varying Covariates*

Variable	B	SE B	P Value (1df)	R	Ex(B)
Time	1.02	.23	.000	.17	2.77
Fixed:					
Antisocial	1.74	.38	.000	.17	5.72
Time-dependent:					
Deviant Peer	1.13	.26	.000	.17	3.10
Constant	−4.28	.30	.000		

childhood for antisocial and deviant peer involvement were significantly related to risk for first arrest at some time during adolescence. Being above the median on antisocial behavior meant that the odds for being arrested during adolescence were more than six times greater than for low-scoring boys. High scores on deviant peer involvement carried almost a doubling of the odds for being arrested. In effect, a single model of an antisocial child who is involved with deviant peers at grade 4 provides an acceptable fit in predicting combined early-onset and late-onset arrest. The findings support the idea of juvenile offending being the outcome of a single dimension of deviancy unfolding over time as presented in the Gottfredson and Hirschi (1990) theory. The fact that deviant peers make a significant contribution to both early and late start does not support the Moffitt (1993) position that deviant peers contribute to the latter but not to the former.

We hypothesized that if time-dependent information concerning early or middle adolescent involvement with deviant peers were added, it would significantly improve the ability of the model to account for risk of first arrest during adolescence. Time-dependent measures of involvement with deviant peers were entered together with fixed-time measures for antisocial behavior and deviant peers. We included age and product terms for the interaction of time with the other independent variables. In keeping with the theoretical model, the covariates in the analysis were lagged by 1 year. Thus, the risk for arrests represented by the dependent variable occurred in the year immediately following the emergence of involvement with deviant peers. This is, of course, a very conservative test of the hypothesis.

The results are summarized in Table 6. Again, the odds of an arrest during the late interval was several times higher than for the early interval. None of the interaction terms that included time were significant. As before, the childhood fixed-time measure of antisocial behavior made the most substantial contribution with an increase in one unit associated with a 5.7-fold increase in risk. The time-varying measure of deviant peer involvement also made a significant contribution with a 1-unit increase associated with an increase in risk of 3.1. The findings are in keeping with the idea that the better model is based on covariates that include both fixed-time and time-dependent variables. The complete model would include covariates that pick up the 20 late-blooming covert antisocial boys.

ADULT ADJUSTMENT

Our future set of modeling studies will test the relation of early-onset and late-onset models to adult adjustment. We can already begin to see the long-term implications of status in one group or the other. For example, only 21% of the early-onset boys graduated from high school as compared to 33% of the late-onset boys and 73% of the nondelinquent groups. Clearly, status in the early-onset group constitutes a major disrupter for adjustment to the transition from public school to the work force.

As a working hypothesis, we assumed that early onset and chronicity constitute the prime predictors of status as adult offenders. The findings from three longitudinal studies reviewed by Blumstein, Cohen, Roth, and Visher (1986) showed that given four juvenile offenses, the likelihoods of adult arrest ranged from .68 to .92. We assumed that the majority of oys chronic juvenile offenders will become adult offenders.

In keeping with Conger and Simons's (1997) formulation, we expected over time that work skills, academic skills, or more positive family relations would begin to provide reinforcements that would result in a relative increase of prosocial behaviors and decrease in antisocial and delinquent behaviors. Presumably these feedback loops will explain why so many late-onset boys drop out of the criminal process and early-onset boys do not.

Implications

A case was made for early and late onset as being two different paths to juvenile offending. In the high-risk oys, 53 boys were arrested prior to the age of 14.0 years, and another 60 were arrested after that time but during adolescence. Capaldi's (1994) report and the current findings showed that the early-onset boys come from more disadvantaged homes and are significantly more deviant and less socially skilled than are late-onset boys. The term *marginally adjusted* seems to be an apt description for the late-onset group.

It has been known for some time that early-onset boys were at greater risk for long-term negative outcomes, such as chronic and violent offending and perhaps adult offending as well. Earlier theories have done little to explicate the process that produces these outcomes. We assume that the proximal variable that accounts for risk of arrest is the overall frequency of antisocial acts. Presumably, the individual is first trained in a variety of overt and covert antisocial acts under the tutelage of the deviant peer group. The antisocial acts are then followed by the emergence of comparable rates of juvenile offending. Engaging in the performance of a wide spectrum of trivial and nontrivial delinquent acts places the child at risk for eventual detection and arrest. In the predictive sense, one precedes the other. The implication is that the process can be interrupted by reducing the level of antisocial behavior. This in turn would be followed by a corresponding decrease in risk for offending as shown in the study by Patterson and Forgatch (1995).

The other facet of the early-onset and late-onset models that is crucial to the understanding of long-term negative outcomes concerns the role of antisocial behavior as a determinant for the timing (as well as the frequency) of juvenile offending. Extremely high levels of antisocial behavior in childhood are associated with the very early emergence of juvenile offending and accompanying risk of earliest police arrest. Presumably this comes about because the extremely deviant child has simply overwhelmed any parental efforts to supervise or control. The young, extremely antisocial child starts earliest and is also the most socially unskilled.

Parenting skills play a key role in both the early-onset and late-onset models. Presumably these parenting practices in turn control the reinforcing and punishing contingencies for the child's behavior. It is the case, of course, that the causal status ascribed to parenting practices cannot be tested in correlational models, even when based on longitudinal data. As pointed out by Forgatch (1991), only experimental manipulation can directly address this issue. She outlines the way in which random assignment prevention designs can be used to provide an experimental test for variables such as parenting practices. Three longitudinal designs that employ random assignment and parental training components are currently underway at the Oregon Social Learning Center and three studies at other sites. Each study is designed to test the assumed causal status for the parenting variables. Thus far, one study has been completed (Dishion et al., 1992). The findings showed that Parent Training Therapy produced significant improvements in parenting scores and that the magnitude of improvements in parenting correlated significantly with the magnitude of improvements in teachers' ratings of antisocial behavior. Forgatch (1995) has summarized unpublished findings from three additional studies that demonstrate support for the causal status of parenting practices.

The late-onset boys not only start later but also perform juvenile offenses at lower rates, as suggested by the research findings reviewed in Patterson and Yoerger (1993b). But the key set of findings has to do with the fact that by the time late-onset boys start offending, they are already moderately skilled in work and relational areas. We predict that, in the long run, the presence of these social skills will generate the relative payoffs that pull them out of the deviancy process (i.e., the relative payoffs for crime are simply less than are the relative payoffs as a member of the nondelinquent community). In passing, we suspect that as adults, as compared to members of the nondelinquent group, the late-onset males are also likely to be marginally adjusted with perhaps higher rates of divorce, illness, unemployment, and alcoholism and substance abuse.

One of the most interesting findings concerned the 20 late-blooming boys who were not antisocial as children but who were perceived during adolescence by one or more adult observers as recently having become antisocial. We suspect that their history centers primarily around the development of covert rather than overt antisocial behavior. Inspection of the intra-individual growth curves shows that although they share the adolescent propensity for arguing, demanding, and bragging (all overt behaviors), the primary growth is in truancy, substance and alcohol use, and stealing. Coercive behaviors, such as threats, temper tantrums, and hitting, do not seem to be a core feature for this group.

The early-onset and late-onset models bear a close resemblance to factor analysis studies of delinquents carried out in the 1940s. These studies produced two (sometimes more) groups labeled "socialized delinquents" and "unsocialized delinquents." The factors appeared when the data consisted of referral symptoms or ratings by the adolescents, teachers, or parents. The findings continue to the present time as shown in recent reviews by Quay (1987). The unsocialized delinquent sounds like the prototype of our early-onset boys. They are not only chronically coercive and antisocial but, in addition, lack the requisite social survival skills. It is interesting to note that Quay speculates, as do we, that it is this group that carries a genetic loading. The socialized delinquent, on the other hand, hangs out with deviant peers, has some modicum of social skills, and tends to have only a transitory career in crime. The current early-onset and late-onset models provide an empirical base for defining the developmental stages and the social interactional processes that lead to one or the other outcomes.

As noted earlier, Moffitt's (1993) life-course persistent and adolescence-limited offending theory of delinquency covers much of the same territory as does the early- and late-onset theory. Both theories emphasize child temperament for disrupted parenting; presumably temperament reflects both genetic and constitutional (birthweight, etc.) processes. In Moffitt's model, neurological signs are also considered prime determinants for child temperament. As noted earlier, the key mechanisms controlling child behavior are internalized controls; but our own efforts to test for these controls in multivariate designs showed that current measures of these mechanisms have not fared well. From the Moffitt perspective, the problem lies within the child and cannot be altered by intervention or prevention trials. In contrast, the early-onset and late-onset models spell out in detail how the parent alters the child's behavior and also specify the means for effectively treating young antisocial children. Reviews of these studies (Kazdin, 1987; Patterson, Dishion, & Chamberlain, 1993) showed replication across sites in Washington, Oregon, and Georgia in well-designed treatment outcome evaluations.

One might well ask how the current set of findings relate to the preeminent model in sociological theories of juvenile crime. Essentially the present findings showed that the training begins in settings where antisocial acts become functional; typically this occurs in the home or in a deviant peer group. At some point for either early-onset or late-onset delinquency, the deviant peer group becomes the proximal cause for a shift to more advanced training in delinquent acts. Regardless of when the training takes place, the same variables (antisocial behavior, deviant peers) are set in motion by disrupted parenting practices.

On the one hand, the early-onset formulation can fit very well within the idea of a general dimension of deviancy unfolded over time. However, there are two problems with the single dimension idea. As noted earlier, it leaves unaccounted the 20 late bloomers. Perhaps a model that fits 93 of all 113 first arrests is acceptable to some.

Our main reservation to a general deviancy framework is that it leaves out almost everything that we require in a theory about juvenile offending. It is analogous to saying that to understand aging all that we require is a concept of time. Yes, of course, it is a necessary condition, but by itself it leaves out all of the details that make up a theory. For example, in the general deviancy theory, what explains why the child is antisocial? Presumably it is a lack of internal social control, but how do you measure that variable? The answer is that if the child is out of control, then he or she lacks inner control. This, of course, is a prime tautology saved occasionally by reference to measures of normlessness, antisocial attitudes, and such. But tests of these constructs have invariably failed to account for much variance. It means that we do not have an explanation for antisocial behavior. That in turn means that we do not really have a theory of general deviancy. We do not know why the training for deviancy begins early for some and late for others. We need specific models that spell out why antisocial behavior moves into peer rejection, academic failure, and depressed mood. If all these "details" are missing, then we do not have a theory. A decade from now when the details have been provided, we may call it a theory; but the current statement of the general deviancy model will be seen as only the first promissory note that provided a basis for the theory. Our own perception is that a functional analysis based on modern learning theory will provide a much stronger base that accounts for juvenile offending. The fact that the theory grew out of earlier efforts to intervene in clinical samples of families of antisocial and delinquent children also implies a natural relevance for prevention trials. The fact that seven different prevention trials currently employ some variant of the parent model clearly speaks to this issue.

The findings show that different models are required to account for different developmental phases of the juvenile crime process. We suggest that it may be useful to build one set of models for early-onset arrest and another set for late-onset arrest.

APPENDIX

Factor Analysis of Covert and Overt Antisocial Behavior Trend Scores

| | Single-Factor Loadings for | |
Covert Items	Linear Trend Scores	Quadratic Trend Scores
1. Hangs around with children who get in trouble	.54	.40
2. Runs away from home	.39	.54
3. Steals outside the home	.43	.50
4. Truancy, skips school	.67	.51
5. Uses alcohol or drugs	.66	.66
Percent of variance accounted for by factor	30.2%	27.9%
Overt Items		
1. Argues a lot	.45	.43
2. Bragging, boasting	.45	.46
3. Cruel to animals	.36	.39
4. Cruelty, bullying, or meanness to others	.57	.39
5. Demands a lot of attention	.59	.48
6. Doesn't get along with other children	.57	.42
7. Doesn't seem to feel guilty after misbehaving	.54	.47
8. Easily jealous	.48	.54
9. Gets in many fights	.52	.36
10. Impulsive or acts without thinking	.54	.36
11. Physically attacks people	.48	.43
12. Screams a lot	.56	.43
13. Showing off or clowning	.43	.34
14. Stubborn, sullen, or irritable	.68	.51
15. Sudden changes in mood or feelings	.65	.48
16. Sulks a lot	.53	.44
17. Swearing or obscene language	.43	.41
18. Teases a lot	.51	.36
19. Temper tantrums or hot temper	.61	.62
20. Threatens people	.67	.54
21. Not liked by other children	.48	.27
Percent of variance accounted for by factor	28.5%	19.5%

REFERENCES

Achenbach, T. M., & Edelbrock, C. S. (1983). *Manual for the Child Behavior Checklist and the revised Child Behavior Profile.* Burlington VT: Thomas M. Achenbach.

————. (1986). *Manual for the Teacher's Report Form and Teacher Version of the Child Behavior Profile.* Burlington VT: University of Vermont.

Achenbach, T. M., Howell, C. T., Quay, H. C., & Conners, C. K. (1991). "National survey of problems and competencies among four- to sixteen-year-olds: Parents' reports for normative and clinical samples." *Monographs of the Society for Research in Child Development, 56*(3), 225.

Bank, L., Dishion, T. J., Skinner, M. L., & Patterson, G. R. (1990). Method variance in structural equation modeling: Living with "glop." In G. R. Patterson (Ed.), *Depression and aggression in family interaction* (pp. 247–279). Hillsdale NJ: Lawrence Erlbaum.

Bank, L., Duncan, T., Patterson, G. R., & Reid. J. B. (1993). Parent and teacher ratings in the assessment and prediction of antisocial and delinquent behaviors. *Journal of Personality, 61*, 693–709.

Bank, L., Forgatch, M. S., Patterson, G. R., & Fetrow, R. A. (1993). Parenting practices of single mothers: Mediators of negative contextual factors. *Journal of Marriage and the Family, 55*, 371–384.

Blumstein, A., Cohen, J., Roth, J. A., & Visher, C. A. (Eds.). (1986). *Criminal careers and career criminals* (Vols. 1 and 2). Washington DC: National Academy Press.

Bollen, K. A. (1989). *Structural equations with latent variables.* New York: Wiley.

Buehler, R. E., Patterson, G. R., & Furniss, J. M. (1966). The reinforcement of behavior in institutional settings. *Behaviour Research and Therapy, 4*, 157–167.

Buss, D. M. (1984). Toward a psychology of person-environment (PE) correlation: The role of spouse selection. *Journal of Personality and Social Psychology, 47*, 361–377.

Cadoret, R. J., Cain, C. A., & Crowe, R. R. (1983). Evidence for gene-environment interaction in the development of adolescent antisocial behavior. *Behavior Genetics, 13*, 301–310.

Cairns, R. B., & Cairns, B. D. (1991). Social cognition and social networks: A developmental perspective. In D. J. Pepler & K. H. Rubin (Eds.), *The development and treatment of childhood aggression* (pp. 249–278). Hillsdale NJ: Lawrence Erlbaum.

————. (1994). *Lifelines and risks: Pathways of youth in our time.* Cambridge: Cambridge University Press.

Capaldi, D. M. (1994, November). *The impact of contextual variables on family process.* Paper presented at a panel for American Society of Criminology, Miami.

Capaldi, D. M., Forgatch, M. S., & Crosby, L. (1994). Affective expression in family problem solving discussions with adolescent boys: The association with family structure and function. *Journal of Adolescent Research, 9*(1), 28–49.

Capaldi, D. M., & Patterson, G. R. (1989). *Psychometric properties of fourteen latent constructs from the Oregon Youth Study.* New York: Springer-Verlag.

————. (1994). Interrelated influences of contextual factors on antisocial behavior in childhood and adolescence for males. In D. Fowles, P. Sutker, & S. Goodman (Eds.), *Progress in experimental personality and psychopathology research* (pp. 165–198). New York: Springer Publications.

Carr, E. G. (1988). Functional equivalence as a mechanism of response generalization. In R. H. Horner, G. Dunlap, & R. L. Koegel (Eds.), *Generalization and maintenance: Life-style changes in applied settings* (pp. 194–219). Baltimore: Paul H. Brookes.

Carr, E. G., Newsom, C. D., & Binkoff, J. A. (1980). Escape as a factor in the aggressive behavior of two retarded children. *Journal of Applied Behavior Analysis, 13*, 101–117.

Carr, E. G., Taylor, J. C., & Robinson, S. (1991). The effects of severe behavior problems in children on the teaching behavior of adults. *Journal of Applied Behavior Analysis, 24*, 523–535.

Caspi, A., & Elder, G. H. (1988). Childhood precursors of the life course: Early personality and life disorganization. In M. Hetherington, R. M. Lerner, & M. Perlmutter (Eds.), *Child development in life span perspective* (pp. 115–142). Hillsdale NJ: Lawrence Erlbaum.

Conger, R. D., Patterson, G. R., & Gé, X. (1995). It takes two to replicate: A mediational model for the impact of parents' stress on adolescent adjustment. *Child Development, 66*, 80–97.

Conger, R. D., & Simons, R. L. (1997). Life-course contingencies in the development of adolescent antisocial behavior: A matching law approach. In T. P. Thornberry (Ed.), *Developmental theories of crime and delinquency* (pp. 55–99). New Brunswick NJ: Transaction.

Cronbach, L. J. (1949). *Essentials of psychological testing.* New York: Harper & Row.

Davison, M., & McCarthy, D. (1988). *The matching law: A research review.* Hillsdale NJ: Lawrence Erlbaum.

Dawes, R. N. (1988). *Rational choice in an uncertain world.* San Diego: Harcourt Brace Jovanovich.

DiLalla, L. R., & Gottesman, I. I. (1989, April). *Early predictors of delinquency and adult criminality.* Paper presented at the meeting of the Society for Research in Child Development, Kansas City MO.

Dishion, T. J., Andrews, D. W., & Crosby, L. (1995). Adolescent boys and their friends in adolescence: Relationship characteristics, quality, and interactional process. *Child Development, 66*, 139–151.

Dishion, T. J., Patterson, G. R., & Griesler, P. C. (1994). Peer adaptation in the development of antisocial behavior: A confluence model. In L. R. Huesmann (Ed.), *Current perspectives on aggressive behavior* (pp. 61–95). New York: Plenum.

Dishion, T. J., Patterson, G. R., & Kavanagh, K. A. (1992). An experimental test of the coercion model: Linking theory, measurement, and intervention. In J. McCord & R. Tremblay (Eds.), *The interaction of theory and practice: Experimental studies of intervention* (pp. 253–282). New York: Guilford.

Dodge, K. A., Bates, J. E., & Pettit, G. S. (1990). Mechanisms in the cycle of violence. *Science, 250,* 1678–1683.

Dodge, K. A., Pettit, G. S., Bates, J. E., & Valente, E. (1995). Social-information-processing patterns partially mediate the effect of early physical abuse on later conduct problems. *Journal of Abnormal Psychology, 104,* 623–643.

Dumas, J. E., & Wekerle, C. (1995). Maternal reports of child behavior problems and personal distress as predictors of dysfunctional parenting. *Development and Psychopathology, 7,* 465–479.

Eddy, M., & Fagot, B. I. (1991, April). *The coercion model of antisocial behavior: Generalization to 5-year-old children and their parents.* Paper presented at the meeting of the Society for Research in Child Development, Seattle.

Elder, G. H. (1980). *Family structure and socialization.* New York: Arno Press.

Elliott, D. S., Huizinga, D., & Ageton, S. S. (1985). *Explaining delinquency and drug use.* Beverly Hills CA: Sage.

Elliott, D. S., & Menard, S. (1996). Delinquent friends and delinquent behavior: Temporal and developmental patterns. In D. Hawkins (Ed.), *Current theories of crime and deviance* (pp. 28–67). Newbury CA: Sage.

Farrington, D. P., & Hawkins, J. D. (1991). Predicting participation, early onset and later persistence in officially recorded offending. *Criminal Behaviour and Mental Health, 1,* 1–33.

Farrington, D. P., & Loeber, R. (1988). RIOC *and Phi as measures of predictive efficiency and strength of association in 2 x 2 tables.* Unpublished manuscript available from R. Loeber, Western Psychiatric Institute and Clinic, Pittsburgh.

Forgatch, M. S. (1991). The clinical science vortex: Developing a theory for antisocial behavior. In D. J. Pepler & K. H. Rubin (Eds.), *The development and treatment of childhood aggression* (pp. 291–315). Hillsdale NJ: Lawrence Erlbaum.

————. (1995, May). *The clinical science vortex revisited.* Paper presented at the Family Research Conference on Marital and Family Therapy Process and Outcome Research, Temple University, Philadelphia.

Forgatch, M. S., Patterson, G. R., & Ray, J. A. (1996). Divorce and boys' adjustment problems: Two paths with a single model. In E. M. Hetherington (Ed.), *Stress, coping, and resiliency in children and the family* (pp. 67–106). Mahwah NJ: Lawrence Erlbaum.

Forgatch, M. S., Patterson, G. R., & Stoolmiller, M. (1994, November). *Progressing toward violence: A replication.* Paper presented at the panel "Oregon Models for Early- and Late-Onset Delinquency" at the meeting of the American Society of Criminology, Miami.

Forgatch, M. S., & Stoolmiller, M. (1994). Emotions as contexts for adolescent delinquency. *Journal of Research on Adolescence, 4,* 601–614.

Glidewell, J. C., Gildea, M. C., Domke, H. R., & Kantor, M. B. (1959). Behavior symptoms in children and adjustment in public school. *Human Organization, 18,* 123–130.

Glueck, S., & Glueck, E. (1940). *Juvenile delinquents grown up*. New York: Commonwealth Fund.

Goldsmith, H. H. (1983). Genetic influences on personality from infancy to adulthood. *Child Development, 54,* 331–355.

Goldsmith, H. H., & Campos, J. J. (1986). Fundamental issues in the study of early temperament: The Denver Twin Temperament Study. In M. E. Lamb, A. L. Brown, & B. Rogoff (Eds.), *Advances in developmental psychology* (Vol. 4, pp. 231–283). Hillsdale NJ: Lawrence Erlbaum.

Gottesman, I. I., & Goldsmith, H. H. (1994). Developmental psychopathology of antisocial behavior: Inserting genes into its ontogenesis and epigenesis. In C. A. Nelson (Ed.), *Minnesota symposia on child psychology: Vol. 27. Threats to optimal development: Integrating biological, psychological, and social risk factors* (pp. 69–104). Hillsdale NJ: Lawrence Erlbaum.

Gottfredson, M. R., & Hirschi, T. (1990). *A general theory of crime*. Stanford: Stanford University Press.

Gottman, J. M., & Roy, A. K. (1990). *Sequential analyses: A guide for behavioral researchers*. New York: Cambridge University Press.

Griest, D., Wells, K. C., & Forehand, R. (1979). An examination of predictors of maternal perceptions of maladjustment in clinic-referred children. *Journal of Abnormal Psychology, 88,* 277–281.

Harris, M. (1979). *Cultural materialism: The struggle for a science of culture*. New York: Random House.

Hayduk, L. A. (1987). *Structural equation modeling with LISREL: Essentials and advances*. Baltimore: Johns Hopkins University Press.

Hirschi, T. (1969). *Causes of delinquency*. Berkeley: University of California Press.

Hoffman, L. W. (1985). The changing genetics/socialization balance. *Journal of Social Issues, 41,* 127–148.

Horner, R. H., & Day, H. M. (1991). The effects of response efficiency on functionally equivalent competing behaviors. *Journal of Applied Behavior Analysis, 24,* 719–732.

Howard, D. V. (1983). *Cognitive psychology: Memory, language, and thought*. New York: Macmillan.

Hoyle, R. H. (1995). *Structural equation modeling: Concepts, issues, and applications*. Thousand Oaks CA: Sage.

Kandel, D., Davies, M., & Baydar, N. (1990). The creation of interpersonal contexts: Homophily in dyadic relationships in adolescence and young adulthood. In L. Robins & M. Rutter (Eds.), *Straight and devious pathways from childhood to adulthood* (pp. 221–241). New York: Cambridge University Press.

Kanfer, R. H. (1987). Self-regulation and behavior. In H. Heckhausen, P. M. Gollwitzer, & F. E. Weinert (Eds.), *Jenseits des rubikon*. Heidelberg: Springer-Verlag.

Kazdin, A. (1987). Treatment of antisocial behavior in children: Current status and future directions. *Psychological Bulletin, 102,* 187–203.

Langer, E. J. (1984). *Rethinking the role of thought in social interaction*. Paper presented at the conference of the Oregon Psychological Association.

Larzelere, R. E., & Patterson, G. R. (1990). Parental management: Mediators of the effect of socioeconomic status on early delinquency. *Criminology, 28,* 301–323.

Loeber, R., & Dishion, T. (1983). Early predictors of male delinquency: A review. *Psychological Bulletin, 94,* 68–99.

Loeber, R., & Schmaling, K. B. (1985). Empirical evidence for overt and covert patterns of antisocial conduct problems: A meta-analysis. *Journal of Abnormal Child Psychology, 13,* 337–352.

Metzler, C. E., & Dishion, T. J. (1992, May). *A model of the development of youthful problem behaviors.* Paper presented at the 18th Annual Convention for Association for Behavior Analysis, San Francisco.

Middlebrook, J. L., & Forehand, R. (1985). Maternal perceptions of deviance in child behavior as a function of stress and clinic versus nonclinic status of the child: An analogue study. *Behavior Therapy, 16,* 494–502.

Moffitt, T. E. (1993). Adolescence-limited and life-course-persistent antisocial behavior: A developmental taxonomy. *Psychological Review, 100,* 674–701.

Montemayor, R., & Flannery, D. (1989). A naturalistic study of the involvement of children and adolescents with their mothers and friends: Developmental differences in expressive behavior. *Journal of Adolescent Research, 4,* 3–14.

Paikoff, R. L., & Brooks-Gunn, J. (1990). Physiological processes: What role do they play during the transition to adolescence? In R. Montemayor, G. R. Adams, & T. P. Gullotta (Eds.), *From childhood to adolescence: A transitional period?* (pp. 310–348). Newbury Park CA: Sage.

Patterson, G. R. (1973). Changes in status of family members as controlling stimuli: A basis for describing treatment process. In L. A. Hamerlynck, L. C. Handy, & E. J. Mash (Eds.), *Behavior change: Methodology, concepts, and practice* (pp. 169–191). Champaign IL: Research Press.

———. (1979). A performance theory for coercive family interaction. In R. B. Cairns (Ed.), *The analysis of social interactions: Methods, issues, and illustrations* (pp. 119–162). Hillsdale NJ: Lawrence Erlbaum.

———. (1982). *A social learning approach: Vol. 3. Coercive family process.* Eugene OR: Castalia.

———. (1983). Stress: A change agent for family process. In N. Garmezy & M. Rutter (Eds.), *Stress, coping, and development in children* (pp. 235–264). New York: McGraw-Hill.

———. (1984). Siblings: Fellow travelers in the coercive family process. In R. J. Blanchard & D. C. Blanchard (Eds.), *Advances in the study of aggression* (pp. 235–264). New York: Academic Press.

———. (1985). Beyond technology: The next stage in developing an empirical base for parent training. In L. L'Abate (Ed.), *Handbook of family psychology and therapy* (Vol. 2, pp. 1344–1379). Homewood IL: Dorsey.

———. (1986). Performance models for antisocial boys. *American Psychologist, 41,* 432–444.

———. (1993). Orderly change in a stable world: The antisocial trait as a chimera. *Journal of Consulting and Clinical Psychology, 61,* 911–919.

————. (1994, November). *Differentiating early- from late-onset delinquency.* Paper presented at the conference panel "Early- and Late-Onset Delinquency" at the meeting of the American Society of Criminology, Miami.

————. (1995). Coercion as a basis for early age of onset for arrest. In J. McCord (Ed.), *Coercion and punishment in long-term perspective* (pp. 81–105). New York: Cambridge University Press.

————. (1996). Some characteristics of a developmental theory for early onset delinquency. In M. F. Lenzenweger & J. J. Haugaard (Eds.), *Frontiers of developmental psychopathology* (pp. 81–124). New York: Oxford University Press.

————. (in press). Expanding the coercion parenting model to include emotional and social cognitive variables. In J. Grusec & L. Kuczynski (Eds.), *The handbook of parenting and the transmission of values.* New York: Wiley.

Patterson, G. R., & Bank, L. (1986). Bootstrapping your way in the nomological thicket. *Behavioral Assessment, 8,* 49–73.

————. (1987). When is a nomological network a construct? In D. R. Peterson & D. B. Fishman (Eds.), *Assessment for decision* (pp. 249–279). New Brunswick NJ: Rutgers University Press.

Patterson, G. R., & Capaldi, D. M. (1991). Antisocial parents: Unskilled and vulnerable. In P. A. Cowan & E. M. Hetherington (Eds.), *Family transitions* (pp. 195–218). Hillsdale NJ: Lawrence Erlbaum.

Patterson, G. R., Capaldi, D., & Bank, L. (1991). An early starter model for predicting delinquency. In D. J. Pepler & K. H. Rubin (Eds.), *The development and treatment of childhood aggression* (pp. 139–168). Hillsdale NJ: Lawrence Erlbaum.

Patterson, G. R., & Cobb, J. A. (1971). A dyadic analysis of "aggressive" behaviors. In J. P. Hill (Ed.), *Minnesota symposia on child psychology* (Vol. 5, pp. 72–129). Minneapolis: University of Minnesota.

Patterson, G. R., Crosby, L., & Vuchinich, S. (1992). Predicting risk for early police arrest. *Journal of Quantitative Criminology, 8,* 333–355.

Patterson, G. R., DeBaryshe, B. D., & Ramsey, E. (1989). A developmental perspective on antisocial behavior. *American Psychologist, 44,* 329–335.

Patterson, G. R., & Dishion, T. J. (1988). Multilevel family process models: Traits, interactions, and relationships. In R. A. Hinde & J. Stevenson-Hinde (Eds.), *Relationships within families: Mutual influences* (pp. 283–310). Oxford: Clarendon.

Patterson, G. R., Dishion, T. J., & Chamberlain, P. (1993). Outcomes and methodological issues relating to treatment of antisocial children. In T. R. Giles (Ed.), *Handbook of effective psychotherapy* (pp. 43–88). New York: Plenum.

Patterson, G. R., & Forgatch, M. S. (1990). Initiation and maintenance of processes disrupting single-mother families. In G. R. Patterson (Ed.), *Depression and aggression in family interaction* (pp. 209–245). Hillsdale NJ: Lawrence Erlbaum.

————. (1995). Predicting future clinical adjustment from treatment outcome and process variables. *Psychological Assessment, 7,* 275–285.

Patterson, G. R., Forgatch, M. S., Yoerger, K.,& Stoolmiller, M. (1997). *Variables that initiate and maintain an early-onset trajectory for juvenile offending.* Manuscript submitted for publication.

Patterson, G. R., & Leve, L. (1996). *Some methodological considerations for twin and adoption designs in behavior genetic research.* Manuscript available from Oregon Social Learning Center, Eugene.

Patterson, G. R., Littman, R. A., & Bricker, W. (1967). Assertive behavior in children: A step towards a theory of aggression. *Monographs of the Society for Research in Child Development, 32*(5), 1–43.

Patterson, G. R., & Moore, D. R. (1979). Interactive patterns as units of behavior. In M. E. Lamb, S. J. Suomi, & G. R. Stephenson (Eds.), *Social interaction analysis: Methodological issues* (pp. 77–96). Madison: University of Wisconsin Press.

Patterson, G. R., & Reid, J. B. (1984). Social interactional processes within the family: The study of moment-by-moment family transactions in which human social development is embedded. *Journal of Applied Developmental Psychology, 5,* 237–262.

Patterson, G. R., Reid, J. B., & Dishion, T. J. (1992). *A social interactional approach: Vol. 4. Antisocial boys.* Eugene OR: Castalia.

Patterson, G. R., & Yoerger, K. (1993a, March). *Adolescent first arrest: One model or two?* Paper presented at the meeting of the Society for Research in Child Development, New Orleans.

———. (1993b). Developmental models for delinquent behavior. In S. Hodgins (Ed.), *Crime and mental disorder* (pp. 140–172). Newbury Park CA: Sage.

———. (1993c, October). *Differentiating outcomes and histories for early and late onset arrests.* Paper presented at the meeting of the American Society of Criminology, Phoenix.

———. (1995). Two different models for adolescent physical trauma and for early arrest. *Criminal Behaviour and Mental Health, 5,* 411–423.

Pierce, W. D., & Epling, W. F. (1995). *Behavior analysis and learning.* Englewood Cliffs NJ: Prentice Hall.

Pulkkinen, L. (1986). Offensive and defensive aggression in humans: A longitudinal perspective. *Aggressive Behavior, 13,* 197–212.

Quay, H. C. (1987). Patterns of delinquent behavior. In H. C. Quay (Ed.), *Handbook of juvenile delinquency* (pp. 118–138). New York: Wiley.

Reid, J. B., Taplin, P. S., & Lorber, R. (1981). A social interaction approach to the treatment of abusive families. In R. Stuart (Ed.), *Violent behavior: Social learning approaches to prediction, management, and treatment* (pp. 83–101). New York: Brunner/Mazel.

Sampson, R. J., & Laub, J. H. (1993). *Crime in the making: Pathways and turning points through life.* Cambridge: Harvard University Press.

Sanson-Fisher, R. W., Poole, A. D., & Thompson, V. (1979). Behaviour patterns within a general hospital psychiatric unit: An observational study. *Behaviour Research and Therapy, 17,* 317–332.

Simons, R. L., Wu, C.-I., Conger, R. D., & Lorenz, F. O. (1994). Two routes to delinquency: Differences between early and late starters in the impact of parenting and deviant peers. *Criminology, 32,* 247–276.

Snyder, J. J. (1995a). Coercion: A two-level theory of antisocial behavior. In W. T. O'Donohue & L. Krasner (Eds.), *Theories in behavior therapy: Exploring behavior change* (pp. 313–348). Washington DC: American Psychological Association.

———. (1995b, June). *Testing the peer group selectivity hypothesis.* Seminar presented at the Oregon Social Learning Center, Eugene.

Snyder, J. J., Edwards, P., McGraw, K., Kilgore, K., & Holton, A. (1994). Escalation and reinforcement in mother-child conflict: Social processes associated with the development of physical aggression. *Development and Psychopathology, 6,* 305–321.

Snyder, J. J., & Patterson, G. R. (1995). Individual differences in social aggression: A test of a reinforcement model of socialization in the natural environment. *Behavior Therapy, 26,* 371–391.

Snyder, J. J., West, L., Stockemer, V., Gibbons, S., & Almquist-Parks, L. (1996). A social learning model of peer choice in the natural environment. *Journal of Applied Developmental Psychology, 17,* 215–237.

Tulkin, S. R. (1977). Social class differences in maternal and infant behavior. In P. H. Leiderman, A. Rosenfeld, & S. R. Tulkin (Eds.), *Culture and infancy* (pp. 495–537). New York: Academic Press.

Tversky, A., & Kahneman, D. (1974). Judgment under uncertainty: Heuristics and biases. *Science, 185,* 1124–1131.

Utting, D., Bright, J., & Henricson, C. (1993). *Crime in the family: Improving child rearing and preventing delinquency* (Vol. 16). London: Family Policy Studies Centre.

Wahlsten, D. (1990). Insensitivity of the analysis of variance to heredity-environment interaction. *Behavioral and Brain Sciences, 13,* 109–161.

West, D. J., & Farrington, D. P. (1973). *Who becomes delinquent?* London: Heinemann Educational Books.

Wiggins, J. S. (1973). *Personality and prediction: Principles of personality assessment.* Reading MA: Addison Wesley.

A Social Interactionist Interpretation of the Motives for Youth Violence

James T. Tedeschi
University at Albany, State University of New York

The topic of youth violence is usually conceived in terms of criminal actions by juveniles. However, fights among siblings, which seldom escalate to a point where the legal system is called upon, have been described as the most frequent type of violence in America (Felson, 1983). Fights on playgrounds, which are often brief because of the intervention of third parties, also occur rather frequently. In their research on youth violence, sociologists focus on youth crime, whereas social psychologists are more concerned with physical aggression. Obviously, these two areas of scholarship overlap. I present a social psychological perspective that borrows from both sociological theories of crime and psychological research on aggression.

Theories of crime have been developed largely to explain demographic differences in crime. One of the most striking statistics is the relationship of age to the prevalence of crimes. There is a sharp increase in the number of incidents of crime at the age of 14, with the largest number of crimes committed by 18-year-olds, and then a substantial decrease in almost all offenses by the mid-20s (Gottfredson & Hirschi, 1990). In 1991, youth under the age of 18 accounted for 17% of arrests for violent crimes (Kantrowitz, 1992). While the proportion of crimes that are committed by juveniles has been rising over the last two decades, they commit fewer serious crimes than do adults

(Wilson & Herrnstein, 1985). Adults are far more likely to kill some-one than are juveniles.

Other demographic factors that criminological theories attempt to explain include gender, race or ethnicity, socioeconomic class, and geographic region. A very high percentage of violent crimes are committed by males. Females commit only about 10% of such crimes. Almost half of violent crimes are committed by African Americans, and the homicide rate of Hispanics is well above that of non-Hispanic whites (Riedel & Zahn, 1985). Criminological theories must explain why minority groups contribute so disproportionately to criminal conduct. It is well known that violent crimes are over-whelmingly performed by members of the lower class (poor people) and more often in highly urbanized communities. Finally, there is evidence that violent crime rates are higher in the southern part of the United States than in other regions (except perhaps for the Rocky Mountain region), and that the U.S. rates are higher than rates in other developed, industrial nations (Nisbett, Polly, & Lang, 1995; Fingerhut, Ingram, & Feldman, 1992).

Criminological Theories

Among the theories that have been proposed to explain these facts about the distribution of crimes are cultural, strain, and control the-ories. While these theories have been reviewed in detail elsewhere (cf. Tedeschi & Felson, 1994, chap. 5), it is worthwhile to provide a short review here.

CULTURAL THEORIES

Cultural theories propose that a few people in society learn a deviant set of values and act upon them. Thus, wayward youth may associ-ate with "bad apples" and become tainted with deviant values as they are socialized into the deviant group (Sutherland & Cressey, 1974). Such values collectively may be referred to as a subculture of delinquency (Miller, 1958) or subculture of violence (Wolfgang & Ferracuti, 1956). These subcultures allegedly promote four sets of values that are directly related to violence—warrior values, excite-ment, fatalism, and autonomy.

First, warrior values emphasize toughness, fearlessness, and skill in combat. Associated with such warrior values is the notion of honor. One should be ready to respond to insults or disrespect with violence, and the failure to respond to provocation will meet with derision from other group members. Toch (1969) noted the desire of violent men to promote themselves as "tough" and as having physical courage. He also observed that such men are prone to tell "war stories" about their aggressive encounters (Toch, 1993). Such positive attitudes toward violent action are central to Wolfgang and Ferracuti's (1956) theory of the subculture of violence, which assumes that warrior values underlie violent behavior.

Secondly, the group seeks out excitement to break up the monotony of everyday life. Third, there is a tendency to believe that one cannot control the future, that whatever happens is fated to be and is unalterable. Thus, teenage boys from violent neighborhoods sometimes report that they expect to die before becoming adults. If people are fatalistic about negative outcomes, they may be more willing to take risks and engage in deviant actions than those who believe outcomes are contingent on their behavior. Finally, there is a general antipathy to authority and an exaggerated concern with autonomy or freedom of action. People with such values may be more prone to have the attitude that no one is going to push them around.

Researchers have tested value theory by examining the attitudes of racial and ethnic groups and people in different socioeconomic classes (Ball-Rokeach, 1973; Erlanger, 1974; Rossi, Waite, Bose, & Berk, 1974). Little or no differences have been found. Blacks, people in the lower class, and members of the white middle class all seem to share a general repugnance for violence. However, Nisbett (1993) found that Southerners were more favorable toward violence if it was used for self-protection and in response to insults.

The evidence is weak for the hypothesis regarding the relationship between deviant values and deviant conduct. The emphasis placed on association with a deviant group by value theory appears to be justified by available evidence. Delinquents do tend to choose delinquents as friends, and most criminal acts by youth are carried out with other youth (Matsueda, 1988). Furthermore, the racial and ethnic composition of youth gangs tends to mirror the prevalence of violent crimes. About one-half of the nation's gangs are composed of African Americans, one-sixth are Hispanic, one-tenth are Asian, and one-tenth are white non-Hispanics (Goldstein, 1994). I examine the impact of group membership on the individual later in the chapter when considering the motivations of group members.

STRAIN THEORY

There are several variants of strain theory, including frustration-aggression, relative deprivation, and blocked opportunity theories. Strain theory stresses the disjunction between the goals of individuals and the opportunities to achieve them. When barriers exist that make it difficult or impossible for people to use legitimate means to achieve goals, they will turn to alternative (deviant) means. Crime is one avenue for achieving such goals. Criminal acts are exciting, require little effort, and provide immediate gratification. As Gottfredson and Hirschi state, criminal acts "provide money without work, sex without courtship, revenge without court delays" (1990, p. 89). Thus, strain theory appears to focus on the social control of others to achieve goals, where normative actions are blocked and the means chosen involve rule violations.

Strain theory seems consistent with the association of dropping out of school and crime, and the fact that poor people are disproportionately represented in committing crimes. Furthermore, the undeniable pattern of discrimination against blacks and Hispanics and their overrepresentation in criminal activities appears to be consistent with strain theory. However, research that attempts to pin down the relationships specified by strain theory is not generally supportive. For example, unemployment is not a good predictor of crime. The small relationship that does exist may only indicate that those who commit crimes have trouble getting or retaining jobs, or that the same characteristic that leads to criminal activity also affects unemployment. It should be expected that youth who have high aspirations but are pessimistic about achieving them by legitimate means would be especially prone to crime. The evidence indicates that students who aspire to go to college engage in less delinquency than those who do not have such aspirations, and that expectations about whether they would actually be able to go to college had no effect on delinquency (Hirschi, 1969; Liska, 1971).

CONTROL THEORY

Social control theory assumes that everyone is tempted to commit crimes, but that most people learn inhibitions that prevent such behavior. Some of the controls on behavior are external to the individual and consist of sources of punishment for misbehavior. Formal control is associated with the legal system and its threat to apprehend and punish those who violate the law. Informal control, which is thought to be more effective than formal control, consists of bonds to conventional others, such as parents, friends, school, and church. Bonds to conventional others make the individual more concerned with their good opinion and more sensitive to their disapproval, and behavior is regulated accordingly. Furthermore, it is proposed that participation in conventional activities—going to school, church, picnics, and so on—leaves less time for criminal activity. Thus, there is less time for the devil to use idle hands.

Routine activities theory (Cohen & Felson, 1979) proposes that conventional activities provide opportunities for crime. According to this theory, most crimes are impulsive, unplanned, and opportunistic. Crimes are therefore more likely to occur in situations where there is a likely offender, a suitable target, and the absence of capable guardians. For example, schools are locales that bring together young males and provide opportunities for many criminal activities. Low parental supervision, college attendance, increased labor force participation by women, and dark parking areas at shopping malls are circumstances that provide opportunities for crime. It would be surprising if some of these circumstances did not contribute to the prevalence of crime. Indeed, unstructured socializing with peers—such as riding around in a car for fun, going to parties, getting together with friends informally, and spending evenings out for fun and recreation—have been found to be strongly related to use of illicit drugs, heavy alcohol use, dangerous driving, and criminal behavior in a national sample of young people between the ages of 18 and 26 years (Osgood, Wilson, Bachman, O'Malley, & Johnston, 1996). In another study, the best predictor of violence against youth was participation in delinquent behaviors (Lauritsen, Laub, & Sampson, 1992). Adolescent victims and offenders are not mutually exclusive groups. The most significant predictors of victimization are the same demographic factors that predict criminal behavior (Cohen, Kluegel, & Land, 1981; Hindelang, 1976).

In Gottfredson and Hirschi's version of control theory, internal controls also play a role in inhibiting criminal activity. Conventional values in support of the law and respect for authorities inhibit illegal actions. Note that unlike cultural theories, which emphasize values that facilitate or promote violence, control theory focuses on values that inhibit such behavior. In addition, the person who commits crimes lacks self-control. Gottfredson and Hirschi (1990) are particularly impressed with the versatility of criminals. While occasionally a criminal will specialize in a particular type of crime—say, a serial rapist or a bank robber—most criminals engage in all kinds of risky and deviant actions. It is not possible to predict with any accuracy what type of crime a person will commit next based on that person's last crime (Blumstein & Cohen, 1979). In addition, repeat offenders engage in other (noncriminal) risky behaviors, such as driving too fast, drinking too much, gambling, and sexual promiscuity. These behaviors indicate a person who is impulsive, shortsighted, and risk taking; in short, a person with low self-control.

The evidence for control theory is mixed. There is little evidence that formal sanctions are effective deterrents of crime. There is an association between low attachment to school and delinquency, but apparently this is due to the fact that delinquent values lead to low interest in school, not the other way around (Liska & Reed, 1985). Job stability and strong marital attachment reduce criminal behavior, but clearly other factors are involved (Sampson & Laub, 1990). Broken homes, conflict in homes, and other measures of bonds to family are not related to criminal activity when attitudes toward breaking the law are controlled (Matsueda & Heimer, 1987). Thus, attitudes rather than the expected costs (inhibitors associated with external controls) of criminal behavior appear to explain the association between family bonds and crime.

The concept of self-control is not fully developed as a psychological process in control theory. Rather, it serves as a summary term to refer to the pattern of versatility highlighted by Gottfredson and Hirschi (1990). They could import Bandura's (1986) theory of self-control into social control theory or flesh out the theoretical aspects of the construct in some other way. On the other hand, it might be that versatility is overrated as a discriminating characteristic of criminals. It seems plausible to suggest that most people who smoke, drink too much, drive too fast, are sexually promiscuous, and gamble do not ever commit a violent crime. The correlations among these forms of deviance are far from perfect. Many criminals are not violent, many sexually promiscuous people are not criminals, and many people who smoke do not drive too fast. One study estimates that half the reliable variance was shared and half was specific for various forms of deviance (Osgood, Johnston, O'Malley, & Bachman, 1988). Thus, there could be considerable value for theories specific to a single form of deviance, such as a theory of violent actions.

CONCLUSIONS REGARDING CRIMINOLOGICAL THEORIES

All three theories described above are controversial in the sense that there is mixed evidence regarding each. A decision theoretic framework provides a basis for integrating some of the aspects of cultural value, strain, and social control theories of crime. A rational choice model (Cornish & Clarke, 1986; Wilson & Herrnstein, 1985) assumes that criminals, like everyone else, make choices among alternative courses of action in a way that maximizes their chances of obtaining desired outcomes (rewards) and minimizes the likelihood of incurring costs (punishments). Cultural value theory emphasizes the high value that some individuals place on fighting skills, physical courage, risk-taking, and defending honor. Such values provide motivation for engaging in physical violence and delinquent behavior. Strain theory points out obstacles that lead the individual to assign a low probability of success to legitimate or nonviolent forms of behavior. Blocked opportunities motivate people to seek other avenues to achieve their goals. Whereas some people may find other legitimate ways to achieve their goals, and some may simply give up their goals, a few people will use illegitimate means to attain the goals. Routine activity theory suggests that individuals are tempted by opportunities to commit crimes, especially when effective guardians are not present to inhibit the behavior. In other words, opportunities suggest alternatives with a high probability of success to individuals. When other alternatives to achieving the goals are blocked, when external controls are not obviously present, and when the individual does not have strong values prohibiting illegal conduct, it is likely the person will engage in the criminal action. Some individual difference factors most likely also contribute to a choice to engage in criminal conduct; if not self-control, then some other dispositional factors. Finally, social control theory points out the many sources of costs that may inhibit criminal behavior. Formal authorities may impose penalties, censure may be forthcoming from family and friends, and guilt may be experienced by the transgressor. As the expected costs for choosing a particular alternative increase, the likelihood of the actor choosing that alternative decreases.

The social interactionist theory of coercive actions presented below focuses on the decision making of the actor and incorporates the various aspects of criminological theories of crime in providing an explanatory system for why an individual uses forms of coercion against other people. This decision framework will also be used to speculate about the individual differences that demark those people who use physical forms of harm doing from people who confine themselves to psychological, social, and economic forms of harm doing. Before this task is undertaken, however, several conceptual issues must be considered.

Some Conceptual Issues

For the most part, sociologists are concerned with demographic and situational factors associated with deviance, while psychologists focus on the cognitions and motives of the individual. Criminologists tend to take a social psychological approach and combine a concern for both remote and proximal causes in their theories. Thus, control theory refers to situational factors and social bonds that inhibit crime and lack of self control, which facilitates crime. However, the basic observational construct for devising criminological theories ("crime") is itself a legal construction. What constitutes a crime varies across jurisdictions, regions, and cultures. It is by no means clear that crime is a unified or useful construct around which to build a sound scientific theory of individual behavior. Deviance is even less specific as a referent to specific types of action than is the concept of crime. Thus, a prediction to deviant behavior is not a very specific prediction. Because the category contains so many possible actions it may be associated with (or correlated with) a large number of conditions. Theories that are confined to more specific actions may uncover causal mechanisms that are missed by theories that use more inclusive action categories.

Gottfredson and Hirschi (1990) have argued that crime includes everything to which psychologists refer when they use the concept of aggression. Such an equation would need to be limited to violent crime, but even with this limitation there is a problem. Clearly much physical harm doing is not criminal. Parental spanking of a child is not a crime in American society, although it is against the law in a number of Scandinavian countries. Indeed, some violent crimes could not be considered aggressive, if by this term we mean, as most psychologists do, behavior that has the intent to do harm (Berkowitz, 1993; Geen, 1990).

It is doubtful that robbers are primarily motivated to harm their victims and are perhaps only secondarily interested in the valuables they take. The most successful robbery, presumably, is one where the robber gets the loot, does not have to physically harm the victim, and gets away cleanly. Furthermore, it is doubtful that robbers even think about the sense of loss or trauma experienced by the victims. Thus, the intent of the robber is get the loot, and there is usually no intent to do harm. Of course, harm is done, and sometimes physical harm accompanies the economic harm, but analysis suggests that at least from the robber's point of view there usually is no intent to do harm. The intention is to gain compliance from the victim so as to acquire the possessions of the victim. If this analysis is correct, then some violent crimes, like robbery, could not be considered aggression.

A number of conceptual issues must be addressed in formulating a theory of youth violence. Psychologists tend to conceptualize harm doing by referring to "aggression" or perhaps to distinctions between legitimate and illegitimate aggression, or predatory and defensive aggression, or reactive and instrumental aggression. Elsewhere I have thoroughly examined the concept of aggression (Tedeschi, Smith, & Brown, 1974; Tedeschi, Melburg, & Rosenfeld, 1981; Tedeschi & Felson, 1994) and concluded that it is so infused with value judgments it cannot be salvaged as a useful scientific term. Aggression theorists clearly focus on "illegitimate" behavior and seem to assume that it has different antecedents or causes than "legitimate" behavior. But of course what is legitimate or illegitimate depends on value judgments, which scientists should not have to make in order to identify a phenomenon. It would be difficult to get all social psychologists in the world to agree on what is or is not legitimate. In any case, aggression theorists clearly are not interested in why judges in criminal trials set different levels of punishment for convicted felons, or why parents impose noncorporal punishments on their children. These socially approved behaviors are assumed to have different causes than the antisocial behaviors of interest to aggression theorists.

One consequence of the way psychologists have conceptualized harmful actions is that attempts to explain them tend to focus on the individual, often at the expense of the social context within which these actions occur. A careful and skeptical examination of laboratory studies of aggression indicates how researchers strip the social context from their explanations of their findings.[1] Typically, a confederate is employed to insult, provoke, or otherwise attack a research participant. The experiment is arranged so that the subject must then deliver some level of noxious stimulation to the confederate, although the intensity or frequency of the harm doing is left up to the discretion of the participant. Researchers provide explanations of the findings that make little or no reference to the prior actions of the confederate and that make generalizations to predatory aggression. These explanations tend to focus on such internal states as negative affect, frustration, and cognitive scripts (Berkowitz, 1993; Dollard, Doob, Miller, Mowrer & Sears, 1939; Huesmann, 1988).

The upshot is that the study of aggression by social psychologists is focused on a flawed concept and limited laboratory techniques. The remainder of this chapter presents a social interactionist perspective that proposes a reconceptualization of the literature in terms of coercive actions. A coercive action is defined as an action taken with the intention of imposing harm on another person or forcing compliance. Threats and punishments are forms of coercive actions. In social interactionist theory, threats are communications stating or implying the intention to harm a target person, usually contingent on noncompliance to some demand. Punishing actions are intended to harm the target person, although sometimes they do not succeed in doing so. Tedeschi et al. (1974) differentiated between forms of harm, including deprivations, physical punishments, and social/emotional punishments. Given this set of definitions, we would want to ask why young males are so prone to using threats and punishments involving physical forms of harm against victims, who frequently are their peers. In my view the answer to this question should be derived from a general theory of coercive actions. The reasons why youth use coercion are not different from those of other people.

The three types of criminological theory reviewed above specify many of the conditions that are associated with crime and thus provide important hints about the psychological processes that mediate violent behavior. However, there are also specific individual difference factors that help determine whether the person will use physical forms of coercion. The social control theory of Gottfredson and Hirschi (1990) makes a stab at providing a psychological mechanism, but it is conceptually underdeveloped. The social interactionist theory of coercive actions proposes that there are individual differences in the way people make decisions, and that there are many dispositional and situational factors, including the influence of third parties, that determine whether a person will use physical forms of coercion. Youth with such dispositions and placed in such circumstances are quite likely to be violent.

A Social Interactionist Theory of Coercive Actions

Social interactionist theory takes the viewpoint of the actor, who makes decisions regarding alternative courses of action. It is assumed that people are interdependent on each other for attaining values—that is, most of the goals of the individual are mediated by other people. Such values as love, status, and esteem are clearly dependent on other people. Material rewards, such as money and goods, and services also are provided by others, often in return for something of value that has been received in exchange (see Foa, 1971, for a theory of resources). The fact of interdependence places the actor in the position of needing to influence others for the purpose of getting them to do (or not do) what the actor wants in order to achieve desired outcomes. Of course, the actor also has the problem of responding to the perceived influence attempts of others.

Tedeschi and Felson (1994) found it useful to couch their theory in the context of expected value theory. The actor, who has social goals, must consider alternative means of achieving them. At any given time the actor will consider what sorts of values can be achieved in the current context, which to a large extent depends both on the situation and the availability (or absence) of particular other people. The actor will choose among the alternatives by considering the likelihood that a given action will lead to the desired outcome and the value of the outcome. The actor must also consider the likelihood of failure and the value of costs for choosing a particular action. The consideration of costs is akin to the concept of inhibition by aggression theorists, and commitment and deterrence by control theorists.[2] The actor calculates (roughly) the net value of each choice alternative, adopts some choice criterion, and undertakes an action. This action is typically some form of influence, such as persuasion, a promise, a reward, a threat, or a punishment. Incorporated within the actor's net value calculation is a procedural value for the type of action considered. It is assumed that people learn to rely on certain forms of action as particularly effective either because such actions have succeeded in gaining interpersonal objectives in the past, or because they have observed someone else in similar circumstances successfully perform them, or because they are unaware of or unskilled at alternative means.

Social interactionist theory views coercive actions—that is, threats and harm doing—as instrumental actions that are intended to change target persons in some way. The expected and valued change in the target person may be a modification of the perceived effectiveness or value of a choice alternative, a change in attitude, a compliant behavior, an induction of an emotional state, or rehabilitation of the target person. Threats and punishments are used to compel or deter behavior, to inflict discomfort, to lower status, and to change dispositions. In other words, coercive actions are forms of social influence and are connected to social motives.

Three major goals are presumed to motivate social behavior: to control the behavior of others, to maintain or restore justice, and to assert and protect identities. Each of these social motives is tied to a particular set of social processes. For example, the sequence of events that are associated with the justice motive are typically different from those that are associated with a self-presentation motive.

All three of these motives appear to be relevant to understanding youth violence.

Threats and harm doing are instrumental in achieving a variety of social goals, including material gain, safety, sexual satisfaction, and services. Of course, these goals can be and usually are achieved by noncoercive forms of influence. Persuasion, requests, appeals to the audience's values, promises of contingent rewards, and many other types of influence tactics are available to a person with good social skills. Formal and informal exchanges can be arranged, such as when people exchange work for money or use money to purchase goods and services. When a person cannot use noncoercive forms of influence to induce a target person to comply with the source's wishes, then the source's ability to achieve an objective may depend on the ability to use bodily force, to immobilize, threaten, injure, or destroy the target (Tedeschi & Bonoma, 1972). Social interactionist theory assumes that the actor examines alternatives and chooses to enact the tactic evaluated by some criterion as the best one available given the perceived circumstances. It is acknowledged that actors sometimes consider only one alternative, but a "go" or "no go" type of decision still needs to be made. For example, aggressive boys perceive fewer solutions to conflict situations than nonaggressive boys (Gouze, 1987). When a single line of conduct is perceived as appropriate in particular situations, the behavior is said to be scripted (Huesmann, 1988). A script is the cognitive equivalent to a habit.

According to social interactionist theory, the actor's decision to use coercion to achieve interpersonal goals involves the estimated probability of success, the value of success, the estimated probability of costs, and the value of costs. Three fundamental postulates can be presented based on these decision factors. They are quite simple and should not be very controversial. Indeed, it could be argued that they are not very enlightening by themselves. However, the remainder of the theory will propose factors that affect each of these postulates and provides an explanation for why people in general and youth in particular use coercive forms of influence.

Postulate 1: The Relative Efficacy Principle. When the probability assigned to the success of using coercion by a decision maker is higher than the probabilities assigned to other means of influence to achieve the same value, a coercive act will be performed.

SOURCE CHARACTERISTICS AND COERCIVE ACTIONS

The relative efficacy principle appears to be self-evidently true in its abstract form, but of course it is necessary to attach it to a social context. Lack of self-confidence in the effectiveness of noncoercive forms of influence is more likely when a person lacks the skills, the experience, or the resources that make them effective. A person who has low intelligence, has little education, and is inarticulate will not have confidence that persuasive arguments will succeed in bringing about desired changes in another person. Violent youth apparently display these characteristics. It is well documented that violent criminals have lower average intelligence than the national average (Wilson & Herrnstein, 1985). While lack of attachment to school is more a consequence of delinquent attitudes than the other way around (Liska & Reed, 1985), the two factors appear to go hand in hand and are most likely associated with lack of articulateness and argumentative ability. The inverse relationship between ability to use persuasion and violence is illustrated by a response to an interview by former middleweight champion Jake Lamotta, on whose life the movie *Raging Bull* was based. When asked by Dick Cavett why he fought so much as a kid on the streets, Jake replied that other guys could argue well, but that he could always win the arguments with his fists. It has been observed that gang members frequently are nonexpressive verbally and have an action orientation toward others. Their reactions to others occur so quickly as to appear to be impulsive (Copeland, 1974).

According to social interactionist theory, the fewer the resources the individual has, the less chance he or she has of influencing others by noncoercive means. This factor might explain why a disproportionate number of violent youth who commit serious violent crimes are from the lower class (Wilson & Herrnstein, 1985). Youths who are poor possess few resources that could be used as bribes, as rewards to make contingent promises effective, or for purposes of exchange. If a lack of resources reduces the effectiveness of noncoercive forms of influence, then it becomes more likely that coercive actions will be taken.

In general, the less confident and effective a person is in using noncoercive forms of influence, the more likely it is that coercive actions will be performed to achieve interpersonal goals. A person's reputation for possessing certain characteristics has an impact on the effectiveness of noncoercive forms of influence. Social psychological research has shown that expertise, attractiveness, status, trustworthiness, and credibility increase the effectiveness of persuasive communications and of promises (see Tedeschi, Lindskold, & Rosenfeld, 1985). A person who lacks these positive characteristics would presumably be relatively unsuccessful in using noncoercive forms of influence. Lack of success should translate into low confidence in using noncoercive forms of influence and thereby make it more likely that some form of coercion will be used.

As American society moves into the so-called information age, failure in school and lack of employable skills make it ever more difficult for youth to move out of poverty and acquire high status or to achieve reputations as experts. Just a decade ago, youth with no more than a high school education could get jobs in factories, making a decent wage and receiving excellent health benefits. Today, many of those jobs have been eliminated by technological change and the export of manufacturing to foreign countries. Furthermore, immigrants have increasingly competed for the low-wage jobs that are available to young and unskilled workers. While some otherwise unemployable youth have sought to develop expertise and achieve status in the military, it is likely that that career path will also be curtailed in the future. Changes in the opportunity structure of American jobs probably has something to do with the increase in the prevalence rates of youth violence in the United States across cohorts in the 1970s and 1980s. There has been increasing membership in gangs, and gangs have increasingly engaged in entrepreneurial activities, primarily in the illegal drug economy (Cervantes, 1992).

An important reputational characteristic that enhances the effectiveness of influence attempts (both noncoercive and coercive) is the credibility of the individual. Credibility refers to the consistency of the individual over time, the person's honesty, and the degree to which deeds match words. A person who makes promises and reliably keeps them and makes statements of fact that usually are correct will gain a reputation as someone who can be taken at his or her word. High credibility is a positive asset when one engages in persuasion or makes promises. The higher the credibility of the source, the more likely the target is to believe influence communications and to be positively affected by them. Attitude change, conformity, and compliance have all been shown to be directly related to the credibility of the source of influence (see Tedeschi, Lindskold, & Rosenfeld, 1985). Credibility is therefore a highly valued reputation, and even the most inveterate liars will grow angry if told that others view them as untruthful or unreliable. A reputation for low credibility decreases the likelihood of success for positive forms of influence. If the values at stake are important to individuals and they lack confidence in the success of noncoercive forms of influence, then there is a greater likelihood that coercion will be used.

The value of maintaining high credibility motivates a person to back up threats with corresponding deeds. In a typical sequence a threatener demands some form of compliance; if the target does not comply, the source is placed in a position of backing up the threat or losing credibility. Since a reputation for high credibility will be associated with the success of future influence attempts, the source would incur a cost for not punishing the target. In this type of situation it has been found that college students playing experimental games display considerable consistency in backing up threats by punishing noncompliant opponents (see Tedeschi, Schlenker, & Bonoma, 1973).

The possession of punitive resources should increase individuals' confidence in the effectiveness of coercion to achieve interpersonal goals. Laboratory research has established that the mere possession of punitive resources increases the frequency of punitive actions (Deutsch & Krauss, 1960), and that the greater the magnitude of available punitive resources, the greater the frequency with which coercive actions are performed (Fischer, 1969; Hornstein, 1965). These findings, combined with the evidence that 20% of children sometimes carry weapons to school and 5% of them carry guns (Callahan, Rivara, & Farrow, 1993), provide an explanation for the increase of violence at schools. Thus, conflicts between adolescents that used to be settled with fists are now escalating into fights with knives and guns. Many of these adolescents report carrying weapons for "defensive" purposes. However, evidence from social psychology indicates that in aggressive incidents both parties tend to believe the other person initiated the hostilities (Mummendey, Linneweber, & Löschper, 1984). In any case, youth who carry weapons will be tempted to use their coercive power to dominate, defend against, and defeat real or imagined antagonists.

SOCIAL CONFLICT AND COERCIVE ACTIONS

Social conflict erodes confidence in noncoercive forms of influence. Conflict typically occurs in a situation of scarcity of resources. If two young males desire exclusive access to the same young female, they will be in conflict with one another. It is doubtful in such a case that one could persuade or bribe the other to desist, or that a third party could be engaged to negotiate the outcome. The conflict takes the form of a zero-sum game in which one party wins and the other loses. Of course, one of the parties may decide that wisdom is the better part of valor and may withdraw from the competition, but if both sides persist, coercion becomes the likely method to use in order to prevail. The greater the values at stake in conflicts, the more intense the conflict is, and the stronger the forms of coercion that will be used. Positive forms of influence will be distrusted during conflict since each protagonist perceives the other as having a stake in winning. In sum, conflicts lower confidence that noncoercive forms of influence will be effective, thereby increasing the likelihood that coercion will be used by the two parties.

Felson (1983) found that conflicts over tangible goods and the division of labor were the bases of fights between siblings. The competition for resources and privileges and the assignment of responsibilities are high within families, and more so the larger the size of the family. Consider that if there are only two children in the family, there can only be one pair of children involved in any conflict. When there are three children, any pair can be involved in a conflict, as can any pair against the third, making for six possible patterns of conflict between the three children. The number of patterns of conflicts increases at a much higher rate than the sheer number of children in a family (or any other group). Children in larger families, then, might be expected to resort to coercion more frequently as a means of resolving conflicts, and presumably they have ample opportunity to observe similar behavior by their siblings. The evidence that the rate of delinquency rises with increasing size of the family is consistent with a social interaction analysis of the effects of family size on the use of coercion by children (Kazdin, 1994).

POWER RELATIONSHIPS AND COERCIVE ACTIONS

Inequality of power in dyadic relationships is associated with the use of coercion. It has been found in laboratory research that both parties to conflict were more apt to use coercion when there was a power inequality than when they were equals in power (Lawler, Ford, & Blegen, 1988). The possession of superior power tempts the individual to use it for predatory advantage. Paradoxically, weakness also encourages the use of coercion. Weak parties may have experienced coercion in the past and expect powerful others to try to exploit them. Acquiescence is perceived as appeasement and only encourages more powerful individuals to continue their attempts at exploitation. Studies of bullies indicate that particular individuals are chronic victims or "whipping boys" (Patterson, Littman, & Bricker, 1967). Whipping boys tend to be socially isolated, anxious, passive, and afraid to defend themselves (Olweus, 1979, 1984). Their appeasing behavior encourages the bullies to continue attacking them. Some weak persons try to discourage attacks by more powerful persons. The latter may expect weak parties to be easy prey to predatory actions. In order to convince the predator that they are determined to resist and perhaps to get in the first blow, weaker actors may engage in preemptive strikes. Relatively weak persons might have to demonstrate their willingness to harm the more powerful person in order to make future deterrent threats believable. The "toughness" of the weak party serves notice to the more powerful adversary of an unwillingness to passively accept attempts at domination or exploitation.

Postulate 2: The Value Principle. It is assumed that people are generally likely to select alternatives that lead to the greatest values. When individuals are faced with choosing among evils, they will prefer the least negative outcome.

TERMINAL AND PROCEDURAL VALUES AND COERCIVE ACTIONS

In addition to commodities, services, love, and other terminal values, people give value to the means used to achieve ends. For example, subjects in experiments perceive coercion as more controlling than promises and rewards (Kite, 1964). One reason why men use more physical coercion than women may be that males value controlling others more than females do (Boldizar, Perry, & Perry, 1989; Schönbach, 1990). Aggressive children report greater expectation of rewards for aggressive behavior than do nonaggressive children (Perry, Perry, & Rasmussen, 1986). Research on school children in Denmark has shown that boys are more likely to use direct forms of coercion, including physical attacks, whereas girls are more likely to use verbal and indirect (third-party) forms of harm doing (Bjorkqvist, Lagerspetz, & Kaukiainen, 1992). There are people, of course, who are socialized to have a strong negative value for using physical forms of coercion. Quakers and the Amish are among American religious groups that are pacifists. They use forms of coercion, such as shunning, to gain conformity and to punish nonconformity, but do not believe in the use of violence.

It may be the case that people in general acquire a strong negative procedural value for violent criminal conduct. Committing the first serious felony may be a threshold that, once crossed, makes it easier to commit subsequent crimes (Paternoster, 1989). The fact that most crimes by youth are carried out with other adolescents and yield very little of value suggests that the tangible benefits to be gained would not be sufficient by themselves to get most juvenile delinquents to cross the crime threshold. Peer pressure, which is strong among most teenagers, is probably at least as strong among delinquent cliques and gangs.

Postulate 3: The Inhibition Principle. A social control theory of crime emphasizes the potential costs that inhibit most people from committing crimes. This relationship can be restated in terms of decision making regarding the use of coercion. The higher the probability that an action will incur costs and the greater the magnitude of the costs, the less likely it is that the actor will perform that action.

EXPECTATION OF COSTS AND COERCIVE ACTIONS

Coercive actions frequently elicit resistance, counterthreats, and retaliation. A history of resistance by a target should reduce the likelihood of subsequent coercion by a source. In general, expectation of retaliation acts as a deterrent. Research indicates that there is less use of physical punishments by male college students when they believe the other person has the capability of retaliating (cf. Donnerstein & Donnerstein, 1973; Shortell, Epstein, & Taylor, 1970; Wilson & Rogers, 1975). Interviews of 1,874 prisoners in 10 states revealed that almost half had decided at least once not to undertake a crime because they believed the potential victim was carrying a gun (Wright & Rossi, 1986).

Expected costs for engaging in aggressive behavior have been shown to be different for aggressive and nonaggressive children (Boldizar et al., 1989). Aggressive children indicated less concern about negative peer evaluations, retaliation by the victim, and negative self-evaluations for engaging in coercive actions than did nonaggressive children. Furthermore, boys indicated less concern about retaliation than did girls. Such differences in expectations and values of costs appear to account for a failure of formal deterrence to inhibit criminal behavior (Claster, 1967). Potential criminals, who more often than not act on the basis of opportunity, expect to avoid punishment for their criminal conduct.

While the expectation of costs tends to inhibit the use of coercion, there are age differences in estimations of the probability of costs. Steadman and Felson (1984) reported a strong negative correlation of age with verbal and physical aggression. As ex-offenders get older, they report an increasing expectation of being apprehended, ending up in prison, or being killed or wounded by police or co-offenders (Cusson & Pinsonneault, 1986). Young people often have a sense of invulnerability and a false sense that they can control events. A tendency to underestimate risks and a belief that one can control events to avoid costs increase the probability that youth will use coercion to achieve interpersonal goals. As discussed later in the chapter, youth also find excitement to be a positive value for engaging in risky actions.

It may be recalled that cultural value theory of crime indicated that an important feature of violence-prone people is that they have a fatalistic outlook. According to Groves, Zuckerman, Marans, and Cohen (1993), among the symptoms of children who have been exposed to violence is a nihilistic, fatalistic orientation to the future, which leads to increased risk-taking behaviors. It is not surprising that many African American youth expect to die at an early age, since homicide is the leading cause of death of young black men. Men who are in constant danger experience great psychological stress and may seek outlets in forms of momentary pleasure. These reactions are commonly observed among military personnel.

RESISTANCE AND COERCIVE ACTIONS

An escalation cycle can occur as a function of miscalculation. If the actor is confident that a target will comply with a threat, and hence the actor does not expect that force will be required, then that actor would also not expect retaliation. Thus, the actor would have the optimistic view that the use of a threat gains compliance without resistance. However, if the target does not comply, and the actor feels compelled to carry through and punish the target, the target may well retaliate. As we have seen, a failure to follow through might make the actor appear weak or bluffing and would lower his or her credibility. This sequence of events may lead the actor to escalate the use of force both to compel compliance and to deter further retaliatory behavior. In this way a low-level threat may escalate to physical violence. This kind of escalation cycle has been documented as occuring in some episodes of child abuse (Patterson, 1976). The parent attempts to discipline the child to gain compliance, the child resists, and the parent escalates the level of punishment used against the child. Indeed, expectation of resistance and retaliation may not inhibit the person but may instead cause this individual to choose a higher level of coercion. Luckenbill (1982) has found that robbers are more likely to physically attack a victim when they anticipate resistance. Women who commit robberies are more likely than men to use force on a victim, probably because they anticipate more resistance than do men (Harlow, 1987).

ALCOHOL AND COERCIVE ACTIONS

Intoxication has been shown to be strongly correlated with the commission of violent crimes (Wolfgang & Strohm, 1956; Shupe, 1954; Virkunen, 1974). There is no direct evidence that drinking causes people to become violent. However, there is reason to believe that imbibing will facilitate or disinhibit the use of coercion. Laboratory evidence indicates that drinking alcohol makes a person less attentive to social cues and contingencies of interpersonal behavior, and more likely to perceive threats in ambiguous circumstances, to attribute hostility to others, and to disregard inhibitions in high-conflict situations (Zeichner & Pihl, 1979; Steele & Southwick, 1985; Schmutte, Leonard, & Taylor, 1979; Taylor, Gammon, & Capasso, 1976). A reduction in sensitivity to social cues may be associated with the likelihood of impolite behavior and of giving offense, which can precipitate an altercation with another person.

Alcohol expectancy effects also increase the likelihood that the imbiber will use coercion. People expect drinking to bolster courage, and its sedating effects contribute to a reduction of fear and anxiety (Brown, Goldman, Inn, & Anderson, 1980). Laboratory studies have shown that subjects who were given alcohol and those given placebos (but who believed they were drinking alcohol) imposed more harm against another person than subjects who were given alcohol but who believed it was a placebo, irrespective of whether the other person provoked them (Lang, Goeckner, Adesso, & Marlatt, 1975). Clearly, drinking alcohol affects psychological and physiological processes that impact on a person's decision making in ways that make the use of coercion more likely.

It is important to note that men drink and get drunk twice as often as women (Cahalan, 1978; Hartford & Gerstel, 1981) and men more often drink in public with same-sex peers (Hartford, 1978; Leland, 1982). According to routine activity theory, these are conditions that should increase the likelihood of some form of antisocial behavior.

The Justice Motive

Coercive actors are often motivated by a value for justice. There are three stages that can be identified with the justice process: perception of injustice, attribution of blame, and the decision by the aggrieved party concerning what to do about the injustice. One of the ways in which people respond to perceived injustice is to punish the perpetrator. Punishments may therefore be a form of retributive justice. Punishments may also be intended to deter the wrongdoer from future norm-violating actions, although recipients of retributive punishment may view it as unjust and may retaliate against the original grievant. In this way an escalation process may be initiated where both parties believe the other person is in the wrong.

A form of blocked opportunity theory that merits attention here is self-help theory (Black, 1983). In this theory the barrier (or belief that there is a barrier) to the use of the legal system may lead people to take the law into their own hands. If a person cannot rely on third parties to maintain or restore justice, then there is an increased likelihood that the person will engage in self-help and will impose punishment on the wrongdoer. Many crimes may be directed toward satisfying grievances against the victims. For example, many youth gangs are involved in illegal drug activities (Spergel, Ross, Curry, & Chance, 1989). Incursions of territory or turf are violations of the gang-imposed rule that outsiders are not allowed in that geographical area. These incursions cannot be reported to the police, so gang members either enforce their own rules or defer to the rule violators. Typically, rule violators are hunted down and punished. Such actions are related to social control but also contain a moral component. The gang members may view their own actions as moralistic or self-righteous and the victim as deserving punishment.

ATTRIBUTIONS AND COERCIVE ACTIONS

Divergent perspectives of actor and victim, hostility biases, and negative reputations that affect expectations about how others will act affect attributions of blame and therefore can increase the likelihood that coercion will be used. Subjects in laboratory experiments view their own punitive actions as reactive to the provocations of others but perceive the others' punitive actions as unprovoked (Mummendey, Linneweber, & Löschper, 1984). Even when actors take responsibility for unjustly harming another person, they view the event as less serious and unjust than do their victims (Mikula & Heimgartner, 1992; Baumeister, Stillwell, & Wotman, 1990). This tendency to blame the other person and to minimize one's own wrongdoing encourages each actor to form a grievance toward the other. These perceptions make it unlikely that either will offer an explanation of or an apology for a precipitating behavior. If either or both individuals seek retributive justice, the problem is compounded and a coercive episode ensues that has a good chance of escalating.

Institutionalized aggressive boys have been found to display a tendency to attribute hostility to other boys (Nasby, Hayden, & DePaulo, 1979). Aggressive boys who made more attributions of hostility were more likely to direct coercive actions against the other boys, which in turn usually brought about retaliation, confirming the original expectation of hostile action. This self-fulfilling process suggests that attacks by aggressive boys are often intended as either preemptive defensive actions or as punitive actions for unfair hostility directed toward them (or both).

People whom we do not like and who have bad reputations may be accused of and judged blameworthy for negative actions on the basis of evidence that would not be considered sufficient if we liked these people or if they had good reputations. The amount of punishment that an offender deserves is also related to our negative or positive impression of him or her (Dion, 1972; Nesdale, Rule, & Hill, 1978; Turkat & Dawson, 1976). Less punishment is recommended for offenders judged similar to us than for dissimilar offenders (Mitchell & Byrne, 1973). In the context of group identification in-group members assign more blame for the same action to out-group members than to in-group members (Schruijer, et al., 1993). All these judgmental biases may contribute to the likelihood and severity of subsequent coercive actions taken by individuals and groups.

ANGER AND COERCIVE ACTIONS

Blame and anger appear to have reciprocal effects on each other. An attribution of blame arouses anger, and anger amplifies the amount of blame attributed to an offender (Quigley & Tedeschi, 1996). The arousal associated with anger intensifies whatever behavior the person performs. Thus, voices are louder, phones and doors are slammed, accelerators on automobiles are pushed further toward the floorboard, and so on (Frick, 1985). Such intense actions violate decorum and rules of politeness and therefore may be perceived by the alleged offender as unwarranted and as constituting an unfair accusation. In this way both parties form grievances against the other, and each is motivated to exact some form of justice in the situation.

Anger also disrupts cognitive functions. The angry person accesses less information, perceives fewer alternative courses of action, engages in either/or thinking, and pays less attention to future costs (Masters, Felleman, & Barden, 1981; Meichenbaum & Gilmore, 1984; White, 1968). Thus, anger makes it more likely that scripted or impulsive behavior will occur because the best-learned behavior for conflict situations will be cognitively accessed, alternatives will not be considered, and future costs will be ignored.

Self-Presentation and Identity

The importance of social identities as a factor in coercive episodes has been recognized by many scholars (Goffman, 1955; Toch, 1969; Wolfgang & Ferracuti, 1956). A person engages in self-presentation to proffer, establish, maintain, or defend a desired identity to audiences. The desire for approval, affection, and attachment and the desire to acquire and exercise social power are the primary bases for self-presentational behavior. Presentation of an identity as a moral, just, cooperative, well-behaved, kind, and friendly person may be inspired by an affiliative motive. Expertise, status, trustworthiness, and credibility are identities associated with the effective use of influence and are often referred to as power bases (French & Raven, 1959). The construction of desired identities is crucial, then, to the achievement of important values, and any attempt by others to discredit or diminish these identities may be perceived as seriously endangering future success. Coercion may be used by individuals to proactively establish identities or used protectively to repair or restore identities that are perceived as under attack.

INTIMIDATION, REP BUILDING, AND COERCIVE ACTIONS

Intimidation tactics may convey to audiences that the actor is a dangerous and powerful person. Intimidation is often used in association with threats so as to increase the likelihood that targets will comply with the source's demands. Staring fiercely into another's eyes, expressions of anger, commands shouted in a loud voice punctuated with expletives and insults, challenges, and displays of weapons are forms of intimidation.

Toch (1969) described some violent men in prison as self-image promoters. These men precipitate violent incidents so they can demonstrate their fighting ability and courage. This kind of "rep building" is similar to the behavior of young gunslingers in western novels, who try to establish a reputation as a "fast gun" by seeking out and dueling with other men. Young initiates in violent gangs need to gain respect from their peers by engaging in some semi-ritualistic violent act. A reputation as a "bad ass" may be a useful and effective identity under some circumstances for maintaining dominance and power over others (Katz, 1988). Rep building appears to be a motivation among bullies, who tend to seek out situations where their dominating behavior can be observed by their peers (Wachtel, 1973).

Identification with a violent model may be an important mediator of antisocial behavior (Bandura, 1986). Indirect support for such a modeling effect is the evidence that parents of delinquents are unusually likely to have criminal records (Rutter & Giller, 1983). Indeed, having parents with a history of criminality is the strongest indicator of a child's future delinquency. A recent case study of violence through several generations of a single family (Butterfield, 1995) describes how a child may promote an identity similar to that of a father figure who is a convicted murderer. The child, whose grandfather also murdered a man, is now in prison convicted of two murders and is kept in solitary confinement because he acts according to his desire to be the "baddest" person who ever lived. It should be noted that this dangerous and uncontrollable person has a very high IQ and can be quite charming on the few occasions he chooses to be.

GENDER AND COERCIVE ACTIONS

The gender role of some men, particularly in the lower classes (Lewis, 1961) and honor-based cultures, involves a set of identities referred to as *machismo*. A person who is highly motivated to show that he is a "man" may want to demonstrate physical courage, willingness to avenge affronts or insults by physically hurting the offender, sexual prowess, and dominance over women and children. Brannon and Juni (1984) identified four clusters of norms adopted by males: avoidance of femininity, independence, achieving status, and aggressiveness. Thompson and Pleck (1987) found essentially the same results. These self-relevant norms of men may explain the fact that altercations between men are more likely to escalate to physical violence than conflicts between women or between a man and a woman (Felson, 1984).

Felson and Liska (1984) found that gender differences in fighting among school children were largely attributable to gender role identities. An observational study of quarrels among 5- to 7-year-old children showed that boys pursue their own agendas and try to win, while girls showed more concern for maintaining social harmony (Miller, Danaher, & Forbes, 1986). The idea that "boys will be boys" was largely demonstrated by these studies. On the other hand, women are more likely to avoid acts that threaten the identity of others (P. Brown, 1980; Connor-Linton, 1986).

Most parents will recall their trepidation when their children began to engage in risky behaviors, such as when they would jump from high places, sled or ski down steep slopes, fail to come to a standstill at stop signs, and a multitude of other actions that place the children at risk for physical injury or failure. Youth (and some adults) tend to be attracted to the excitement of risky behaviors. Often they want to show off to their friends and ask others to "watch me." These commonsense observations have been supported by laboratory research.

Risk takers are perceived as more fearless, less easily scared, and tougher than more conservative decision makers (Dahlbäck, 1978). Experimental subjects who value the macho identity associated with engaging in risky behavior are more likely to engage in coercive behavior (Weigold & Schlenker, 1991). Furthermore, there is abundant evidence that people in groups make riskier decisions than individuals (e.g., Isenberg, 1986). Young men appear to be especially uninhibited by physical danger (Bell & Bell, 1993; Gove, 1985; Jonah, 1986). Most youth who engage in delinquency act in consort with peers, and the presence of others most likely increases both self-presentational concerns and associated risk-taking behavior. Several criminologists have noted that much dangerous and violent behavior by young men is a form of self-presentation intended to impress others (Daly & Wilson, 1988; Jackson & Gray, 1976; Rothe, 1987).

CHARACTER CONTESTS AND COERCIVE ACTIONS

When identities are challenged, threatened, or attacked, the person may respond in a protective way. While proactive self-presentation is often concerned with asserting an identity of strength, protective self-presentation is motivated by the desire to avoid an appearance of weakness. Individuals can restore face by retaliating, an action that shows that they are not weak, lacking in courage, or willing to tolerate disrespect. However, retaliation casts its target into a negative or weak identity, which often motivates a counter-counterattack, and a conflict spiral ensues. According to studies by Felson and Steadman (1983) and Luckenbill (1977), such "character contests" sometimes result in physical assaults and homicides.

The prospect of losing a fight might not inhibit retaliation. While it might lower status, the status loss can be minimized or even eliminated by putting up a courageous fight. The loser of a fight can display courage and "guts" and can gain the respect of both antagonists and onlookers. Short and Strodtbeck (1965) reported that in fights between members of different gangs both fighters enhanced their reputations.

HONOR, RESPECT, AND COERCIVE ACTIONS

The cultural value theory of crime suggests that affronts to honor may precipitate violence by members of particularly violent groups. Honor-based societies encourage physical attacks to uphold the honor of one's own identity and that of one's family or social group (Nisbett et al., 1995). Violence between gangs may occur when a member of one gang "disses" a member of another gang, bringing the honor of the gang into play. As Horowitz and Schwartz (1974) describe the process, perceived violation of right treatment is interpreted as a threat to manhood and requires the individual to retaliate in kind. A very simple slight can ignite quickly into a physical attack. Gang youth tend to be hypersensitive to any signs of disrespect (Moore, Garcia, Garcia, Cerda, & Valencia, 1978). Wolfgang's (1958) study of homicides in Philadelphia indicated that the most common episode was some trivial triggering event, such as a curse, insult, jostling, and so on. Thirty years later, Daly and Wilson (1988) found similar results. Indeed, in many homicidal incidents, either party could have killed the other (Wilson & Daly, 1985).

A challenge to autonomy tends to be resisted (psychological reactance) because acquiescence might be perceived as appeasement or weakness and might encourage further encroachments by others (Tedeschi, Schlenker, & Bonoma, 1971). This process is illustrated by instances of barroom violence that begin when the bartender refuses to serve a customer, who perceives this constraint as an affront (Felson, Baccaglini, & Gmelch, 1986). Police officers who ask questions, give orders, and make accusations may elicit negative reactions by civilians who resist the role of suspect and perceive the officer as disrespectful and exceeding his or her authority (Brent & Sykes, 1979; Hudson, 1970). Assaults against police officers often occur when a citizen challenges their commands (Toch, 1969). An officer might tell young men standing on a street corner to "move on"; they might respond that it is a free country and they are not doing anything wrong. This challenge may lead the officer to convert the situation into a confrontation because he or she is motivated to maintain credibility and authority on the street, and a fight may then occur. Such a scenario is more likely in neighborhoods where the legitimacy or fairness of the police is questioned by the citizens.

DEMOGRAPHIC FACTORS AND COERCIVE ACTIONS

The motivation to assert and protect identities also suggests an explanation for demographic differences in youth violence. Consistent with a cultural value theory of crime, social interactionist theory assumes that there are differences between people in the kinds of identities they aspire to, construct, and protect. Gender differences in the use of physical forms of coercion may reflect the masculine ideal in a culture and the models presented to and admired by young males. Furthermore, there may be subcultural and regional

variations both in the identities that are admired and the kinds of behavior that are scripted for young men. Evidence indicates that machismo is an important identity among poor white, African American, and Hispanic men, especially in the southern and mountain
regions of the United States, and in most gangs. Scripts that pre-
scribe physically punitive actions in response to affronts and threats
to family and significant others appear to be associated with machismo identities and prescriptions about how a man defends his
honor.

It might be assumed that poor and disenfranchised people who
feel alienated from society are apt to experience more injustice and
to have less access to remedies than more advantaged people. According to Black (1983), these are the conditions that foster self-help,
and we represent this condition in our theory of coercive actions by
the justice motive. If a person is robbed, physically attacked, or otherwise harmed by someone and does not expect the legal system to
exact justice by prosecuting and punishing the perpetrator, the victim may seek to impose retributive justice himself or herself. People
who distrust the police or other third parties to help them in their
disputes will more often take matters into their own hands. For example, gang members cannot expect the police to help them protect
their turf against intrusion from other gangs. The justice motive can
help explain why some alienated minorities and poor people resort
to coercion more frequently than other citizens.

INDIVIDUAL DIFFERENCES AND COERCIVE ACTIONS

An interesting and important crime statistic is that 6% of individual
offenders commit half of all crimes (Wolfgang, Figlio, & Sellin, 1972).
Similarly, West and Farrington (1977) found that half of all criminal
convictions were accounted for by the families of 5% of the individual criminals. Thus, there are a very few people who commit a large
percentage of all the crimes in our society. A reasonable question is
what individual difference factors help to explain this deviant pattern of behavior.

Aggressiveness and antisocial behavior in childhood is one of
the best predictors of criminal behavior by adults (Eron & Hues-

mann, 1990; Gove, 1985). However, most antisocial and aggressive children do not become adult criminals, and most adult criminals have no record of juvenile delinquency (McCord, 1980). Rivera and Widom (1990) found that one-third of adult violent offenders had been arrested for a violent action before the age of 18. However, longitudinal studies have found no important individual differences between violent and nonviolent criminal offenders (Farrington, 1991). All these crime statistics, along with the evidence of the versatility (i.e., lack of specialization) of criminals, have led some criminologists to conclude that a disposition to engage in antisocial actions underlies criminal behavior and the propensity to be violent.

Gottfredson and Hirschi (1990) argued that learning theory fails to explain the versatility of criminal behavior because patterns of reinforcement should encourage repetition of successful crimes and hence lead to specialization. They proposed that lack of self-control is the individual difference factor that can account for these findings. Gottfredson and Hirschi's view of learning theory is couched in terms of old-fashioned behaviorism: Aggressive behaviors that are reinforced are repeated. However, people may develop other forms of behavior that increase the likelihood of friction and conflict with others. Children may learn forms of interpersonal behavior that initiate conflicts with others (Patterson, DeBaryshe, & Ramsey, 1989), and may value identities that are associated with scripts prescribing that the response to any slight by others should be physical forms of punishment. In tandem with learning coercive scripts, irritating, impolite, and norm-violating behaviors, and the value of macho identities, failure to learn particular skills may impact decision making and lead to violent actions. Failure to learn delay of gratification is most likely associated with strong temptation to take advantage of immediate opportunities to obtain rewards and to disregard long-term costs of engaging in illegitimate actions. Failure to learn complex social scripts about negotiation, the lack of social skills and knowledge, and other factors that would encourage noncoercive ways of achieving values also contribute to decisions to use coercion.

In general, the social interactionist theory of coercive actions suggests that researchers should focus more attention on individual difference factors that affect decision making by youth. Recent development of prevention programs for high-risk youth appear to recognize many of these factors. Thus, youths identified as having a high risk for violence are being taught social skills, social problem solving, social perspective taking, and consideration of the costs of their actions (Guerra, Tolan, and Hammond, 1994). The important roles of identity and justice in the likelihood and intensity of violence have not been addressed in prevention programs.

Conclusion

Social interactionist theory assumes that the same conditions motivate the use of coercion by parents, children, youth, and adults; by African American, Hispanic, and white people; by men and women; by Southerners and Northerners; and by Americans, Europeans, and Asians. There are, of course, some people who use coercion much more frequently than others, and a few who are violent. Thus, while some people might respond to an insult by shunning the rude person, and still others might subject her or him to counter-insults, there are a few people who might respond with a physical attack. The strategy of explanation offered here is first to understand the general conditions that lead most people to use coercion and then to ask why physical rather than nonphysical forms of coercion are used.

It has been proposed that the decision processes of the actor must be examined in the context of his or her social motivations if we are to understand why threatening or punitive actions are performed. When the net expected gains associated with a particular alternative are greater than for other alternatives, and when expected costs are held constant, the actor will act to maximize gains. However, the decision maker also considers expected costs. As expected costs increase, the actor becomes less likely to choose a particular course of action.

All people are motivated to achieve values that must be provided or mediated by other people. Among the means available to influence others to act in desired ways are threats, bodily force, and punitive actions. In the scheme of things, each of us is also likely to be a target of influence attempts by others. One way to deter others is to use coercion. Consistent with such an "offensive-defensive" distinction, Dodge and Coie (1987) found that proactive and reactive aggression are two separate factors in predicting behavior. In addition, any factor that increases the procedural value of coercion or decreases the individual's confidence in the effectiveness of noncoercive forms of influence will increase the likelihood that coercion will be used.

Most people are socialized to expect that rewards and punishments are generally consistent with principles of "just deserts." Anyone who violates rules, laws, and norms should be punished. Such expectations may encourage both conformity and the performance of punitive actions, a pattern that is consistent with the conceptualization of an authoritarian personality (Adorno, Frenkel-Brunswick, Levinson, & Sanford, 1950). A justice process begins with a perception of an injustice, an attribution of blame, the experience of anger, and the development of a grievance. A grievant is motivated to restore justice. There are a number of alternative ways in which a grievant could act, such as doing nothing, forgiving the wrongdoer, asking for an apology or restitution, and engaging in an act of retributive justice. A social interactionist theory of coercive actions focuses on those factors that cause decision makers to choose alternatives that directly or indirectly lead to violent encounters.

Finally, people are motivated to assert and protect their identities, particularly those that enhance the effectiveness of social influence and that gain the love and affection of others. Threats and punishments may be used to establish a reputation as a tough and dangerous person. Coercion may also be used in response to slights, affronts, or insults that are believed to damage or threaten desired identities. Character contests may then ensue, and an escalation of increasing intensities of punitive actions is likely to occur, as each party wants to end the contest by being one up.

The frequency with which a person uses coercion is also addressed by the theory. People who do not possess characteristics that enhance the effectiveness of noncoercive forms of influence, such as expertise and attractiveness, will use coercion more frequently than those who possess such characteristics. A person who is inarticulate and possesses few material resources is also likely to use coercion more often than a verbally skilled person who has valuable possessions. These considerations indicate why lack of attachment to school and failure in school are such important indicators of subsequent aggression and delinquency.

The application of our theory to the problem of youth violence is in the context of the motives for social control, for justice, and to establish and protect identities. Special factors that may affect youth—such as desire for excitement, peer influence and insecure identities, feelings of invulnerability, and short-time perspectives—should increase the likelihood that they will use coercion. The versatility of antisocial behavior by youth should not blind us to the overall thematic (i.e., motivational) unity to their actions. Several antisocial behaviors may serve the same purpose. Thus, a pattern of apparently versatile behaviors may all be directed to obtaining money or to gain the respect of peers (Jessor & Jessor, 1977). Antisocial and violent behaviors of youth may come in packages linked to specific social motives.

In their contribution to this symposium, Heimer and Matsueda have proposed a symbolic interactionist theory of deviance that is similar in many respects to the present theory. Of course, both symbolic interactionist and social interactionist theories must explain the same set of data. Many of the apparent similarities are traceable more to the facts of delinquency and crime (and deviance) than to the mechanisms specified by the two theories. These theories are alike in that both view the actor as a decision maker who evaluates the gains and costs of engaging in alternative actions. Also, both theories include the motive of actors to achieve tangible rewards, status, group acceptance, and positive identity. However, an important difference is that symbolic interactionist theory views the self-concept as playing a central role in regulating behavior, including deviant behavior. The individual's conduct is based on self-definitions and attitudes. Actions are consistent with self-definitions, self-attitudes, and roles. While the self is clearly constructed out of interactions and expectations regarding others, actions are largely generated and controlled by the self.

Social interactionist theory views the individual as embedded in a matrix of other people. Most important rewards are obtainable only through the mediation of other people. Social influence is a central process because the only way for a person to get what she or he wants is to get other people to engage in desired actions. Thus, the focus of social interactionist theory is on social motivation and social influence. Coercive actions are types of influence, as are persuasion, promises, exhortation, and other actions. Social motives depend on the person's values and the opportunity structure of the social environment. Among the most important social motives specified by social interactionist theory are the desire for compliance, a concern for justice, and a positive social identity. What form of influence will be chosen depends on the social situation, the relationship with the target, source characteristics, factors that affect the expectations of success in using various forms of influence, and the values and costs that are associated with various alternatives.

Another important difference is that the dependent variable for symbolic interactionist theory is deviance. Social interactionist theory more specifically focuses on the use of threats and punishments by individuals against other individuals. Everyone engages in coercive actions. Parents make demands of their children, judges sentence convicted felons to jail, supervisors may penalize workers, and robbers make contingent threats to targeted victims. Whereas each of these actions is coercive, only the robbery is a deviant action. Thus, each theory has its own domain to explain, and they overlap only with regard to coercive actions that are deviant in nature. Social interactionist theory was not designed to explain deviance, nor was symbolic interactionist theory designed to explain coercive actions.

Some directions for future research are suggested by the social interactionist theory of coercive actions. The theory proposes that high aspirations (i.e., strong social motivation) combined with lack of certain personal attributes or resources limit the effectiveness of noncoercive forms of influence. Lack of confidence in noncoercive forms of influence should be related to either withdrawal or more frequent use of coercion, depending on the effectiveness of inhibiting factors. Furthermore, any factor that contributes to the disregard of future costs of engaging in coercive actions would be associated with "impulsive" actions. For example, among such disinhibiting factors are the use of alcohol, the experience of strong emotions, and fatalistic attitudes. In addition, it would be important to understand why coercion takes a violent form. Rep building, a procedural value for risk taking and violent actions, a concern for honor and a macho identity, and a desire to defend oneself against the real or imagined threats of others are some possible bases for understanding the choice of violent action by youth. In general, the orientation suggested by social interactionist theory emphasizes social motivations of youth, who choose among alternative possible means of influencing others to get what they want. Like everyone else, young people want material things, services, excitement, justice, love, and a positive social identity.

NOTES

1. See Tedeschi and Quigley (1996) for a critique of laboratory paradigms for studying human aggression.
2. Deterrence refers to formal controls, such as legal sanctions. Commitment refers to a sort of investment that could be lost by engaging in deviant actions. Thus, the rewards associated with doing well in school could be lost by engaging in delinquent actions.

REFERENCES

Adorno, T. W., Frenkel-Brunswick, E., Levinson, D. J., & Sanford, R. N. (1950). *The authoritarian personality.* New York: Harper.

Ball-Rokeach, S. J. (1973). Values and violence: A test of the subculture of violence thesis. *American Sociological Review, 38*, 736–749.

Bandura, A. (1986). *Social foundations of thought and action: A social cognitive theory.* Englewood Cliffs NJ: Prentice-Hall.

Baumeister, R. F., Stillwell, A., & Wotman, S. R. (1990). Victim and perpetrator accounts of interpersonal conflict: Autobiographical narratives about anger. *Journal of Personality and Social Psychology, 59*(5), 994–1005.

Bell, N. J., & Bell, R. W. (Eds.), (1993). *Adolescent risk taking.* Newbury Park CA: Sage.

Berkowitz, L. (1993). *Aggression: Its causes, consequences, and control.* New York: McGraw-Hill.

Bjorkqvist, K., Lagerspetz, K. M. J., & Kaukiainen, A. (1992). Do girls manipulate and boys fight? Developmental trends in regard to direct and indirect aggression. *Aggressive Behavior, 18*, 117–127.

Black, D. (1983). Crime as social control. *American Sociological Review, 48*, 34–45.

Blumstein, A., & Cohen, J. (1979). Estimation of individual crime rates from arrest records. *Journal of Criminal Law and Criminology, 70*, 561–585.

Boldizar, J. P., Perry, D. G., and Perry, L. C. (1989). Outcome values and aggression. *Child Development, 60*, 571–579.

Brannon, R., & Juni, S. (1984). A scale for measuring attitudes about masculinity. *Psychological Documents, 14*, 6–7.

Brent, E. E., & Sykes, R. E. (1979). A mathematical model of symbolic interaction between police and suspects. *Behavioral Science, 24*, 388–402.

Brown, P. (1980). How and why are women more polite? Some evidence from a Mayan community. In S. McConnell-Ginet, R. Borker, & N. Furman (Eds.), *Women and language in literature and society.* New York: Praeger.

Brown, S. A., Goldman, M. S., Inn, A., & Anderson, L. R. (1980). Expectations of reinforcement from alcohol: Their domain and relation to drinking patterns. *Journal of Counseling and Clinical Psychology, 48,* 419–426.

Butterfield, F. (1995). *All God's children.* New York: Knopf.

Cahalan, D. (1978). Implications of American drinking practices and attitudes for prevention and treatment of alcoholism. In G. A. Marlatt & P. E. Nathan (Eds.), *Behavioral approaches to alcoholism.* (pp. 6–26). New Brunswick NJ: Rutgers Center for Alcohol Studies.

Callahan, C. M., Rivara, F. P., & Farrow, J. A. (1993). Youth in detention and handguns. *Journal of Adolescent Health, 14,* 350–355.

Cervantes, R. C. (Ed.). (1992). *Substance abuse and gang violence.* Newbury Park CA: Sage.

Claster, D. S. (1967). Comparison of risk perception between delinquents and nondelinquents. *Journal of Criminal Law, Criminology, and Police Science, 58,* 80–86.

Cohen, L. E., & Felson, M. (1979). Social change and crime rate trends: A routine activity approach. *American Sociological Review, 44,* 588–608.

Cohen, L. E., Kluegel, R., & Land, K. (1981). Social inequality and predatory criminal victimization: An exposition and test of a formal theory. *American Sociological Review, 46,* 505–524.

Connor-Linton, J. (1986). Gender differences in politeness: The struggle for power among adolescents. In J. Connor-Linton, C. J. Hall, & M. McGinnis (Eds.), *Southern California Occasional Papers in Linguistics, 11,* 64–98.

Copeland, A. D. (1974). Violent black gangs: Psycho- and sociodynamics. *Adolescent Psychiatry, 3,* 340–353.

Cornish, D. B., & Clarke, R. V. (Eds.). (1986). *The reasoning criminal: Rational choice perspectives on offending.* New York: Springer-Verlag.

Cusson, M., & Pinsonneault, P. (1986). The decision to give up crime. In D. B. Cornish and R. V. Clarke (Eds.), *The reasoning criminal: Rational choice perspectives on offending* (pp. 72–82). New York: Springer-Verlag.

Dahlbäck, O. (1978). Risktagande ["Risk taking"]. Unpublished doctoral dissertation (in Swedish), University of Stockholm.

Daly, M., & Wilson, M. (1988). *Homicide.* New York: Aldine.

Deutsch, M., and Krauss, R. M. (1960). The effect of threat upon interpersonal bargaining. *Journal of Abnormal and Social Psychology: 61,* 181–189.

Dion, K. K. (1972). Physical attractiveness and evaluation of children's transgressions. *Journal of Personality and Social Psychology, 24,* 207–213.

Dodge, K. A., & Coie, J. D. (1987). Social-information-processing factors in reactive and proactive aggression in children's peer groups. *Journal of Personality and Social Psychology, 53,* 1146–1158.

Dollard, J., Doob, N., Miller, N. E., Mowrer, O. H., & Sears, R. R. (1939). *Frustration and aggression.* New Haven: Yale University Press.

Donnerstein, E., & Donnerstein, M. (1973). Variables in interracial aggression: Potential ingroup censure. *Journal of Personality and Social Psychology, 27,* 143–150.

Erlanger, H. S. (1974). The empirical status of the subculture of violence thesis. *Social Problems, 22,* 280–291.

Eron, L. D., & Huesmann, L. R. (1990). The stability of aggressive behavior—even into the third generation. In M. Lewis & S. M. Miller (Eds.), *Handbook of developmental psychopathology* (pp. 207–217). New York: Plenum Press.

Farrington, D. P. (1991). *Childhood aggression and adult violence: Early precursors and later-life outcomes.* Cambridge: Cambridge University Press.

Felson, R. B. (1983). Aggression and violence between siblings. *Social Psychology Quarterly, 46,* 271–285.

———. (1984). Patterns of aggressive interaction. In A. Mummendey (Ed.), *Social psychology of aggression: From individual behavior to social interaction* (pp. 107–126). Berlin: Springer-Verlag.

Felson, R. B., Baccaglini, W., & Gmelch, G. (1986). Bar-room brawls: Aggression and violence in Irish and American bars. In A. Campbell & J. J. Gibbs (Eds.) *Violent transactions.* Oxford: Basil Blackwell.

Felson, R. B., & Liska, A. E. (1984). Explanations of the sex-deviance relationship. *Deviant Behavior, 5,* 1–10.

Felson, R. B., & Steadman, H. J. (1983). Situational factors in disputes leading to criminal violence. *Criminology, 21,* 59–74.

Fingerhut, L. A., Ingram, D. D., & Feldman, J. J. (1992). Firearm homicide among black teenage males in metropolitan counties: Comparison of death rates in two periods, 1983 through 1985 and 1987 through 1989. *Journal of the American Medical Association, 267,* 3054–3058.

Fischer, C. S. (1969). The effect of threats in an incomplete information game. *Sociometry, 32,* 301–314.

Foa, U. G. (1971). Interpersonal and economic resources. *Science, 171,* 345–351.

French, J. R. P., Jr., & Raven, B. (1959). The bases of social power. In D. Cartwright (Ed.), *Studies in social power.* Ann Arbor: University of Michigan Press.

Frick, R. W. (1985). Communicating emotion: The role of prosodic features. *Psychological Bulletin, 97,* 412–429.

Geen, R. G. (1990). *Human aggression.* Pacific Grove CA: Brooks/Cole.

Goffman, E. (1955). On face-work: An analysis of ritual elements in social interaction. *Psychiatry, 18,* 213–231.

Goldstein, A. P. (1994). Delinquent gangs. In J. Archer (Ed.), *Male violence* (pp. 87–104). New York: Routledge.

Gottfredson, M., & Hirschi, T. (1990). *A general theory of crime.* Stanford: Stanford University Press.

Gouze, K. R. (1987). Attention and social problem solving as correlates of aggression in preschool males. *Journal of Abnormal Child Psychology, 15,* 181–197.

Gove, W. (1985). The effect of age and gender on deviant behavior: A biopsychological perspective. In A. S. Rossi (Ed.), *Gender and the life course.* New York: Aldine.

Groves, B. M., Zuckerman, B., Marans, S., & Cohen, D. J. (1993). Silent victims: Children who witness violence. *Journal of the American Medical Association, 269,* 262–263.

Guerra, N. G., Patrick, H., Tolan, P. H., & Hammond, W. R. (1994). Prevention and treatment of adolescent violence. In D. Eron, J. H. Gentry, & P. Schlegel (Eds.), *Reason to hope: A psychosocial perspective on violence and youth.* Washington DC: American Psychological Association.

Harlow, C. (1987). *Special report: Robbery victims.* Washington DC: Bureau of Justice Statistics.

Hartford, T. C. (1978). Contextual drinking patterns among men and women. In F. A. Seixas (Ed.), *Currents in alcoholism* (Vol. 4, pp. 287–296). San Francisco: Grune & Stratton.

Hartford, T. C., & Gerstel, E. K. (1981). Age-related patterns of daily alcohol consumption in metropolitan Boston. *Journal of Studies on Alcohol, 42,* 1062–1066.

Hindelang, M. J. (1976). *Criminal victimization in eight American cities.* New York: Ballinger.

Hirschi, T. (1969). *Causes of delinquency.* Berkeley: University of California Press.

Hornstein, H. A. (1965). The effects of different magnitudes of threat upon interpersonal bargaining. *Journal of Experimental Social Psychology, 1,* 282–293.

Horowitz, R., & Schwartz, G. (1974). Honor, normative ambiguity and gang violence. *American Sociological Review, 39,* 238–251.

Hudson, J. R. (1970). Police-citizen encounters that lead to citizen complaints. *Social Problems, 18,* 179–193.

Huesmann, L. R. (1988). An information processing model for the development of aggression. *Aggressive Behavior, 14,* 13–24.

Isenberg, D. J. (1986). Group polarization: A critical review and meta-analysis. *Journal of Personality and Social Psychology, 50,* 1141–1151.

Jackson, T. T., & Gray, M. (1976). Field study of risk-taking behavior of automobile drivers. *Perceptual and Motor Skills, 43,* 471–474.

Jessor, R., & Jessor, S. L. (1977). *Problem behavior and psychosocial development: A longitudinal study of youth.* New York: Academic Press.

Jonah, B. A. (1986). Accident risk and risk-taking behaviour among young drivers. *Accident Analysis and Prevention, 18,* 255–271.

Kantrowitz, B. (1992, August 2). Wild in the streets. *Newsweek.*

Katz, J. (1988). *Seductions of crime: Moral and sensual attractions of doing evil.* New York: Basic Books.

Kazdin, A. E. (1994). Interventions for aggressive and antisocial children. In D. Eron, J. H. Gentry, & P. Schlegel (Eds.), *Reason to hope: A psychosocial perspective on violence and youth.* Washington DC: American Psychological Association.

Kite, W. R. (1964). *Attributions of causality as a function of the use of reward and punishment.* Unpublished doctoral dissertation, Stanford University.

Lang, A. R., Goeckner, D. J., Adesso, V. J., & Marlatt, G. A. (1975). Effects of alcohol on aggression in male social drinkers. *Journal of Abnormal Psychology, 84,* 508–518.

Lauritsen, J. L., Laub, J. H., & Sampson, R. J. (1992) Conventional and delinquent activities: Implications for the prevention of violent victimization among adolescents. *Violence and Victims, 7,* 91–108.

Lawler, E. J., Ford, R., and Blegen, M. A. (1988). Coercive capability in conflict: A test of bilateral deterrence versus conflict spiral theory. *Social Psychology Quarterly, 51,* 93–107.

Leland, J. (1982). Gender, drinking and alcohol abuse. In I. Al-Issa (Ed.), *Gender and psychopathology* (pp. 201–220). San Francisco: Academic Press.

Lewis, O. (1961). *The children of Sanchez: Autobiography of a Mexican family.* New York: Random House.

Liska, A. E. (1971). Aspirations, expectations and delinquency: Stress and additive models. *Sociological Quarterly, 12,* 99–107.

Liska, A. E., & Reed, M. D. (1985). Ties to conventional institutions and delinquency: Estimating reciprocal effects. *American Sociological Review, 50,* 547–560.

Luckenbill, D. F. (1977). Criminal homicide as a situated transaction. *Social Problems, 25,* 176–186.

———. (1982). Compliance under threat of severe punishment. *Social Forces, 60,* 810–825.

Masters, J. C., Felleman, E. S., & Barden, R. C. (1981). Experimental studies of affective states in children. In B. Lahey & A. E. Kazdin (Eds.), *Advances in clinical child psychology* (Vol. 4, pp. 91–114). New York: Plenum.

Matsueda, R. L. (1988). The current state of differential association theory. *Crime and Delinquency, 34,* 277–06.

Matsueda, R. L., & Heimer, K. (1987). Race, family structure, and delinquency: A test of differential association and social control theories. *American Sociological Review, 52,* 826–840.

McCord, J. (1980). Patterns of deviance. In S. B. Sells, R. Crandall, M. Roff, J. S. Strauss, and W. Pollin (Eds.), *Human functioning in longitudinal pespective* (pp. 157–165). Baltimore: Williams & Wilkins.

Meichenbaum, D., & Gilmore, J. B. (1984). The nature of unconscious processes: A cognitive-behavioral perspective. In K. Bowers & D. Meichenbaum (Eds.), *The unconscious reconsidered* (pp. 273–298). New York: Wiley.

Mikula, G., & Heimgartner, A. (1992). *Experiences of injustice in intimate relationships.* Unpublished manuscript, University of Graz, Austria.

Miller, P., Danaher, D., & Forbes, D. (1986). Sex-related strategies for coping with interpersonal conflict in children aged five and seven. *Developmental Psychology, 22,* 543–548.

Miller, W. B. (1958). Lower class culture as a generating milieu of gang delinquency. *Journal of Social Issues, 14,* 5–19.

Mitchell, R., and Byrne, D. (1973). The defendant's dilemma: Effects on juror's attitudes and authoritarianism on judicial decisions. *Journal of Personality and Social Psychology, 25,* 123–129.

Moore, J. W., Garcia, R., Garcia, C., Cerda, L., and Valencia, F. (1978). *Homeboys, gangs, drugs, and prison in the barrios of Los Angeles*. Philadelphia: Temple University Press.

Mummendey, A., Linneweber, V., & Löschper, G. (1984). Actor or victim of aggression: Divergent perspectives—divergent evaluations. *European Journal of Social Psychology, 14*, 291–311.

Nasby, W., Hayden, B., & DePaulo, B. M. (1979). Attributional bias among aggressive boys to interpret unambiguous social stimuli as displays of hostility. *Journal of Abnormal Psychology, 89*, 459–468.

Nesdale, A. R., Rule, B. G., & Hill, K. A. (1978). The effect of attraction on causal attributions and retaliation. *Personality and Social Psychology Bulletin, 4*, 231–234.

Nisbett, R. E. (1993). Violence and U.S. regional culture. *American Psychologist, 48*, 441–449.

Nisbett, R. E., Polly, G., & Lang, S. (1995). Homicide and U.S. regional culture. In R. B. Ruback & N. A. Weiner (Eds.), *Interpersonal violent behaviors: Social and cultural aspects* (pp. 135–152). New York: Springer.

Olweus, D. (1979). Stability of aggressive reaction patterns in males: A review. *Psychological Bulletin, 86*, 852–875.

———. (1984). Aggressors and their victims: Bullying at school. In N. Frude & H. Gault (Eds.), *Disruptive behaviors in schools* (pp. 57–76). New York: Wiley.

Osgood, D. W., Johnston, L. D., O'Malley, P. M., & Bachman, J. G. (1988). The generality of deviance in late adolescence and early adulthood. *American Sociological Review, 53*, 81–93.

Osgood, D. W., Wilson, J. K., Bachman, J. G., O'Malley, P. M., & Johnston, L. D. (1996). Routine activities and individual deviant behavior. *American Sociological Review, 61*, 635–655.

Paternoster, R. (1989). Absolute and restrictive deterrence in a panel of youth. *Social Problems, 36*, 289–309.

Patterson, G. R. (1976). The aggressive child: Victim and architect of a coercive system. In L. A. Hamerlynck, E. J. Mash, & L. C. Handy (Eds.), *Behavior modification and families: Vol. 1. Theory and research. Vol. 2. Applications and developments*. New York: Brunner/Mazel.

Patterson, G. R., DeBaryshe, B. D., & Ramsey, E. (1989). A developmental perspective on antisocial behavior. *American Psychologist, 44*, 329–335.

Patterson, G. R., Littman, R. A., & Bricker, W. (1967). Assertive behavior in children: A step toward a theory of aggression. *Monographs of the Society for Research in Child Development, 32* (5), Serial No. 113).

Perry, D. G., Perry, L. C., & Rasmussen, P. (1986). Cognitive social learning mediators of aggression. *Child Development, 57*, 700–711.

Quigley, B. M., & Tedeschi, J. T. (1996). The mediating effects of blame attributions of feeling of anger. *Personality and Social Psychology Bulletin, 22*, 1280–1288.

Riedel, M., & Zahn, M. A. (1985). *The nature and patterns of American homicide*. Washington DC: U.S. National Institute of Justice.

Rivera, B., & Widom, C. S. (1990). Childhood victimization and violent offending. *Violence and Victims, 5*, 19–35.

Rossi, P. H., Waite, E., Bose, C. E., & Berk, R. E. (1974). The seriousness of crime: Normative structure and individual differences. *American Sociological Review, 39*, 224–237.

Rothe, J. P. (1987). *Rethinking young drivers*. North Vancouver: Insurance Corporation of British Columbia.

Rutter, M., & Giller, H. (1983). *Juvenile delinquency: Trends and perspectives*. New York: Penguin Books.

Sampson, R. J. & Laub, J. H. (1990). Crime and deviance over the life course. *American Sociological Review, 55*, 609–627.

Schmutte, G. T., Leonard, K. E., & Taylor, S. P. (1979). Alcohol and expectations of attack. *Psychological Reports, 45*, 163–167.

Schönbach, P. (1990). *Account episodes: The management or escalation of conflict*. New York: Cambridge University Press.

Schruijer, S., Blanz, M., Mummendey, A., Tedeschi, J. T., Banfai, B., Dittmar, H., Kleibaumhuter, D., Mahjoub, A., Mandrosz-Wroblewska, J., Molinari, L., & Petillon, X. (1993). The group-serving bias in evaluating and explaining harm-doing behavior. *Journal of Social Psychology, 134*, 47–54.

Short, J. F., & Strodtbeck, F. L. (1965). *Group process and gang delinquency*. Chicago: University of Chicago Press.

Shortell, J., Epstein, S., & Taylor, S. P. (1970). Instigation to aggression as a function of degree of defeat and the capacity for massive retaliation. *Journal of Personality, 38*, 313–328.

Shupe, L. M. (1954). Alcohol and crime: A study of the urine-alcohol concentration found in 882 persons arrested during or immediately after the commission of a felony. *Journal of Criminal Law & Criminology, 44*, 661–664.

Spergel, I. A., Ross, R. E., Curry, G. D., & Chance, R. (1989). *Youth gangs: Problem and response*. Washington DC: Office of Juvenile Justice and Delinquency Prevention.

Steadman, H. J., & Felson, R. B. (1984). Self-reports of violence: Ex-mental patients, ex-offenders, and the general population. *Criminology, 22*, 321–342.

Steele, C. M., & Southwick, L. (1985). Alcohol and social behavior: Part 1. The psychology of drunken excess. *Journal of Personality and Social Psychology, 48*, 18–34.

Sutherland, E. H., & Cressey, D. R. (1974). *Criminology*. New York: Lippincott.

Taylor, S. P., Gammon, C. B., & Capasso, D. R. (1976). Aggression as a function of alcohol and threat. *Journal of Personality and Social Psychology, 34*, 938–941.

Tedeschi, J. T., & Bonoma, T. V. (1972). Power and influence: An introduction. In J. T. Tedeschi (Ed.), *The social influence processes*. Chicago: Aldine.

Tedeschi, J. T., & Felson, R. B. (1994). *Violence, aggression, and coercive actions*. Washington DC: American Psychological Association.

Tedeschi, J. T., Lindskold, S., & Rosenfeld, P. (1985). *An introduction to social psychology.* St. Paul: West.

Tedeschi, J. T., Melburg, V., & Rosenfeld, P. (1981). Is the concept of aggression useful? In P. Brain & D. Benton (Eds.) *A multi-disciplinary approach to aggression research.* New York: Elsevier North Holland, Biomedical Press.

Tedeschi, J. T. & Quigley, B. (1996). Limitations of laboratory paradigms for studying aggression. *Aggression and Violent Behavior: A Review Journal, 1,* 163–177.

Tedeschi, J. T., Schlenker, B. R., & Bonoma, T. V. (1971). Cognitive dissonance: Private ratiocination or public spectacle. *American Psychologist, 26,* 685–695.

———. (1973). *Conflict, power, and games.* Chicago: Aldine.

Tedeschi, J. T., Smith, R. B., III, & Brown, R. C., Jr. (1974). A reinterpretation of research on aggression. *Psychological Bulletin, 89,* 540–563.

Thompson, E. H., & Pleck, J. H. (1987). The structure of male role norms. In M. S. Kimmel (Ed.), *Changing men: New directions in research on men and masculinity.* Newbury Park CA: Sage.

Toch, H. H. (1969). *Violent men: An inquiry into the psychology of violence.* Chicago: Aldine-Atherton.

———. (1993). Good violence and bad violence: Self-Presentations of aggressors through accounts and war stories. In R. B. Felson & J. T. Tedeschi (Eds.), *Aggression and violence: Social interactionist perspectives* (pp. 193–208). Washington DC: American Psychological Association.

Turkat, D., & Dawson, J. (1976). Attributions of responsibility for a chance event as a function of sex and physical attractiveness of target individual. *Psychological Reports, 39,* 275–279.

U.S. Department of Justice. Bureau of Justice Statistics. (1993). *Sourcebook of criminal justice statistics, 1992.* Washington DC: Author.

Virkunen, M. (1974). Alcohol as a factor precipitating aggression and conflict behavior leading to homicide. *British Journal of Addictions, 69,* 149–154.

Wachtel, P. L. (1973). Psychodynamics, behavior therapy, and the implacable experimenter: An inquiry into the consistency of personality. *Journal of Abnormal Psychology, 83,* 324–334.

Weigold, M. F., & Schlenker, B. R. (1991). Accountability and risk taking. *Personality and Social Psychology Bulletin, 17,* 25–29.

West, D. J., & Farrington, D. P. (1977). *The delinquent way of life.* London: Heinemann.

White, R. K. (1968). *Nobody wanted war: Misperception in Vietnam and other wars.* Garden City NY: Doubleday.

Wilson, J. Q., & Herrnstein, R. J. (1985). *Crime and human nature.* New York: Simon & Schuster.

Wilson, L., & Rogers, R. W. (1975). The fire this time: Effects of race of target, insult, and potential retaliation on black aggression. *Journal of Personality and Social Psychology, 32,* 857–864.

Wilson, M. I., & Daly, M. (1985). Competitiveness, risk taking, and violence: the young man's syndrome. *Ethology and Sociobiology, 6,* 59–73.

Wolfgang, M. E. (1958). *Patterns in criminal homicide*. Philadelphia: University of Pennsylania Press.

Wolfgang, M. E., & Ferracuti, F. (1956). *The subculture of violence: Toward an integrated theory of criminality*. London: Tavistock.

Wolfgang, M. E., Figlio, R. M., & Sellin, T. (1972). *Delinquency in a birth cohort*. Chicago: University of Chicago Press.

Wolfgang, M. E., & Strohm, R. B. (1956). The relationship between alcohol and criminal homicide. *Quarterly Journal of Studies on Alchohol, 17*, 108–123.

Wright, J. D., & Rossi, P. H. (1986). *Under the gun: Weapons, crime, and violence in America*. Hawthorne NY: Aldine.

Zeichner, A., & Pihl, R. O. (1979). Effects of alcohol and behavior contingencies on human aggression. *Journal of Abnormal Psychology, 88*, 153–160.

A Symbolic Interactionist Theory of Motivation and Deviance: Interpreting Psychological Research

Karen Heimer
Ross L. Matsueda
University of Iowa

Recent research in sociological criminology has examined several questions of traditional importance to psychologists, including the following: What motivates individuals to engage in antisocial and deviant behavior? To what extent are criminal acts the result of rational decision making? How do social roles and life-course transitions influence antisocial behavior? Within sociology, the studies addressing these questions are framed by a variety of criminological theories, including social control, social learning, subcultural strain, and labeling theories. Many of these theories are rooted, implicitly or explicitly, in a broader set of principles derived from symbolic interactionism, a traditional sociological perspective on social psychology. We have argued elsewhere for developing a symbolic interactionist theory of crime and deviance and for viewing other sociological theories of deviance as special cases of this more general theoretical per-

This paper is based on research supported in part by grants from the National Science Foundation (sbr-9311014), the National Institute of Justice (87-ij-cx-0028), and the Central Investment Fund for Research Enhancement at the University of Iowa. The funding agencies bear no responsibility for the arguments in this paper. We thank Kathleen Anderson and Stacy De Coster for research assistance.

spective (Heimer & Matsueda, 1994). In this chapter, we expand this view by showing that an interactionist perspective can address questions of traditional concern to psychology.

We begin by contrasting psychological research on antisocial behavior with its counterpart in sociology. Despite some commonalities, there are major distinctions: sociological work tends to emphasize the effects of social structure, in general, and the self as a product of that social structure, in particular. This echoes Stryker's (1987) observation regarding the differences between sociological and psychological versions of social psychology. We next discuss a theory of deviance and crime based on symbolic interactionism, show how it can incorporate predictions from traditional criminological theories, and then discuss how it may be consistent with some psychological theory and research on aggression and other antisocial behavior. Throughout our discussion, we highlight an important tenet of the symbolic interactionist perspective—that individuals are embedded within groups, social systems, and the broader social structure, and that the actions of individuals are essential for reproducing those very group, system, and structural arrangements.

The Two Social Psychologies and Motivations to Deviant Behavior

Commentary on social psychology often notes that it is, in reality, two fields, with one located within psychology and the other within sociology (e.g., House, 1977; Stryker, 1977, 1983). While psychological social psychology focuses on the influence of the environment on individuals' behavioral, affective, and cognitive processes, sociological social psychology focuses on the dynamic interplay between individuals and the society in which they are embedded (Stryker, 1989). In terms of motivation, then, psychological theories tend to emphasize the way that affect, cognition, personality, interpersonal interactions, and developmental learning processes motivate behavior. Sociological social psychology, by contrast, focuses on the reciprocal influence of social structure and the individual in producing motivations to act. This focus offers the potential for a unique contribution from sociology (Stryker, 1987). The divergent foci of the two social psychologies is apparent in research on aggressive, anti-social, and criminal behavior. In this section, we highlight these differences in foci, first discussing the major themes in psychological work on aggressive and deviant behavior and then mentioning the major themes in sociological research on this topic.

PSYCHOLOGICAL PERSPECTIVES ON THE SOCIAL PSYCHOLOGY OF ANTISOCIAL BEHAVIOR

Within contemporary psychological social psychology, much of the work on deviant behavior focuses on aggression. Research in this area typically draws a distinction between *angry aggression,* which is motivated by an affective or emotional reaction, and *instrumental aggression,* which may or may not involve an emotional reaction but which is presumed to be motivated by the attempt to attain some goal (Geen, 1990). Research on angry aggression often begins with the premise that situational conditions—such as provocation, aversive conditions, and physical discomfort—can trigger aggressive behavior. There are at least two major lines of work that take this approach. The first maintains that unpleasant conditions—such as an insult, goal blockage, or physical pain—evoke negative affect, which *itself* can precipitate hostile and aggressive behavior (e.g., Berkowitz, 1989, 1993). The link between negative affect and aggression, from this perspective, can appear rather automatic and can exist independently of deep-level cognitive processing. Consequently, any situational conditions that create sufficient negative affect can prompt hostile behavior. Research shows that these conditions include frustration and insult or attack (Geen, 1968), physical pain (Berkowitz, Cochran, & Embree, 1981), and physical discomfort due to high room temperatures (Baron & Bell, 1975), exposure to air pollution (Rotton & Frey, 1985), or uncontrollable noise (Geen, 1978). Building on these arguments, Berkowitz (1989, 1993) has proposed a *neoassociationist theory* of aggression, which argues that the negative affect created by aversive situations can trigger or prime any or all of the following processes: emotions, such as anger or fear; cognitions, such as thoughts about hostility or flight; and expressive behavior patterns, such as aggressive actions or escape. In addition, each of these processes can stimulate the other processes. This means, for example, that hostile thoughts can evoke the emotion of anger or aggressive actions, independent of negative affect induced by aversive environmental stimuli (Berkowitz & Heimer, 1989). In short, the neoassociationist theory considers emotion, cognition, and behavior to be parallel processes that stem from negative affect; each process may influence the others but does not necessarily evoke the others (Berkowitz, 1989). The assumption of the independence of these processes implies that the emotion of anger is not necessary for aggression to occur (Geen, 1995).

The second major line of psychological research on angry aggression differs from the neoassociationist view by emphasizing higher-level cognitive processing and by maintaining that anger is indeed a necessary precursor to aggressive behavior (Geen, 1995). Zillmann (1988), for example, argues that anger precedes aggression, and that both are affected by physiological arousal and cognitive evaluations. The *arousal-cognition* process operates as follows: When situational conditions threaten one's well-being in some way, they evoke physiological arousal. This arousal prompts a cognitive process whereby the individual assesses the situation, which, in turn, determines the individual's behavioral response. Interestingly, research shows that the level of physiological arousal is key; indeed, people who experience identical situations of provocation behave more aggressively when they are physiologically aroused than when they are not aroused—even when the source of the arousal is irrelevant to the provocation to aggression (Zillmann, Katcher, & Milavsky, 1972). Other research has focused greater attention on the specifics of the cognitive processes that prompt aggression in response to aversive situational conditions. For example, some work examines the *causal attributions* that lead to angry aggression as retaliation for some harm or imagined harm by others, typically finding that when individuals attribute hostile intent to others, their aggressive retaliation is enhanced (Dyck & Rule, 1978; Dodge, 1991). Other research finds that in cases where harm is judged to be unintended, people are more likely to blame the offender when they determine that the harm could have been foreseen than when they think the harm was unforeseeable (Rule & Nesdale, 1976).

A third line of psychological research on angry aggression focuses on how *personality factors* mediate the relationship between anger and aggression. Most of this work argues for a stable personality style that fosters aggressive, violent, and criminal behavior (e.g., Olweus, 1979, 1980; Huesmann, Eron, Lefkowitz, & Walder, 1984; Farrington, Loeber, & Van Kammen, 1990; Robins & Rutter, 1990). Presumably, some personality characteristics predispose individuals to respond to aversive situational conditions with aggression, whereas other individuals may not be so quick to enact hostile lines of action. Some researchers argue that this personality characteristic takes the form of a cognitive predisposition, whereby the individual holds in memory a great number of cognitive scripts, or schemata, that suggest aggressive measures for dealing with problems in one's environment (Huesmann & Eron, 1984). Solving problems via aggression, of course, adds to aggressive scripts in memory and makes such behavior more likely in the future. In addition, a hostile or aggressive personality can influence the kinds of attributions that people are likely to make about situations, and thereby influences the chances that individuals will respond to the situation with aggressive behavior. For example, research shows that youths who have hostile personality styles are more likely than other youths to respond aggressively to an intrusion from another youth when the motives for the intrusion are unclear (Dodge, 1980). Presumably, those youths who responded aggressively are more likely to think that the intrusion of the other youth is motivated by malice or hostility.

Other psychological research focuses on the cognitive processes that lead individuals to engage in goal-directed or *instrumental* aggression, deviance, or crime. Such behavior is motivated by some extrinsic purpose, rather than the pleasure that is inherent in the deviance itself (Berkowitz, 1993, p. 11). In the case of instrumental aggression, these extrinsic goals can include attempts to manage or improve one's image or social status, to coerce others, and to restore justice (e.g., Patterson, 1982; Tedeschi, 1983; Felson & Tedeschi, 1993a). In instances of instrumental property deviance, such as financial dishonesty and minor theft, research most often portrays the cognitive processes leading to the deviance as rational analyses of situations, where the potential costs and benefits of the deviance are weighed (e.g., Piliavin, Hardyck, & Vadum, 1968; Farrington & Kidd, 1977; Cornish & Clarke, 1986). Psychological research in this tradition is often rooted in *subjective expected utility theory* (e.g., Edwards, 1961). From this perspective, subjective expected utility is the product of one's estimate of the likelihood of the outcome and the utility or subjective value given to the outcome (see Cornish & Clarke, 1986).

Another line of psychological research on aggression and anti-social behavior focuses on social interaction, interdependence, and social influence. Here the focus is on analyzing aggressive interactions as goal-directed utilitarian behavior, which renders the distinction between angry and instrumental aggression irrelevant (Tedeschi & Felson, 1994). Instead, acts of aggression and violence are seen as tinged with emotion, while also directed toward some extrinsic goal, such as coercion, impression management, or obtaining some other desired reward. For example, when an individual is insulted or injured, she or he may aggress against the offender based on anger as well as on the desire to save face or protect one's sense of self. Recently, Tedeschi and Felson have proposed a *social interactionist* approach to violence, which rests on the following four assumptions: all violence is motivated by the pursuit of goals; people decide to enact violent behavior based on a decision-making process that takes into account expectations of costs, benefits, and the value of the outcome, as well as morals; situational factors are key to decisions about enacting violence; and aggressors often view their own behavior as legitimate and moral (Felson & Tedeschi, 1993a, 1993b; Tedeschi & Felson, 1994). From this perspective, although acts of violence may be accompanied by anger, they are motivated primarily by a rational decision-making process. Yet, some aggressive interactions may be motivated by a "weak" form of rationality, such as those that involve hasty decisions or strong emotions. In essence, these situations involve a circumscribed consideration of alternatives (see Simon, 1957). The social interactionist perspective also maintains that violence can at times become scripted or habitual and can occur without giving the decision much thought. This approach has the advantage of recognizing both the emotional and rational bases of aggression and violence, as well as explicitly incorporating inhibitions to violence in the form of individuals' perceptions of cost. This approach considers situational contingencies for aggression, theorizes about the role of emotions, and incorporates notions of subjected expected utilities. The social interactionist approach, therefore, can be viewed as an integrative approach in psychology.

A final line of psychological research on antisocial behavior focuses on social learning and developmental socialization. Early work in this tradition emphasized operant and social learning mechanisms. Burgess and Akers (1966) revised differential association theory, a prominent sociological theory of crime, to incorporate principles of operant conditioning. Bandura (1977) modified behaviorist arguments by showing that aggression can be the result of modeling, imitation, and vicarious reinforcement, as when one becomes aggressive after viewing the reinforcement of another person's aggressive behavior. More recently, Bandura (1986) has specified the role of social cognition more completely, and Akers (1985) has incorporated social learning principles into a sociological theory of crime. Other research on the social learning of deviance and crime focuses on the influence of parenting practices on antisocial and criminal behavior (Trasler, 1960; McCord, 1979). Another research program that fits within the developmental learning tradition is Patterson's work on the reciprocal effects of parents' and children's coercive behaviors (e.g., Patterson, Reid, & Dishion, 1992; Patterson & Yoerger, this volume). Finally, Jessor and his colleagues elaborate the developmental socialization process leading to deviant behavior by proposing that personality (i.e, aspects of self, attitudes about deviance, personal motivations) and environmental factors (i.e., parent and peer influences) combine to produce a social-psychological context, which, in turn, operates within a broader social context (i.e., social-structural and group factors) to produce deviant behavior (Jessor & Jessor, 1977; Jessor, Donovan, & Costa, 1991).

In sum, the major psychological perspectives on aggressive and deviant behavior tend to focus on five categories of motivational factors: affective, cognitive, personality, social interaction, and social learning-socialization processes. Theories often propose that some combination of these factors operates in tandem to produce deviance.

SOCIOLOGICAL PERSPECTIVES ON THE SOCIAL PSYCHOLOGY OF DELINQUENT BEHAVIOR

Sociological work on individuals' motivations toward antisocial and deviant behavior, which most often appears in the criminological literature, offers themes that depart somewhat from those that characterize psychological research. Much of this research is theory-driven and differs by the underlying assumptions of the theoretical perspective. We can categorize these social-psychological perspectives into three groups, which differ in their treatment of deviant motivation. First, control and disorganization theories argue that deviant behavior is natural, requires no special motivation, and, therefore, focuses on the motivation to conform. Second, learning and subculture theories argue that criminal and deviant behavior must be learned and that a principal part of this learning involves acquiring criminal versus conforming motivations. Third, labeling theories typically eschew etiological questions of primary deviance—including motivations to deviate—and instead focus on the determinants and consequences of labeling.

The first set of sociological theories of crime, control theories, make the Hobbesian assumption that all human beings are inherently hedonistic and self-seeking, all people are equally motivated to engage in criminal and deviant behavior, and all deviant and antisocial behaviors are natural in the absence of restraints (Hirschi, 1969; Kornhauser, 1978). Therefore, crime is explained not by individual differences in deviant motivation—since there are no such differences—but instead by the absence of social controls or restraints. In this way, control theories are consistent with Freudian theories of motivation, in which deviant motivations arise in the conflict between natural impulses of the id and the civilizing restraints of conventional institutions through the superego. For *social* control theory, the restraints consist of affiliations to conventional institutions, such as attachments to others, commitments to conventional lines of action, involvements in conventional activities, and beliefs in common morality (Hirschi 1969). For *self*-control theory, restraint consists of early child rearing, in which parents identify and punish antisocial behavior, which leads to a stable trait of high self-control (Gottfredson & Hirschi, 1990). Such individuals are able to plan, delay gratification, and consider the long-term consequences of their actions. Individuals who fail to receive such parental disciplining develop the stable trait of low self-control. Throughout their lives, they will tend to be impulsive, thrill seeking, and unable to plan, delay gratification, and consider the long-term consequences of their actions. They will always be at higher risk of crime.

The structural-level analogue of control theory is social disorganization theory. Shaw and McKay (1969) originally specified two concepts to explain delinquency. Social disorganization, the institutional form of lack of restraint, refers to weak institutional controls, such as families, schools, and communities. Cultural transmission, the motivation and learning process, refers to the process of transmitting deviant cultures through deviant groups. Criminologists have extracted a "pure" disorganization model that de-emphasizes cultural transmission (Kornhauser, 1978, pp. 70–72; Bursik, 1988) and focuses on weak institutional controls. This version of disorganization theory is consistent with restraint or control theories.

The second set of criminological theories, learning and subculture theories, parallels work in psychology by focusing on the *social learning* mechanisms that lead to criminal behavior. Unlike most psychological theories, however, social learning theories in sociology attend to the embeddedness of individuals within social groups and within social-structural locations, as reflected in social class, race, and gender stratification. The earliest learning theory of crime, Sutherland's (1947) *differential association theory*, posits that crime is rooted in normative conflict. High crime rates in modern industrial societies result from conflicting structures of norms, behavior patterns, and definitions about the appropriateness of crime and delinquency. At the group level, normative conflict is translated into group crime rates through differential social organization, the extent to which groups are organized for and against crime. At the individual level, normative conflict is translated into individual acts of crime through differential association.

Through interaction with primary groups, individuals learn criminal behavior, which includes learning criminal techniques and skills, as well as definitions favorable and unfavorable to crime. Definitions of crime as appropriate behavior include attitudes toward crime, Cressey's (1953) "verbalizations about crime," Sykes and Matza's (1957) "techniques of neutralization of the law," and McCord's (this volume) "potentiating reasons." When a person learns an excess of definitions favorable to crime, he or she will engage in criminal behavior, assuming the opportunity is present and techniques are known (Sutherland, Cressey, & Luckenbill, 1992). Because definitions are learned from organized groups, the content of learning crime will reflect the organization of one's reference groups. Moreover, reference groups are embedded within broader social-structural arrangements; therefore, learning crime is indirectly shaped by social-structural factors. For instance, individuals in crime-ridden, impoverished neighborhoods may be more likely to encounter groups organized in favor of crime; these individuals, then, would be more likely than others to learn criminal definitions and techniques and to engage in criminal behavior (Matsueda, 1988).

The social-learning reformulation of differential association theory adds an analysis of the reinforcement mechanisms through which techniques and definitions are learned (Burgess & Akers, 1966; Akers, 1985). Thus, according to Akers (1985), initial acts of crime are learned through modeling, imitation, and vicarious reinforcement. Subsequent acts of crime are learned through differential reinforcement, the process of pairing rewards and punishments with criminal behavior. Definitions favorable and unfavorable to crime serve as important cues that discriminate for reinforced criminal or noncriminal behavior.

A third sociological approach to deviance is the *labeling* approach. Labeling theories represent a heterogeneous group and thus are difficult to characterize. Nevertheless, they all tend to de-emphasize the causes of initial acts of delinquent behavior, assuming they are randomly distributed across the population, harmless acts of mischief, or, given certain epistemological assumptions, beyond causal explanation. Instead, labeling theories focus on the causes and consequences of labeling individuals as deviant and criminal (e.g., Tannenbaum, 1938; Lemert, 1951; H. Becker, 1963; Schur, 1971). Thus, according to labeling theories, children typically view their initial acts of primary deviance as "mischief" or "play"; however, from the standpoint of the larger community, the behavior may be seen as "evil," "bad," or even "criminal." An important proposition of labeling theory is that deviant labels are differentially applied to members of society, so that those who are disadvantaged, impoverished, or minority, or who otherwise fit the image of deviant stereotypes, are more likely to be labeled as deviant—even independent of their actual deviance. Moreover, once individuals are labeled as deviant, they are likely to be ostracized by others, viewed as "bad" or "deviant" by society, and in general cut off from conventional society. This, in turn, increases the likelihood of subsequent crime, or "secondary deviance," causing more labeling and more deviance (Lemert, 1951). This spiraling process can lead an individual into the hands of the criminal justice system. In short, labeling sets in motion a potential self-fulfilling prophecy: an otherwise conforming youth may end up confirming the deviant label through a process of deviance amplification.

From these major sociological approaches, we can extract two themes that depart from those in psychological explanations of motivations for antisocial and deviant behavior: a view of individuals as embedded within groups and broader social-structural arrangements, and a focus on self processes as key motivations to deviate. More generally, these two themes distinguish psychological from sociological social psychology (see House, 1977; Stryker, 1977). They also indicate important ways in which sociological work can augment psychological work. Yet, there is an important theme within sociological social psychology that is not fully captured by the sociological approaches to antisocial and deviant behavior described above. Specifically, these approaches do not fully capture the primacy of the group or society, in which the individual is an abstraction from the group, rather than the group being merely an abstract aggregation of individuals. Thus, there is a dynamic interplay, or reciprocal influence, between individuals and the society in which they are embedded. It is this theme—which is central to the symbolic interactionist perspective—that may offer the greatest potential for the unique contribution of sociological social psychology (Stryker, 1987, 1989).

In the remainder of this chapter, we lay out a symbolic interactionist theory of crime and delinquency. We have argued elsewhere (Heimer & Matsueda, 1994) that this perspective provides a broad theoretical framework that allows one to view the major sociological explanations of crime and deviance as special cases. Here, we reiterate and expand this argument by showing that the major psychological perspectives on antisocial and deviant behavior can be reinterpreted using our interactionist theory of crime and delinquency.

A Symbolic Interactionist Theory of Delinquent Motivations

Symbolic interactionism is one of the more enduring theories of sociological social psychology. Its intellectual roots lie in the tradition of the Scottish moral philosophers (e.g., Hume, Smith) and in the tradition of American pragmatism (e.g., James, Dewey, Cooley, and G. H. Mead). By the mid-20th century, symbolic interactionism achieved a dominant position among sociological theories through the work of numerous scholars who collectively became known as the Chicago School of Sociology. Ideas stemming from the Chicago School—such as the concepts of social (dis)organization, subcultural transmission, differential association, and labeling—have had a great impact on sociological studies of crime and deviance. In this section, we discuss our interactionist theory of delinquency (Matsueda, 1992; Heimer & Matsueda, 1994; Heimer, 1996; Matsueda & Heimer, 1997), which traces its roots to the Chicago School tradition, as well as symbolic interactionism more generally. Although our work so far has concentrated on juvenile delinquency, the interactionist perspective that we describe here should apply to antisocial behavior more generally, including adult criminal behavior, aggression, and minor deviance.

ROLE-TAKING AND DELINQUENT TRANSACTIONS

For symbolic interactionism, social systems, groups, individuals, and situations constitute an ongoing social process, mutually influencing one another and merging imperceptibly in the web of daily interactions. This is captured in George Herbert Mead's (1934) analysis of the social act, which is the basis of most versions of contemporary symbolic interactionism. Building on the social act as the unit of analysis, we begin with the immediate situation of delinquency, which consists of a social transaction between two or more individuals (Matsueda, 1992; Heimer & Matsueda, 1994). The situation can influence delinquent behavior in two ways. First, the specific situations that individuals encounter may present opportunities for delinquency. For example, a situation in which two antagonistic street gangs are present on controversial turf is highly conducive to violence (Short & Strodtbeck, 1965). Second, and more importantly, the immediate situation influences delinquency through its effects on the direction and content of social interaction.

The important mechanism of social interaction is role-taking, which refers to the process of projecting oneself into the role of other persons and, from their standpoint, appraising the situation, one-self in that situation, and possible lines of action (Mead, 1934; Blumer, 1969). For example, individuals confronted with delin-quency as a possible line of action take the role of each other through verbal and nonverbal communication, and thereby fit their lines of action together into joint delinquent behavior. Delinquent transac-tions are built up through a dynamic process of reciprocal role-tak-ing: One youth signals the intention to break the law, or actually be-gins a delinquent line of action; other youths in the situation consider the first youth's perspective and then respond; the first youth then takes the perspectives of these other youths and reacts to the response. This reciprocal role-taking process continues until ei-ther the youths jointly negotiate the delinquent line of action or the interaction terminates (Matsueda, 1992).

Role-taking is also the basis for an interactionist theory of cogni-tion. Cognitive processes arise in problematic situations when an in-dividual's impulse or ongoing line of action is temporarily blocked by a physical or social barrier. This results in a discontinuity in the interaction. The situation becomes problematic, and the individual engages in an imaginative rehearsal (Dewey, 1922; Mead, 1934). Spe-cifically, the blocked impulse is transformed into an image of self (the self as an object, or the "me"), which consists of alternative lines of action, anticipated reactions of others to alternatives, and a view of the self from the standpoint of others. This image of self ("me") is responded to by another impulse ("I"), which either enacts the cur-rent line of action through overt behavior or blocks the line of action, causing the situation to remain problematic and eliciting another self-image. This internal conversation between the "I" and the "me," which constitutes the serial process of cognition, continues until the problem is solved or the transaction ends. Cognition, then, is identical to role-taking between interactants, except that it occurs in the mind of the individual between phases of the self. Through role-taking, self-conscious thinking, or imaginative rehearsals, so-cial groups control the behavior of their members.

In carrying out this imaginative rehearsal, individuals consider three important elements. First, they consider attitudes toward a potential line of action; these attitudes are symbols that are shared by others and serve as plans to act or pivots for redirecting action (Dewey, 1922; Mead, 1938; Miller, 1982). Second, they anticipate the likely reactions of others to a possible line of action and the implications of these reactions for tangible rewards, self-image, and maintaining status and group memberships (McCall & Simmons, 1978). Third, they assess how others appraise them (Cooley, 1922) and consider the implications of these reflected appraisals of self for behavior (Kinch, 1963; Felson, 1985). Therefore, individuals are more likely to engage in delinquency when they share attitudes favorable to delinquency, participate in groups that condone delinquent acts, and have significant others who view them as delinquents.

Early in the socialization process, children take the role of concrete significant others one at a time. Later, individuals are able to take the role of the entire community or reference group and thereby cognitively construct a generalized other, which includes the norms, rules, and expectations governing various positions and roles of the group (Mead, 1934). This form of role-taking represents the most effective mode of social control because it integrates the individual into organized sets of roles and institutions. Whether taking the role of the generalized other increases or decreases the likelihood of delinquent or deviant behavior depends on the nature of the generalized other, the role of the individual within the group, and the norms, rules, and expectations of the individual's role. For example, Short and Strodtbeck (1965) found that a gang leader, in contemplating joining a delinquent gang fight, takes the role of the gang, considers how they would view him (given his role as leader) if he were to refrain from the fight, and consequently decides to join the action for fear of losing his leadership status.

As problematic situations are repeatedly encountered and resolved in consistent ways, they eventually cease to be problematic, and behavior becomes nonreflective, habitual, or scripted (Mead, 1934; Dewey, 1922). This proposition is supported by psychological research, which finds that cognitive processing tends to be automatic rather than reflective in routine settings (Shiffrin & Schneider, 1977; Langer, 1989). Furthermore, individual and joint behavior is not completely determined by each individual's prior socialization histories (learned attitudes, views of self, etc.). Instead, social transactions allow for an element of emergence, novelty, and creativity, which cannot be predicted entirely from the contributions of each interactant. For example, group forms of delinquency may be less structured and determined, and more fluid and chaotic, as youth present situationally induced motives to each other (Briar & Piliavin, 1965). Through a conversation of gestures, best characterized as a tentative, probing trial-and-error process, youth may innovate delinquent solutions to their problems of low status (Cohen, 1955). In short, group delinquency may unfold as an instance of collective behavior (Short & Strodtbeck, 1965).

This analysis of the social act implies five features of role-taking that affect the likelihood that problematic situations will be resolved through delinquent behavior (Heimer & Matsueda, 1994). First, when individuals call up attitudes that favor law violation, they will be predisposed to consider delinquent solutions to problematic situations (see also Heimer, 1996). Second, when role-taking leads individuals to perceive that crime will bring tangible rewards, social rewards, or positive consequences for self-image, they will be more likely to engage in delinquency. This is particularly pertinent for adolescents, given that they enter many situations offering illegal ways to satisfy common adolescent needs—including the need for spending money, autonomy and power, status among peers, and thrills (cf. Greenberg, 1977; Coleman, 1961; Stinchcombe, 1964; Hagan, 1989). Third, when role-taking leads individuals to see themselves from the standpoint of others as delinquents, troublemakers, and lawbreakers, they will be more likely to solve problems using delinquency or violence (Matsueda, 1992). Fourth, delinquent peers can foster delinquency both directly and indirectly. Directly, peers increase delinquency by pressuring, influencing, and presenting motives within delinquent situations. Indirectly, peers affect delinquency through role-taking by influencing attitude formation, anticipated consequences of behaviors, and views of the self. Fifth, delinquency can occur in the absence of reflective thought through habitual or scripted responses that result from previous experiences. Thus, when similar problematic situations are repeatedly solved with delinquency, the situations become increasingly unproblematic, and delinquency becomes increasingly nonreflective and habitual (Matsueda, 1992; Heimer & Matsueda, 1994). This is most likely in institutionalized delinquent situations, such as fights between gangs.

This description of role-taking has been conditional on a given situation, which thus far we have treated as exogenous to the interaction process. To some extent, opportunities are exogenous to role-taking, resulting from either chance factors or elements of social structure, like social class, residential neighborhood, and urbanicity, which in part determine proximity to suitable targets, capable guardians, and the like (Cohen & Felson, 1979). But situations and opportunities are also in part endogenous to the social process of role-taking and cognition because one may solve a problematic situation by selecting into a criminal opportunity. Moreover, even given an individual within a situation, objective situations interact with role-taking because perception is selective, and different individuals perceive identical situations differently based on their prior role-taking experience and group participation.

In sum, this discussion implies that self-control is social control. Individuals control their own behavior by participating in social groups, engaging in role-taking, and forming habits, attitudes, motives, and images of self from the standpoint of others. Such control enables individuals to fit their lines of action into an ongoing social process. Whether those lines of action are delinquent versus conventional is determined by the direction of social control exerted by groups and the social-structural context in which individuals and groups are embedded. We use the term *differential social control* to describe this process of conflicting or competing controls.

THE SOCIAL-STRUCTURAL CONTEXT: SOCIAL SYSTEMS AND ORGANIZED GROUPS

According to symbolic interactionism, social-structural arrangements—the configuration of groups, positions within groups, social systems, and communication networks—are produced through the cooperative social action of individuals and thus are products of the meaning that individuals give to situations through role-taking. Yet, the social organization of groups, positions, and communication networks themselves constrains the form, content, and participants of interaction (Shibutani, 1986). This creates regularities in the outcomes of role-taking when interactants occupy similar positions and share communication networks (Fine & Kleinman, 1979; Shibutani, 1986). Thus, role-taking is ultimately rooted in the social-structural context in which it is embedded, but it also reproduces that social-structural context (Stryker, 1980). In other words, role-taking at the individual level of analysis and social-structural arrangements mutually influence one another, and neither can exist apart from the other.

Organized social systems and groups influence cognition and behavior when members take the role of the generalized other (Mead, 1934; Shibutani, 1955, 1961). In its simplest form, this entails taking the role of the social system or group and applying its general standards or expectations to one's own behavior. In a more complex form, taking the perspective of the generalized other entails taking the role of the social system or group as a whole, locating one's position within it, and adjusting one's behavior to fit with the complex constellation of positions within the system or group. This means that through role-taking, individuals must consider the multiplicity of norms, expectations, and appraisals that govern and organize positions in the social system or group. Furthermore, taking the role of the generalized other influences the kinds of situations in which members place themselves. Structuralist versions of symbolic interactionism emphasize the relative stability of roles in organized systems and groups, including the stability of selection into situations and the stability of outcomes of role-taking (Stryker, 1968, 1980; McCall & Simmons, 1978).

In our work on an interactionist theory of delinquency, we argue that the control exerted by organized groups and social systems varies in *efficacy*, or probability of successful control, as well as *content* of control, or direction with regard to the law (Heimer & Matsueda, 1994). When an individual is strongly invested in or committed to a role in a particular group or social system, we can expect that the group will be effective in controlling this individual's behavior. But whether or not that behavior deviates from or conforms to widely accepted norms and laws depends on the orientation of the particular group. Some groups are characterized by roles that encourage conformity to the law and to core social norms, such as the importance of honesty and responsibility. Other groups are characterized by roles that encourage—or at least fail to discourage—deviant behavior. Thus, the probability of deviance will reflect an individual's relative commitments to groups organized in favor of, versus against, deviant behavior. We refer to this as *differential organizational control* to emphasize the organizational nature of the control and the dual processes of efficacy and content of control (Heimer & Matsueda, 1994).

In the case of juvenile delinquency, the most important roles in organized systems and groups are those of families, peer groups, and schools (Heimer & Matsueda, 1994; Matsueda & Heimer, 1997). Families are perhaps the earliest social system to influence delinquency, operating through early parental socialization and supervision. Because most families do not explicitly promote delinquency by their children, the focus of regulation is on the effectiveness of conventional controls. The important locus of control resides in parent-child relationships. Parents control the behavior of their children through role-taking, as the youth takes the role of the parent, forms an image of self as an object from the standpoint of parents, considers attitudes about deviance, and appraises parental reactions to delinquency. It follows that families that are cohesive, communicative, and stable should be more effective in controlling members because children are more likely to consider the family as generalized other. Moreover, families also control delinquent behavior directly by monitoring and controlling their children's peer group interactions.

Most peer groups are organized to dissuade members from delinquent acts by sharing conventional or law-abiding norms, motives, and roles. But some peer groups are organized in ways that foster delinquent acts by sharing delinquent norms, motives, and roles. The delinquency rate of a given group is determined by the extent of this differential organizational control (Sutherland, 1947). Individuals who belong to peer groups organized in favor of delinquency are more likely than other youths to break rules and laws because peer groups are an important generalized other for most youths. This occurs via the role-taking process: When considering unlawful behavior, an individual will take the role of the peer group and consider the self as an object from the standpoint of the group. Members of conventional groups are more likely to see themselves as conformers and refrain from law violation; members of deviant or delinquent groups are more likely to see themselves as rule breakers or law violators and, hence, are more likely to behave accordingly.

Schools operate similarly to influence youths' delinquency, although they are more formally organized. The overall orientation of a school with regard to law violation, therefore, should account for varying rates of crime across schools. Schools are organized against delinquent behavior when conventional rules governing students' behavior are salient, respected, and enforced, and when students are committed to scholastic and extracurricular school activities (Hirschi, 1969). Commitment to school results when students are motivated to learn, rewarded for achievement, and inculcated with high-achievement aspirations. Youths who repeatedly succeed in scholastic or extra-curricular activities are likely to form self-images premised on commitments to conventional school roles. Such youths are motivated to maintain these self-images and role commitments and are likely to continue to seek good grades and pursue extracurricular activities (Schafer & Polk, 1967; Wiatrowski, Hansell, Massey, & Wilson, 1982). In this way, conforming students are encouraged to take the role of conventional classmates, teachers, and the school organization, considering views of self from their standpoint and assessing the cost of losing an investment in scholarship. Thus, youths who are committed to conventional roles in schools are less likely than others to break rules.

The flip side of these processes can lead to the school organization fostering delinquency. Repeated failure in scholastic and extra-curricular activities is likely to tarnish one's self-image from the perspectives of teachers, conventional students, and the school. This is likely to reduce commitment to student roles, lessen motivation to perform well academically, and increase alienation from school. Uncommitted and alienated students are likely to be viewed negatively by teachers and committed students, which can further tarnish self-images and increase alienation. These youths are also prime targets for selection into peer groups of other alienated students (Menard & Morse, 1984), perhaps because such companionship helps them to repair damaged views of self (Kaplan, 1980). The reference groups and generalized others for these youths are less likely to include teachers, principals, and conforming students and more likely to include delinquent peers. In this way, schools can encourage peer interactions that increase delinquent behavior.

As this last point indicates, commitments to roles in families, peer groups, and schools have implications for commitments to roles in other groups. For example, alienation from school not only can foster commitments to deviant peer groups but may also damage relationships with family members. Conversely, strong commitment to roles in conventional families can foster strong commitments to roles in school and in conventional, rule-following peer groups. The point is that commitments to roles in each of these three groups mutually influence one another.

Moreover, role commitments during adolescence establish trajectories that often persist in adulthood. Negative experiences in families (such as conflict and estrangement) and schools (such as failure, alienation, and dropping out) can have negative consequences for adult roles, increasing the likelihood of employment difficulties and marital problems. For example, assortative mating patterns based on homogamy increases the likelihood that youth with poor family and school backgrounds are more likely to marry partners with similar disadvantaged backgrounds. Such conditions impair labor market chances and produce strain on a marriage. Some empirical research supports these arguments: people with histories of temperamental behavior during childhood are less likely to succeed in educational and occupational realms, are more likely to marry people with similar problems, and thus are more likely to experience unhappy marriages (Caspi, Elder, & Bem, 1987; Elder, Caspi, & Downey, 1986). These conditions may also increase the chances of criminal and deviant behavior in young adulthood (Sampson & Laub, 1993).

When labor market success is hampered by deficits in educational background, skills, abilities, and social network connections (Hagan, 1993), role-taking may lead to roles in criminal groups, such as drug dealing or larceny rings (Sullivan, 1989; Anderson, 1990), and to identities, goals, and morals favoring property and street crimes as viable solutions to financial problems. Young adults who become committed to criminal roles often experience restricted networks that afford less access to legitimate jobs in the future (Hagan, 1993). In short, early involvement in crime can restrict legitimate labor market options (Sullivan, 1989), which sets in motion a self-fulfilling prophecy of sorts, whereby prior involvement in crime begets future crime. This occurs because the longer one derives income and other benefits through crime, the less likely one is to maintain ties to law-abiding groups and the more likely one is to consider criminal groups as generalized others in the role-taking process.

Of course, individuals can be simultaneously committed to both legitimate and criminal groups, and role-taking will reflect these dual commitments. At times, these commitments can be quite compatible. For example, Sullivan's (1989) study of three neighborhoods in New York finds young men working in legitimate auto garages by day and simultaneously stripping stolen cars in chop shops by night. Here, views of the self center more on the common features of the work—working on automobiles—and less on the legal-illegal dimension of work.

At times, even roles in conventional, stable jobs can encourage crime and deviance. Given that some studies estimate that over 75% of employees in legitimate jobs are involved in employee theft of some kind (Henry, 1981; Comer, 1985), employee theft is perhaps seen as justified, or even as a "job perk" that is simply passed on to the customer (Ditton, 1977). Similarly, pressure to deviate may be a stable component of other conventional occupations, including bank tellers, high-level finance administrators, corporate executives, and solo law practitioners (e.g., Sutherland, 1949; Cressey, 1953; Clinard & Yeager, 1980; Arnold & Hagan, 1992).

In sum, not only do commitments to organized groups and social systems affect other commitments during the same stage of life, but role commitments in one period have consequences for roles in later periods. This begins to illuminate the reciprocal nature of the relationship between individuals and the social organization of groups and social systems. In addition, role commitments, organized groups, and social systems themselves are embedded within a broader social-structural context. For example, research finds that gender, race, and social class stratification have important consequences for commitments to delinquent groups (e.g., Matsueda & Heimer, 1987; Sampson, 1987; Hagan, 1989; Hagan & Peterson, 1995). Moreover, when certain characteristics of communities— such as high rates of crime, drug use, female-headed households, and geographical mobility—combine to create ecological, economic, and political marginalization (Vigil, 1985), a social context emerges that is more likely to foster role commitments to delinquent groups than to law-abiding groups (see Wilson, 1987). Social-structural context is important because it shapes commitments to roles in deviant versus conventional groups and social systems and thus influences role-taking processes in which individuals consider attitudes or predispositions to delinquent acts, anticipate the consequences for such actions, and consider reflected appraisals of self as delinquent.

CLASSICAL SOCIOLOGICAL THEORIES OF CRIME AND DEVIANCE AS SPECIAL CASES OF AN INTERACTIONIST THEORY

A long tradition of theorizing in criminology is rooted in the Chicago School of Sociology, specifically in the ideas of symbolic interactionism. Thus, principles of symbolic interactionism underlie many classical theories, including social disorganization and control theories (Shaw & McKay, 1969; Kornhauser, 1978; Hirschi, 1969), differential association and social learning (Sutherland, 1947; Akers, 1985); and labeling theories (Lemert, 1951; H. Becker, 1963). Consequently, these theories can be viewed as special cases of a broader symbolic interactionist perspective. Elsewhere, we have developed and empirically assessed the argument that the classical theories of crime are special cases of a symbolic interactionist theory (Heimer & Matsueda, 1994). Here we briefly review our arguments with regard to the major motivational perspectives on crime and deviance.

Social disorganization theories hypothesize that community self-regulation thwarts crime through institutional controls. Communities with strong conventional institutions, like schools and families, discourage youth from delinquency through close supervision, socialization to conventional values, and commitments to conventional activities. The major disorganization theorists, Shaw and McKay (1969), included the concept of cultural transmission to explain how unsupervised and disaffiliated youth turn to crime by learning delinquent values and traditions. Kornhauser (1978) extracted a "pure disorganization theory" from Shaw and McKay by assuming that delinquent organizations and subcultures are ineffectual in motivating delinquency; all that is needed to explain delinquent acts is social disorganization (Matsueda, 1988; Heimer & Matsueda, 1994). Social disorganization theory can be seen as a special case of differential organizational control in which rates of delinquency are explained solely by absence of conventional organizational control. Delinquent organizational control is assumed to be irrelevant.

Similarly, social control theories can be viewed as a special case of differential social control. Social control theories assume that "(1) society is characterized by consensus; (2) the motivation to deviate is identical across persons; and (3) deviant subcultures and groups are impotent to control behavior" (Heimer & Matsueda, 1994, p. 371). Control theories become a special case of differential social control when the following three conditions hold for society: because of widespread consensus, groups are organized only against delinquency; systems of attitudes and motives conducive to crime either do not exist or are ineffectual; and delinquent groups do not foster criminal behavior. Empirically, this implies that delinquency is determined by the absence of conventional controls, and not by the presence of delinquent learning and delinquent peers.

The differential association–social learning tradition in sociology is based on the same group conflict assumptions as symbolic interactionism. But, according to differential association theory, the cause of crime is the learning of an excess of definitions favorable to crime over definitions unfavorable to crime (Sutherland et al., 1992). Social learning theories add operant conditioning, modeling, and vicarious reinforcement to this learning mechanism (Akers, 1985). From a symbolic interactionist standpoint, differential association's concept of definitions of rules and laws constitute one aspect of role-taking leading to deviant and criminal behavior, but this is not the sole mechanism. Symbolic interactionism also differs from social learning theories of crime by emphasizing the centrality of the self as an object and the cognitive process of role-taking, and de-emphasizing the role of nonsocial reinforcement. We argue that role-taking includes the concept of definitions of delinquency, as well as reflected appraisals, anticipated reactions of others, situational group processes, and prior habitual behavior. Consequently, we can view a "pure" differential association–social learning approach as a special case of a more general interactionist theory, in which the social self, cognition, and role-taking is de-emphasized.

Labeling theories of deviance are most explicitly based on symbolic interactionism. Indeed, in Lemert's (1951) version, the concepts of secondary deviance, self-identity, and stigmatization are drawn directly from symbolic interactionism. Although labeling theories represent a diverse group and are difficult to characterize, they typically make one or more of the following arguments that contradict our perspective of differential social control (Heimer & Matsueda, 1994). First, they assume that deviance is a status conferred by a social audience and not by objective behavior (H. Becker, 1963). Second, they focus on only secondary deviance and treat primary deviance as a random phenomenon, beyond causal explanation (e.g., H. Becker, 1963; Lemert, 1951). Third, they emphasize the negative effects of labeling by the criminal justice system and slight the impact of labeling by significant others and primary groups (see Schur, 1971; Rains, 1975). Fourth, they focus on developing sensitizing concepts to describe the process of negotiating and constructing deviant labels, while explicitly rejecting the quantitative study of the etiology of crime. In contrast, a more general interactionist perspective tries to explain primary as well as secondary deviance, defines delinquency as objective behavior, and focuses on informal social controls by significant others and reference groups, in addition to official labeling. The labeling approach offers two hypotheses that can be viewed as special cases of a more general symbolic interactionist theory of deviance: deviant labels are more likely to be applied to disadvantaged members of society; and deviant labels can increase future deviance by affecting one's self-image—or reflected appraisals—resulting in a self-fulfilling prophesy.

In sum, we can conceptualize several major sociological explanations of the motivations leading to crime and deviance as special cases of a symbolic interactionist perspective. The interactionist perspective provides a more complete explanation than the separate classical theories of crime, unifies their separate predictions within a single, internally consistent theoretical framework, and allows us to test the explanatory power of the more general perspective against the more parsimonious individual theories.

MAJOR EMPIRICAL RESULTS FROM STUDIES OF JUVENILE DELINQUENCY

As part of our research program, we have conducted a series of empirical tests of a symbolic interactionist theory of delinquency. These studies derived specific hypotheses from the theory and subjected them to empirical examination using structural equation models and survey data from national samples of adolescents. Overall, the results provide support for a symbolic interactionist explanation of juvenile delinquency.

In an initial study, Matsueda (1992) examined the core relationships of a symbolic interactionist view of the self, labeling, and delinquency. Following Mead's (1934) view of the self as an object from the standpoint of others and Cooley's (1922) view of the self as a looking glass, he conceptualized the self as a reflection of appraisals made by significant others. He examined adolescents' views of themselves—from the standpoint of parents, peers, and teachers—as rule violators, sociable, distressed, and likely to succeed. Matsueda found strong support for a symbolic interactionist theory. First, supporting the hypothesis of differential social control, reflected appraisals of the self as a rule violator were strongly related to future delinquency and were strongly predicted by prior delinquency. Second, consistent with the notion of a looking-glass self, reflected appraisals were significantly predicted by their corresponding parental appraisals. Third, consistent with the hypothesis of role-taking and self-control, the effects of parental appraisals on delinquency were largely indirect, operating through reflected appraisals. Matsueda also found modest support for labeling theory: holding constant their delinquent behavior, youth who were nonwhite and urban residents were more likely to be labeled as rule violators by their parents.

Heimer and Matsueda (1994) extended this model by incorporating additional elements of role-taking and differential social control, specifying links between role-taking and social structure through the concept of *role commitment*, and testing the perspective against the classical theories viewed as special cases. Specifically, they argued that delinquency is controlled not only by reflected appraisals of the self as delinquent but also by other features of role-taking, including anticipated reactions of significant others to delinquency, evaluative attitudes favorable to delinquency, and delinquent peer groups. They found support for the propositions: delinquency was significantly explained by reflected appraisals, delinquent peers, and attitudes favorable to delinquency. They also found that role-taking is affected by commitments to roles in deviant and conforming groups, communication networks, and thus, broader social-structural arrangements. Heimer and Matsueda found support for a general interactionist theory over classical theories of crime when the causal mechanisms of the latter are viewed as a special case of the former. Delinquency was found to be a function of delinquent organizational and social controls, rather than solely a function of conventional controls and organization, as implied by disorganization and control theories. Delinquency was predicted by other aspects of role-taking, such as reflected appraisals and prior behavior, rather than definitions of delinquency alone, as implied by differential association theory. Further, primary delinquency was structured by role-taking processes, rather than being random or beyond explanation, as implied by some labeling theories.

In a series of papers, we have extended the interactionist perspective to account for gender differences in the process leading to delinquency. Bartusch and Matsueda (1996) developed an explanation of gender differences in the reflected appraisal process leading to offending by combining principles from symbolic interactionism, labeling theory, and research on gender socialization. They found that, overall, the model supported an interactionist explanation of delinquency for both males and females, but that some significant gender differences existed. Specifically, males were more likely than females to be falsely labeled as troublemakers by their parents, and parents' labels and youths' reflected appraisals had larger effects on delinquency among boys than girls. In addition, when their model considered both the mean levels of independent variables and the magnitude of effects of the variables, it explained a substantial portion of the gender gap in delinquency.

Heimer (1996) also assessed the usefulness of interactionist arguments for explaining gender differences in delinquency. She developed an integrated theory of cross-gender differences in delinquency by integrating gender socialization, feminist, and symbolic interactionist perspectives. Specifically, she conceptualized gender from a symbolic interactionist perspective, arguing that gender is an important aspect of the self and thus that people try to negotiate lines of action that are consistent with their definitions of gender. She predicted that when girls incorporate traditional gender definitions or beliefs into their views of self, they would be inhibited from breaking the law. By contrast, boys who incorporate traditional gender definitions would be no more likely to break the law than other boys. This gender difference presumably arises because the dominant culture in our country treats deviant behavior by females as more problematic than similar behavior by males. In essence, deviance by females is "doubly deviant" (Heimer, 1996). The results of Heimer's study were consistent with this argument: holding traditional gender definitions reduced delinquency among females but not among males. Heimer concluded that the meaning of gender is key for controlling delinquency by females but not by males. Overall, the results demonstrated the usefulness of a symbolic interactionist perspective for explaining delinquency by girls as well as by boys.

In a study of race and gender, Heimer (1995) specified other outcomes of role-taking as important in the interactionist process leading to gender and race differences in four types of adolescent deviance: school deviance, drug use, theft, and violent delinquency. Drawing on feminist and interactionist perspectives on delinquency, she argued that gender definitions, attitudes about risk taking, and self-esteem are important outcomes of the role-taking process leading to deviance. The results of this study showed that gender differences in all four types of deviance studied occurred largely because attitudes favorable to risk-taking had a much stronger positive effect on deviance by boys than by girls. Also, low self-esteem operated differently across gender, encouraging attitudes favorable to risk-taking among boys but reducing them among girls. Furthermore, race operated differently across gender. Black males— but not black females—were more likely to engage in violent delinquency than their white counterparts. Heimer (1995) interpreted this gender-race pattern of violence as consistent with a combined feminist-interactionist argument, that black males—but not black females—are afforded physical power based on their gender, and use this physical power to cope with situations where their legitimate social and economic power is restricted based on their race.

All in all, these findings support an interactionist perspective on juvenile delinquency. Moreover, this work shows that individuals' role-taking is influenced by commitments to organized groups and social systems. As the studies of the influence of gender and race emphasize, patterns of interactions within groups and social systems combine to create broader social-structural arrangements, which in turn have implications for the role-taking process leading to deviance and crime.

A Symbolic Interactionist Interpretation of Psychological Research on Antisocial Behavior

Psychological research on aggressive and antisocial behavior has identified important theoretical propositions and empirical regularities. In this section, we interpret the major themes of psychological research from the standpoint of a symbolic interactionist perspective. These themes involve the following five sets of motivational factors: affective/emotional, cognitive, personality, social interaction, and social learning–developmental factors. Explaining the psychological findings using a symbolic interactionist theory offers some advantages. First, it allows divergent themes in the psychological literature to be conceptualized under a single, unified theoretical framework. Second, it makes clear the overlap and links between psychological and sociological research on this topic. Third, it opens the door for the work of sociologists to contribute to psychological lines of research. These contributions may include a specification of the self as a process, and recognition of the impact of the self on motivations to deviate; the development of a unified theoretical model of individuals as embedded within reference groups, which in turn combine to build up broader social-structural arrangements; and a recognition of the dynamic interplay (reciprocal influence) between individuals and the social structural arrangements in which they are embedded (see House, 1977; Stryker, 1977, 1987, 1989).

AFFECT AND EMOTION

Psychological and sociological research typically distinguishes between emotion and other related constructs, such as feeling and affect. Affect often is defined as a positive or negative evaluative reaction that is quite general (Smith-Lovin, 1989, p. vi; Thoits, 1989, p. 318). Feelings are physical or emotional drive states, and emotion is often defined as an affect or feeling state that involves an appraisal of the situation, physiological sensations, expressive gestures, and cultural labeling (Thoits, 1989, p. 318). Consequently, emotion is considered to be a refined, differentiated state; affect and feelings are less differentiated.

Psychological studies of emotion typically adopt one of two perspectives: Some take a constructionist view, following the classic work of Schachter and Singer (1962), which maintains that when the source of physiological arousal is ambiguous, individuals seek to evaluate and understand their feelings by labeling them using available cues in the situation. Other research follows the work of Ekman (1982; Ekman & Friesen, 1986), which argues that the basic emotions are automatic responses to arousal and are physiologically based and species specific. The major perspectives on affect and angry aggression differ in their views of the origin of affect and emotion.

The *neoassociationist theory* of aggression, for example, argues that unpleasant events give rise to negative affect and, thus, to biologically programmed expressive motor reactions, feelings, thoughts, and memories that are associated with either fight or flight tendencies (Berkowitz, 1993, p. 57). The fight tendency includes an inclination to strike out and harm someone. When the individual becomes aware of his or her initial, automatic "fight" reactions, a rudimentary form of anger emerges. In the next stage, these rudimentary feelings can be repressed or elaborated through additional thought to become more specific emotions, like jealousy or hatred. From this perspective, although the original fight reactions to an unpleasant situation are determined physiologically, the complete emotional experience is constructed cognitively. In other words, a parallel process leads to both anger and aggression; therefore, anger is a correlate but not a cause of aggression (p. 59). This theory thus argues for physiological determinism with regard to the instigation of angry aggression and argues for a parallel process of cognitive constructionism with regard to the full-blown emotion of anger.

The *arousal-cognition model* of angry aggression (Zillmann, 1988), by contrast, clearly takes a constructionist approach. According to this model, physiological arousal is necessary to trigger a cognitive process, whereby the individual evaluates the situation and the source of arousal, which leads to the formation of a specific emotion, such as anger. This experience of anger prompts an aggressive behavioral response to the situation. Unlike the neoassociationist theory, therefore, the arousal-cognition model makes anger a necessary prerequisite for aggression.

Within sociology, the symbolic interactionist perspective has become a central theoretical paradigm in the study of emotion. This perspective is most closely associated with the cognitive constructionist approach in psychology (Shott, 1979; Thoits, 1989). Indeed, according to symbolic interactionism, emotional experiences are social experiences in that they arise and are given meaning through interaction with others (Hewitt, 1991; Hochschild, 1979). Through role-taking, individuals view emotions as meaningful objects to be interpreted and managed in interactions (Thoits, 1989). More specifically, emotions are significant gestures or symbols that influence the course of social transactions and the cognitive dialogue between the "I" and the "me" (Mead, 1914/1982; Miller, 1973). Through role-taking, individuals negotiate the expression of emotions according to culturally prescribed rules about feelings, just as they negotiate the other elements of the social act and the formation of the social self (see Hochschild, 1979). Some emotions, such as pride, guilt, and shame, arise when individuals respond reflexively to their own attitudes and behaviors; these emotions can motivate self-control, as individuals attempt to bring behavior into line with the expectations of others (Mead, 1934; Shott, 1979; Miller, 1982). Other emotions, such as empathy, sympathy, and pity, arise when individuals experience the emotions of others vicariously; these emotions can motivate prosocial behaviors (Shott, 1979). For example, in a situation where a youth initiates a potentially violent line of action, he or she may come to feel shame through taking the perspectives of parents or conventional peers and therefore may abandon the violent action. Or, in the same situation, the youth may empathize with the victim through role-taking, which would lead him or her to abandon the violence and, perhaps, make amends through prosocial behavior. In short, the *full* emotional experience is a social product.

Yet, some symbolic interactionist perspectives also acknowledge what might be considered a precognitive phase of affect, which serves as a precursor to the full-blown emotional experience. Some theorists argue that "physical sensations," such as excitement, grief, or anger, are rather spontaneous responses (Hewitt, 1991, pp. 192–193) that can take the form of expressive gestures, such as smiling, crying, or grimacing (Mead, 1934; Miller, 1982). These sensations and expressions can be viewed as "tendencies to act in certain ways or the beginnings of acts," but they are not true emotional experiences or conscious attempts to express emotion (Miller, 1982, pp. 9–

10). Sensations and spontaneous expressions, however, can initiate the social act. For Mead (1914/1982, 1934), when an ongoing line of action is blocked, the individual may emit a gesture, such as a grimace, but this gesture is nonsignificant (not shared) until it evokes a response from others; it is this response that gives the grimace meaning or makes it a shared symbol (Miller, 1982). Once others respond, the gesture takes on meaning to the actor as well. At this point, a reciprocal role-taking process unfolds and the individual forms and refines his or her emotional experience in the situation (Mead, 1914/1982).

These arguments have implications for addressing the roles of affect and emotion in situations of crime and deviance. We illustrate these implications using the example of a violent interaction between two youths in school. The impetus that sets in motion the social act occurs when one of the boys does something that temporarily disrupts the action of the other youth. This may be a physical interruption, such as tripping the other boy as he walks along, or a verbal disruption, such as calling the other boy a name. In some instances, the other youth may respond immediately, without thinking, by lashing out at the first youth. In other instances, the interruption will evoke negative affect in the target youth, which may be accompanied by a grimace or some other expressive gesture. When the offending youth responds to the grimace—either with an apology or hostility—and the target youth recognizes this response, then the target's original grimace becomes a significant symbol in that it becomes a symbol shared by the two boys. Through reciprocal role-taking, in which the boys take the perspectives of one another as well as their reference groups and generalized others, they can refine their own responses and thus create a full emotional experience. In addition, each youth will consider other factors through role-taking. The target boy may consider whether the offending youth intended to trip him, for example, or whether it was an accident. If the target boy determines that the offending youth indeed intentionally tripped or insulted him, this may amplify his emotional experience of anger. Interactions such as these can evolve into character contests, as actors attempt to save face in the situation and manage impressions, and thus can culminate in fist fights, assaults, or even homicide (Luckenbill, 1977). Such encounters can lead the interactants to change their future behavior by encouraging them to relinquish claims to identities in certain groups—such as conventional law-abiding groups—and to lay claims to identities in other groups—such as a delinquent or fighting gang. This, of course, implies that emotions are an impetus for changes in groups and communication networks, which ultimately implies changes in social-structural arrangements (see Stryker, 1988).

The neoassociationist and arousal-cognition theories of angry aggression can be viewed from the standpoint of a symbolic interactionist framework. Indeed, the neoassociationist view is compatible with the interactionist perspective outlined here. As in the interactionist analysis above, the neoassociationist theory argues that unpleasant situations—which likely disrupt ongoing action in some way—can trigger behavioral responses, such as lashing out at another person, and can also trigger a negative affective response, which can be further refined through deeper-level cognition to become a full-blown emotional experience. Both perspectives differentiate between the initial sensation or affect and the subsequent formation of the full emotional experience; both propose that the full emotional experience of anger is not necessary for a precognitive, aggressive response; both also allow for aggressive behavior after a deeper-level cognitive process and the development of the emotional reaction of anger. Symbolic interactionism can further specify the precise mechanisms giving rise to emotions, specify the role of organized groups in this process, and show how the outcomes of interactions affect future interactions, communication networks, and, ultimately, social-structural arrangements. Similarly, the arousal-cognition model of aggression can be conceptualized within a symbolic interactionist theory because it focuses on a subset of the interactionist process—the cognitive processes leading to the emotional experience and aggressive behavior. Again, adopting a symbolic interactionist theory allows us to specify more completely the dynamics of this cognitive process, as well as how it affects and is affected by groups, communication networks, and social-structural arrangements.

PERSONALITY AND TEMPERAMENT

Until recently, sociological theories of crime and deviance have neglected the role of personality, temperament, and other stable individual characteristics. This is in part a historical negative response to early psychological theories of crime, which attributed all criminal behavior to a defective personality type. In their influential book, *A General Theory of Crime*, Gottfredson and Hirschi (1990) have resurrected the notion of a stable individual characteristic as a principal determinant of crime. Building in part on psychological research that finds delinquency fairly stable throughout the life course (e.g., Olweus, 1979), Gottfredson and Hirschi (1990) argue that all crime is the result of low self-control, a stable individual trait characterized by impulsivity, insensitivity to the suffering of others, and inability to plan, delay gratification, and avoid risky behaviors. Persons low on self-control are free of conventional restraints and therefore are susceptible to crime when opportunities and incentives present themselves. Gottfredson and Hirschi have distinguished themselves from psychological theories of personality, maintaining that low self-control is best measured by prior crime, rather than psychologists' personality inventories.

The psychological and psychiatric research on personality and antisocial behavior is too voluminous to review or even characterize here (for a more detailed discussion see Rutter, this volume). For our purposes, two views of temperament and personality are particularly useful. Both regard personality and temperament as stable individual characteristics that predict antisocial and criminal behavior. One view, however, looks at temperament as an unmotivated noncognitive trait that affects crime and other forms of psychopathology (Garrison & Earls, 1987). Here, personality predisposes some individuals to react to aversive stimuli immediately with aggressive, hostile responses. The second view treats personality as a cognitive predisposition: personality consists of cognitive scripts or schemata that are used to adjust to one's environment (Huesmann & Eron, 1984). Individuals with impulsive violent personalities are likely to use aggressive scripts to deal with aversive situations. The important point is that personality is translated into behavior through a cognitive process of activating cognitive scripts.

From a symbolic interactionist standpoint, each of these two views is correct under two different conditions: nonproblematic situations in which personality affects behavior noncognitively; and problematic situations in which personality affects behavior through a cognitive process. Personality, from our perspective, is the relatively stable, enduring component of the self, consisting of constellations of "I's" and "me's" (or impulses and organized responses) derived from generalized others. Although personality is somewhat stable over time, it is not necessarily fixed at any time; rather, it is constantly subject to change as the individual makes adjustments to a changing environment. With each interaction—particularly those involving reflective behavior—personality is modified, sometimes imperceptibly, sometimes radically. However, because most individuals develop strong commitments to groups and maintain consistent generalized others, personality tends to be stable across situations. When confronting problematic situations, the organized responses making up the personality are available for use in taking the role of the other, engaging in an imaginative rehearsal, and employing a serial process of cognition to solve the problem. Here, the relationship between personality and behavior is mediated by cognition, using organized responses or, to use the psychological term, *cognitive scripts*. The organized responses making up personality are also available for use in habitual behavior. As similar problematic situations are repeatedly solved in similar ways, the situation becomes increasingly nonproblematic, and the behavior increasingly automatic, habitual, and unreflective. Habitual behavior, then, is determined by organized responses, but in an automatic, noncognitive way.

Although personality is rooted in role-taking, it is not merely a social construction. Rather, it is also conditioned by the biological makeup of the individual. Thus, some individuals may be constitutionally incapable of delaying an immediate response to a stimulus and may have difficulty controlling their behavior through role-taking and cognition. Laboratory research on cognition suggests that for persons scoring high on psychopathic inventories, a key impediment to using cognitive processes to solve problematic situations is an inability to delay an immediate response to the problem (Newman, Patterson, & Kosson, 1987). From an interactionist standpoint, the individual here is unable to delay an initial impulse to a problematic situation, or unable to perceive that the situation is problematic in the first place. Such problems can originate from organic deficits, learning deficits, or both. Other individuals, by virtue of an inherited characteristic, like race or gender, may be selected into delinquent gangs and peer groups that influence long-term changes in personality and foster criminal behavior. Selection based on individual characteristics can be selection by others, self-selection, or more likely a combination of the two in social interaction. Here, the important mediating process by which individual characteristics are expressed in criminal behavior is the participation in organized groups through role-taking (for a more detailed discussion, see Matsueda & Heimer, 1997).

Studies of development, personality, and deviance illustrate this view of personality, biological makeup, and social interaction (see Rutter, this volume). For example, Caspi et al. (1987) find that early onset of temper tantrums can lead to later problems in life through one of two mechanisms: cumulative continuity, in which the maladaptive behavior selects individuals into negative environments (e.g., dropping out of school or affiliating with a delinquent peer group) that perpetuate the maladaptation; and interactional continuity, in which reciprocal interaction with the environment leads to sustained maladaptive behaviors. From our standpoint, these two mechanisms derive from a continuous social process in which reciprocal role-taking produces a self that selects future environments and is then affected by those environments (Matsueda & Heimer, 1997). As another example, Caspi, Lynam, Moffitt, and Silva (1993) find that early onset of puberty increases female delinquency in coed schools but not in all-girl schools. In coed schools, early maturing girls are selected by older delinquent boys, whose influence leads to delinquent behavior. In all-girl schools, however, older boys are not present to influence the early-maturing girls. From our standpoint, the early maturing girls engage in role-taking with older delinquent boys, learn to view delinquency as justified in certain situations, and come to identify with the older boys.

RATIONAL CHOICE AND COGNITION

Recent years have witnessed a resurgence of interest in rational choice theories of crime. This is due partly to the rise of economic models to explain criminal behavior (G. Becker, 1968) and partly to the connection between policies of deterrence and rational actor models—indeed, the criminal justice system is itself based on the utilitarian assumptions of classical theorists such as Beccaria and

Bentham. In criminology, studies of deterrence led to interest in rational choice theories, which in turn evolved from formal expected utility models to models of limited rationality. Expected utility models begin with the assumption that criminals and noncriminals are rational actors, and that their behavior can be explained by expected utility models under conditions of risk and uncertainty. Typically, these models assume that criminal behavior occurs when the expected utility of crime is greater than the expected utility of legal pursuits. Expected utility of crime, in turn, is a function of the returns to crime minus the costs, which is then weighted by perceived probability of getting caught, plus the returns to crime (which includes monetary and psychic returns) times the probability of getting away with it. This, of course, leads to the prediction that crime will be a monotonically decreasing function of the certainty and severity of formal sanction. Whether risk or severity is more important depends on the criminal's taste for risk: if a criminal is not risk averse, then the utility function is convex and certainty of punishment will be more effective than severity. There are a variety of specifications of the utility function, including time-allocation models and portfolio models, but all are rooted in these basic assumptions.

These models have several strengths: They are powerful models of consumer choices and market behavior, so it is natural to apply them to other domains of behavior. They provide a very parsimonious model of crime stated in mathematical form and subject to empirical test. They have direct policy implications. But the rational choice models have also been criticized on at least three grounds. First, many have questioned the assumption that criminals are rational, engaging in the complex calculations required by the theory. Proponents, however, counter that the models do not assume perfect rationality or perfect information; rather, the models assume only that actors act *as if* they are rational, or that actors respond to incentives and punishments, or that behavior appears rational in the aggregate (although individual actors may not behave rationally). Second, most of the empirical research finds weak or qualified support for formal economic models of behavior in general (e.g., Lichtenstein & Slovic, 1971) and crime in particular (e.g., Piliavin, Gartner, Thornton, & Matsueda, 1986). Third, economic models appear to de-emphasize what many regard as critical to crime: the structural distribution of information, and individuals' preferences, motivations, and values.

To avoid the unrealistic assumptions of expected utility models, criminologists have turned to theories of limited rationality. Here the idea is to specify a more realistic decision-making model by relaxing the assumption of optimal decisions. This follows from the work of Herbert Simon (1957), who long ago argued that limitations in the capacities of people to process information forces them to use heuristics and shortcuts to solve complex problems. The hypothesis of bounded rationality specifies that behavior is rational within constraints set by people's cognitive capacities. Moreover, rather than seeking to maximize utility, actors are said to "satisfice," that is, to select the first alternative that passes a set of criteria. Therefore, the order of consideration of an alternative may be important in a decision.

Kahneman and Tversky's (1984) prospect model identifies common rules of thumb and shortcuts to decision making used by actors. Thus, actors edit, code, combine, segregate, simplify, and cancel alternatives; then they evaluate prospects, using subjective decision weights (which replace probabilities) and subjective value functions (which replace utility), and choose the alternative that has the highest prospect for success (see also Edwards, 1955). Subjective probabilities, therefore, do not necessarily correspond linearly to objective probabilities but can be biased or distorted by the actor's emotional state, intoxication, or inability to imagine certain outcomes. Also, subjective value functions vary by initial reference point and other considerations (see Lattimore & Witte, 1986). The result may be systematic biases in decision making.

With respect to crime, criminals may discount those consequences that have a low probability of occurring or have a long time horizon, such as formal sanction (Lattimore & Witte, 1986). Or noncriminals may adopt "standing decisions" to refrain from crime, which are invoked in the absence of extraordinary events (for empirical support see Carroll, 1978). Or criminals may have information on the potential returns from crime, but lack information on the threat of punishment. Such information is tied to communication, personal experience, and observation of peers (Cook, 1980).

Clarke and Cornish (1985) have developed perhaps the most elaborate rational choice model, beginning with a limited rationality assumption—that criminal acts have a measure of rationality within the constraints of time, cognitive ability, and information available to the actor (see also Lattimore & Witte, 1986). They decompose the decision-making process into three decision points: the criminal's recognition of "readiness" to commit a specific criminal act (e.g., burglary for money); the decision to carry out the crime (e.g., situational factors making an opportunity attractive); and the decision to victimize a specific target (e.g., unoccupied middle-class home). Readiness is a function of a broad range of variables, including background factors (temperament, IQ, personality, upbringing, demographics), prior learning experiences (learning attitudes toward crime, self-perception, and foresight), general needs, evaluations of solutions (sanctions, moral costs, effort required), and perceived solutions (legitimate versus illegitimate alternatives). Readiness can undergo modification, as life circumstances (marriage, new job, new criminal opportunities) change, and thus can account for desistance from crime. Once an individual is ready to commit a crime, the factors leading to a criminal decision are situational chance events—such as when an easy opportunity presents itself, an urgent need arises, a friend persuades the individual to commit the crime, or the individual gets drunk. Finally, the decision to select a particular target involves situational opportunity factors, such as routine activity theory's suitable targets and capable guardians.

A symbolic interactionist perspective provides a general framework for addressing these issues and questions. First, symbolic interactionism implies a decision-making model in which individuals are adapting to a changing environment or social process, rather than optimizing some utility function. Thus, it is consistent with the notion of "satisficing": the first alternative considered that solves the problematic situation is the one used, unless blocked by an internal impulse. These impulses are social and derived from groups. It follows that group participation explains individual variation in the extent to which internal impulses block lines of action, which in turn causes further role-taking and searches for solutions. Adolescents in impulsive turf gangs may have little patience in considering alternatives, whereas members of professional theft rings may engage in exhaustive searches. In extreme cases the search for a solution is also affected by constitutional factors, such as organic brain deficits that impede the ability to delay and engage in cognition. Research on psychopathy suggests that some individuals are unable to consider alternatives because they cannot delay their initial response (e.g., Newman et al., 1987).

When an impulse is delayed, the serial process of cognition occurs, in which the individual engages in an imaginative rehearsal before continuing the act. Here the alternatives and potential consequences considered are derived from general attitudes of organized groups (generalized other). It follows that rationality derives from the generalized other, which determines the alternatives and potential consequences considered, as well as their importance or weight. Therefore, the salience and meaning of formal sanctions derive from groups—and range from a law-abiding adolescent feeling terrified at the thought of being caught by police to a gang member submerged in a criminal subculture gaining prestige from doing time in prison. Group differences in meaning may help explain why formal sanctions generally fail to show the consistently strong effect predicted by deterrence theory and expected utility models.

This implies that responses to formal sanctions should be patterned across social groups: groups that share communication and interaction networks should show similar evaluations of the meaning and salience of formal sanctions. It also implies that, all else being equal, informal sanctions by primary groups (serving as generalized others) should be more effective in controlling individual behavior. Moreover, both criminal and conventional organization is important in the process of social control. Because most individuals participate in multiple groups, their store of alternatives and evaluations are multifaceted, making predictions difficult. We might hypothesize that if all factors are constant, individuals will be more rational when they participate in groups that value carefully planned decisions and when they participate in a broad range of groups that offer multiple perspectives and alternatives. Because of these two factors, we might expect criminals to be less rational on average than their conventional counterparts.

Participation in organized groups through role-taking also helps explain information and information processing. Information about criminal and conventional alternative lines of action and their consequences is learned through reciprocal role-taking and communication within social interactions. Moreover, both successful and unsuccessful solutions to problematic situations involving crime provide very salient information for future transactions. For symbolic interactionism, information processing is driven by the alternatives, evaluations, and attitudes of the group, but it is not limited to those evaluations since the impulsive response always contains an element of novelty. Which reference group will be invoked in role-taking depends on the group's relevance to the problematic situation at hand and the extent to which the person is committed to the group. This model of cognition and role-taking should apply to all phases of decision making including readiness, criminal decisions, and target selection. Also, the formation of habits through repeated solutions to a given problematic situation helps explain the origins of "standing decisions."

Finally, the degree to which individuals engage in rational cognitive processes varies by the situation and the individual. Of course, situations are in part selected by individuals through conscious decision making and in part conditioned by social-structural constraints on opportunities. Given a specific situation, some individuals will not view criminal situations as problematic; therefore, their behavior will be immediate and nonreflective. As stated earlier, other individuals may have organic deficits that impede their ability to perceive situations as problematic or delay their initial impulsive responses. In both cases, these individuals will be unlikely to engage in elaborate rational calculations specified by utility maximization theories.

SOCIAL INTERACTION

Psychological research on the immediate situation leading to adolescent aggression and antisocial behavior focuses on social interactions, social influence, and interdependence. Tedeschi and Felson (1994) develop a *social interactionist* approach, which argues that aggression is a coercive behavior resulting from a decision-making process in which individuals weigh the costs, benefits, and values of outcomes in given situations (Felson, 1993; Felson & Tedeschi, 1993a; Tedeschi & Felson, 1994; for a complete presentation of this perspective see Tedeschi, this volume). According to the theory, coercive actions often begin when an individual feels he or she has been wronged by another party, giving rise to a perception of injustice and a grievance. Depending on the costs, benefits, and values of outcomes, the individual may attempt to restore justice by absolving the other party of blame or by claiming restitution. In the latter case, the first party then engages in a similar decision-making process in responding to the claim. Such coercive interactions often escalate into character contests in which interactants attempt to manage impressions, save face, and maintain certain desired identities. Finally, although the theory is based on a rational decision-making model, Tedeschi and Felson (1994) argue that some behaviors are scripted or habitual and that rationality can be limited by strong emotions, alcohol and drugs, or the urgency of making a snap decision.

These propositions are consistent with our symbolic interactionist perspective; in fact, the perspective evolved in part from sociological work on impression management (e.g., Goffman, 1959), which is rooted in symbolic interactionist principles and in part from psychological work on social influence. Indeed, the empirical analyses of face-to-face coercive interactions, which underlie the social interactionist perspective, provide valuable insights into role-taking, the negotiation of meanings, and violence (e.g., Short & Strodtbeck, 1965; Felson, 1978; Luckenbill, 1977; Luckenbill & Doyle, 1989). Nevertheless, this perspective also differs from our symbolic interactionist theory of crime in at least one fundamental way. Whereas Tedeschi and Felson appear to follow the psychological tradition of viewing the group as an abstraction comprised of interacting individuals, symbolic interactionism begins with the primacy of the group, viewing the individual as an abstraction from the group. For symbolic interactionism, all that is social is derived from participation in organized groups. Thus, role-taking, reflected thought and cognition, shared meanings, and coordinated behavior are social because they all derive from group organization. This implies that social groups, and consequently larger social structures and organizations, are always implicated in social behavior, including criminal and delinquent behavior.

SOCIAL LEARNING AND SOCIALIZATION

A final important psychological tradition in studies of aggressive, antisocial, and deviant behavior focuses on social learning and developmental socialization. The theoretical perspectives on social learning and socialization are many and varied, but all share the following three characteristics: a view of deviance as emerging through a developmental socialization process; an attention to the role of primary groups such as families and peers in this socialization process; and an attention to the role of direct reinforcement or observation and vicarious reinforcement in the process leading to deviant behavior. Consequently, for the present purposes, we treat the various social learning and socialization approaches together.

Early applications of learning theory to crime and delinquency focused on the direct reinforcement of illegal behavior. Burgess and Akers (1966), for example, restated Sutherland's (1947) differential association theory using principles of operant conditioning. Crime was said to be learned directly in social and nonsocial situations that were reinforcing or discriminating for behavior. Trasler (1960) also proposed an associationist model, arguing that when parents consistently punish children for counternormative behavior, the anxiety and pain associated with the disapproved behavior become associated with the counternormative behavior, thereby inhibiting future deviance.

Contemporary social learning theories, by comparison, typically propose that aggressive and other deviant behaviors are acquired through vicarious as well as direct reinforcements. Individuals learn deviant behaviors directly when they enact such behaviors and are either rewarded or not punished. They learn deviance indirectly, or vicariously, when they observe another person's deviant behavior receive rewards or escape punishment. According to Bandura's (1977) early specifications of observational learning, when we watch modeled behavior, we form symbolic representations of that behavior, and these representations serve as guides for our future action. The symbolic process includes attending to the behavior, encoding it cognitively, rehearsing it mentally, and recognizing reinforcement contingencies. Akers (1985) has proposed a reformulation of his earlier work with Burgess by incorporating some of the cognitive elements of Bandura's (1977) work on learning theory, as well as aspects of the symbolic interactionist view of the self; he thus achieves a more integrated social learning theory of crime and delinquency.

Other explanations of antisocial behavior within the learning-socialization tradition emphasize the long-term consequences of child rearing. McCord (1979), for example, reports that poor supervision, lack of strong affection between parent and child, and conflict between parents can increase a child's chances of criminality later in life. In later work, McCord maintains that children who experience high levels of coercion and punishment are more likely to have behavioral problems, such as crime and deviance, in the future (McCord 1995; see also McCord, this volume).

Patterson and his colleagues expand on this theme by emphasizing the reciprocal influence of parents' and children's coercive behaviors. Specifically, Patterson shows that parents' use of coercive discipline—such as threats, scolding, and physical punishment—increases the probability that their children enagage in antisocial behavior. But children's antisocial behaviors also evoke high levels of coercive discipline from parents (Patterson, 1982, 1996; Patterson et al., 1992). In short, coercive behavior in parent-child interactions begets coercive behavior, regardless of the source and the target of the coercion. More recently, Patterson and his colleagues have identified types of families in which early coercive behaviors (e.g., temper tantrums) and later covert antisocial acts (e.g., stealing) become functional within the family (Patterson & Yoerger, this volume). Other recent work indicates that coercive parenting practices are influenced by social-structural arrangements, such as socioeconomic stratification, and lead to cultural definitions that encourage youths to use coercion to solve problematic situations (Heimer, 1997). There is also evidence that the relationships between socioeconomic stratification, parenting practices, and problem behavior vary across gender (Heimer & De Coster, 1996).

These perspectives on learning and socialization are generally consistent with a symbolic interactionist perspective (see also Akers 1985). At the most general level, both perspectives focus on the development of attitudes or predispositions to act and anticipated social and nonsocial consequences for behavior; from a symbolic interactionist perspective, these evolve through an internal dialogue or cognitive process of serial role-taking in problematic situations. Both perspectives also allow for reciprocal interactions, such as Patterson's mutually coercive parent-child interactions; from a symbolic interactionist perspective, this reflects the process of reciprocal or serial role-taking among actors in the situation. Both the learning and symbolic interactionist perspectives allow for behavior to become scripted or nonreflective over time.

Bandura's (1986) recent respecification of his original social learning arguments as social cognitive theory creates additional links between the learning-socialization tradition and symbolic interactionism. Consistent with symbolic interactionism, Bandura's social cognitive approach emphasizes the use of symbols to exercise forethought, among other things, and thereby regulate one's own conduct. In addition, social cognitive theory acknowledges the importance of the process by which people reflect on their own thinking. Indeed, Bandura argues that "(a)mong the types of thought that affect action, none is more central or pervasive than people's judgements of their capabilities to deal effectively with different realities" (p. 21). For Bandura as well as for symbolic interactionism, self-control is possible because we contemplate and act upon our own cognitions and behaviors. As Bandura (p. 410) recognizes, however, his view could be extended by conceiving of other self processes, such as self-concepts and self-esteem. Perhaps a fruitful avenue for accomplishing this would be to draw on a symbolic interactionist formulation of self processes.

In addition, symbolic interactionism allows us to explicate the relationships among social-structural arrangements, social groups, and individuals, a procedure that receives relatively scant attention in most social learning perspectives. Although some psychological explanations of development and socialization—most notably that of Jessor and his colleagues—argue that social system factors (e.g., demographic characteristics, group memberships, and control structures) combine with personality factors (e.g., motivations, personal belief structures, personal control structures) to increase the chances of problem behavior (Jessor & Jessor, 1977; Jessor et al., 1991), they do not present a theory of the precise social-psychological *mechanism* linking these factors. Bandura's (1986) social cognitive theory moves further in this direction by viewing individuals as embedded within social groups and networks, but it does not have a developed explanation of how these link to broader social-structural arrangements. Symbolic interactionism, by contrast, clearly specifies that social-structural arrangements, groups, and individuals are intertwined through the process of role-taking: Individuals incorporate the perspectives of groups via role-taking, and group perspectives, in turn, can be influenced by the novelty that emerges through role-taking between individuals. The communication and interaction patterns between groups create social-structural arrangements, such as social class differences, and in turn, group perspectives and individuals' role-taking can be constrained by these arrangements. In short, symbolic interactionism can offer to psychological perspectives the specification of an internally consistent, theoretical model of the links among social structures, groups, and individuals.

This advantage may be associated with a distinction that we raised earlier between symbolic interactionism and psychological theories, in general. On the one hand, because psychological theories usually begin with a model of the individual and view groups as abstractions from or aggregates of individuals, the precise mechanisms by which individuals are linked to groups, and by which both are linked to social-structural arrangements, often are not explicitly stated. On the other hand, a symbolic interactionist perspective begins with a model of the social group and treats the individual as an abstraction from the group. Indeed, the role-taking process through which individuals are socially constituted is inconceivable in the absence of significant others and organized social groups. Moreover, through role-taking, individuals and groups construct the communication and interaction patterns that become broader social-structural arrangements (such as systems of social class and racial stratification); conversely, role-taking is constrained by such structural systems.

Concluding Remarks

The theme of this chapter is that cross-disciplinary fertilization in the study of crime and deviance can enrich our research and increase the rate at which knowledge grows. In sociology, empirical social psychological research based on symbolic interactionism has led to an accumulation of important findings, such as articulating the relationships between individual behavior, group processes, and social-structural arrangements. In psychology, empirical research on aggressive and antisocial behavior has also led to an accumulation of important findings on factors relevant to motivation, including affect, cognition, personality, social influence and interactions, and social learning and socialization processes. In this chapter, we articulate a symbolic interactionist theory of crime and deviance and attempt to show how it might incorporate, interpret, and account for research findings in the psychology of aggression and antisocial behavior. We hope that this will help stimulate cross-disciplinary discourse by providing a sociological framework for interpreting important psychological principles and empirical research. Moreover, a symbolic interactionist perspective offers a route for expanding psychological perspectives to specify links among individuals, groups, communication networks, and social-structural arrangements (Stryker, 1987).

Future research on symbolic interactionism and delinquency is needed to advance this integration of psychological and sociological perspectives. We can identify six directions for future research. First, an explicit theory of social structure is needed to guide empirical research on the larger patternings of role-taking and delinquency. Such a theory would focus on neighborhood effects and residential patterns, family structures, and school organization, as well as larger class structures that influence allocation to neighborhoods and schools. Symbolic interactionism implies that such structures affect delinquency through their effects on communication channels, interaction patterns, and, most importantly, peer group interactions.

Second, research is needed to articulate communication networks and the diffusion and innovation of information relevant to delinquent behavior. Symbolic interactionism provides a framework for analyzing innovation, creativity, and diffusion of delinquent identities, attitudes, information, perceptions of the threat of sanction, and so on.

Third, further research is needed to identify additional unique dimensions of role-taking that are important to delinquency beyond those we have investigated here, which include identities, reflected appraisals, definitions of delinquency, anticipated reactions, habits, and delinquent peer processes. Furthermore, inductive research is needed to identify the content of such dimensions as identities, definitions of delinquency, and attitudes toward formal sanction. What are the major definitions or justifications that motivate delinquent behavior within subcultures? How are they diffused to other groups? How do delinquents view themselves, how do their peers view them, and how does this bring them status?

Fourth, additional research should examine the reciprocal effects of selection into roles—both delinquent and conforming roles—and illegal behavior throughout the life course. To what extent is selection into roles self-selection, other-selection, or purely structurally driven? How does early problem behavior influence interaction patterns, labeling, and role trajectories? How do genetic differences affect this selection process?

Fifth, additional research is needed to identify individual variations in role-taking, such as organic deficits and impulsivity, that may alter some individuals' role-taking abilities (e.g., Rutter, this volume).

Sixth, more research is needed to examine the dynamics of criminal and delinquent transactions (e.g., Tedeschi & Felson, this volume). Symbolic interactionism provides an analytical framework for investigating social transactions and role-taking processes. How are individuals sorted into potentially delinquent situations? Once there, what individual and situational elements may impede a criminal act from transpiring?

Research on topics such as these will contribute to a symbolic interactionist theory of delinquency and help integrate psychological and sociological perspectives on deviant and antisocial behavior.

REFERENCES

Akers, R. L. (1985). *Deviant behavior: A social learning approach.* (3d. ed.). Belmont CA: Wadsworth.

Anderson, E. (1990). *Streetwise: Race, class, and change in an urban community.* Chicago: University of Chicago Press.

Arnold, B. L., & Hagan, J. (1992). Careers of misconduct: Prosecuted professional deviance among lawyers. *American Sociological Review, 57,* 771–780.

Bandura, A. (1977). *Social learning theory.* Englewood Cliffs NJ: Prentice-Hall.

———. (1986). *Social foundations of thought and action: A social cognitive theory.* Englewood Cliffs NJ: Prentice-Hall.

Baron, R. A., & Bell, P. A. (1975). Aggression and heat: Mediating effects of prior provocation and exposure to an aggressive model. *Journal of Personality and Social Psychology, 31,* 825–832.

Bartusch, D. J., & Matsueda, R. L. (1996). Gender, reflected appraisals, and delinquency: A cross-group model. *Social Forces, 75,* 145–177.

Becker, G. S. (1968). Crime and Punishment: An Economic Approach. *Journal of Political Economy, 78,* 189–217.

Becker, H. S. (1963). *Outsiders: Studies in the sociology of deviance.* New York: Free Press.

Berkowitz, L. (1989). Frustration-aggression hypothesis: Examination and reformulation. *Psychological Bulletin, 106,* 59–73.

———. (1993). *Aggression: Its causes and consequences.* Philadelphia: Temple University Press.

Berkowitz, L., Cochran, S. T., & Embree, M. C. (1981). Physical pain and the goal of aversively stimulated aggression. *Journal of Personality and Social Psychology, 40,* 687–700.

Berkowitz, L., & Heimer, K. (1989). On the construction of the anger experience: Aversive events and negative priming in the formation of feelings. In L. Berkowitz (Ed.), *Advances in experimental social psychology* (Vol. 22, pp. 1–28). Orlando FL: Academic Press.

Blumer, H. (1969). *Symbolic interactionism: Perspective and method.* Englewood Cliffs NJ: Prentice-Hall.

Briar, S., & Piliavin, I. (1965). Delinquency, situational inducements, and commitment to conformity. *Social Problems, 13,* 35–45.

Burgess, R. L., & Akers, R. L. (1966). A differential association-reinforcement theory of criminal behavior. *Social Problems, 14,* 128–147.

Bursik, R. J., Jr. (1988). Social disorganization and theories of crime and delinquency: Problems and prospects. *Criminology, 26,* 519–552.

Carroll, J. S. (1978). A psychological approach to deterrence: The evaluation of crime opportunities. *Journal of Personality and Social Psychology, 36,* 1512–1520.

Caspi, A., Elder, G. H., Jr., & Bem, D. J. (1987). Moving against the world: Life-Course patterns of explosive children. *Developmental Psychology, 23,* 308–313.

Caspi, A., Lynam, D., Moffitt, T. E., & Silva, P. A. (1993). Unraveling girls' delinquency: Biological, dispositional, and contextual contributions to adolescent misbehavior. *Developmental Psychology, 29,* 19–30.

Clarke, R. V., & Cornish, D. B. (1985). Modeling offenders' decisions: A framework for research and policy. In M. Tonry & N. Morris (Eds.), *Crime and justice: An annual review of research* (Vol. 6, pp. 147–185). Chicago: University of Chicago Press.

Clinard, M. B., & Yeager. P. C. (1980). *Corporate crime.* New York: Macmillan.

Cloward, R. A., & Ohlin, L. E. (1960). *Delinquency and opportunity.* New York: Free Press.

Cohen, A. K. (1955). *Delinquent Boys.* Glencoe IL: Free Press.

Cohen, L. E., & Felson, M. (1979). Social change and crime rate trends: A routine activities approach. *American Sociological Review, 44,* 588–608.

Coleman, J. S. (1961). *The adolescent society.* Glencoe IL: Free Press.

Comer, M. J. (1985). *Corporate fraud.* London: McGraw-Hill.

Cook, P. J. (1980). Research in criminal deterrence: Laying the groundwork for the second decade. In N. Morris & M. Tonry (Eds.), *Crime and justice:*

An annual review of research (Vol. 2, pp. 211–268). Chicago: University of Chicago Press.

Cooley, C. H. (1922). *Human nature and the social order.* New York: Scribners.

Cornish, D. B., & Clarke, R. V. (Eds.) (1986). *The reasoning criminal: Rational choice perspectives on offending.* New York: Springer-Verlag.

Cressey, D. R. (1953). *Other people's money: A study in the social psychology of embezzlement.* Glencoe IL: Free Press.

Dewey, J. (1922). *Human nature and conduct.* New York: Modern Library.

Ditton, J. (1977). *Part-time crime.* New York: Macmillan.

Dodge, K. A. (1980). Social cognition and children's aggressive behavior. *Child Development, 51,* 162–170.

Dodge, K. W. (1991). The structure and function of reactive and proactive aggression. In D. J. Pepler & K. H. Rubin (Eds.), *The development and treatment of childhood aggression* (pp. 201–218). Hillsdale NJ: Lawrence Erlbaum.

Dyck, R. J., & Rule, B. G. (1978). The effect on retaliations of causal attributions concerning attack. *Journal of Personality and Social Psychology, 36,* 521–529.

Edwards, W. (1955). The prediction of decision among bets. *Journal of Experimental Social Psychology, 50,* 201–214.

———. (1961). Behavioral decision theory. *Annual Review of Psychology, 12,* 473–498.

Ekman, P. (Ed.) (1982). *Emotion in the human face.* Cambridge: Cambridge University Press.

Ekman, P., & Friesen, W. V. (1986). A new pancultural facial expression of emotion. *Motivation and Emotion, 10,* 159–168.

Elder, G. H., Jr., Caspi, A., & Downey, G. (1986). Problem behavior and family relationships: Life course and intergenerational themes. In A. B. Sorenson, F. E. Weinert, & L. R. Sherrod (Eds.), *Human development and the life course: Multidisciplinary perspectives* (pp. 293–340). Hillsdale NJ: Lawrence Erlbaum.

Farrington, D. P., & Kidd, R. F. (1977). Is financial dishonesty a rational decision? *British Journal of Clinical Psychology, 16,* 139–146.

Farrington, D. P., Loeber, R., & Van Kammen, W. B. (1990). Long-term criminal outcomes of hyperactivity-impulsivity-attention deficit and conduct problems in children. In L. Robins & M. Rutter (Eds.), *Straight and devious pathways from childhood to adulthood* (pp. 62–81). New York: Cambridge University Press.

Felson, R. B. (1978). Aggression as impression management. *Social Psychology Quarterly, 41,* 205–213.

———. (1985). Reflected appraisal and the development of self. *Social Psychology Quarterly, 48,* 71–77.

———. (1993). Predatory and dispute-related violence: A social intractionist approach. In R. V. Clarke & M. Felson (Eds.), *Advances in criminological theory* (Vol. 5, pp. 103–125). New Brunswick NJ: Transaction Press.

Felson, R. B., & Tedeschi, J. T. (1993a). A social interactionist approach to violence: Cross-cultural applications. *Violence and victims, 8,* 295–310.

————. (Eds.) (1993b). *Aggression and violence: Social interactionist perspectives.* Washington DC: American Psychological Association.

Fine, G. A., & Kleinman, S. (1979). Rethinking subculture: An interactionist analysis. *American Journal of Sociology, 85,* 1–20.

Garrison, W. T., & Earls, F. J. (1987). *Temperament and child psychopathology.* Beverly Hills CA: Sage.

Geen, R. G. (1968). Effects of frustration, attack, and prior training in aggressiveness on aggressive behavior. *Journal of Personality and Social Psychology, 9,* 316–321.

————. (1978). Effects of attack and uncontrollable noise on aggression. *Journal of Research in Personality, 12,* 15–29.

————. (1990). *Human aggression.* Pacific Grove CA: Brooks-Cole.

————. (1995). Human aggression. In A. Tessler (Ed.), *Advanced social psychology* (pp. 383–417). New York: McGraw-Hill.

Goffman, E. (1959). *The presentation of self in everyday life.* New York: Anchor.

Gottfredson, M. R., & Hirschi, T. (1990). *A general theory of crime.* Stanford: Stanford University Press.

Greenberg, D. F. (1977). Delinquency and the age structure of society. *Contemporary Crises: Crime, Law, and Social Policy, 1,* 189–223.

Hagan, J. (1989). *Structural criminology.* New Brunswick NJ: Rutgers University Press.

————. (1993). The social embeddedness of crime and unemployment. *Criminology, 31,* 465–491.

Hagan, J., & Peterson, R. (1995). *Crime and inequality.* Stanford: Stanford University Press.

Heimer, K. (1995). Gender, race, and the pathways to delinquency: An interactionist explanation. In J. Hagan and R. Peterson (Eds.), *Crime and Inequality* (pp. 140–173). Stanford: Stanford University Press.

————. (1996). Gender, interaction, and delinquency: Testing a theory of differential social control. *Social Psychology Quarterly. 59,* 39–61.

————. (1997). Socioeconomic status, subcultural definitions, and violent delinquency. *Social Forces, 75,* 799–833.

Heimer, K., & De Coster, S. (1996). *The gendering of violent delinquency.* Paper presented at the annual meeting of the American Sociological Association, New York.

Heimer, K., & Matsueda, R. L. (1994). Role-taking, role-commitment, and delinquency: A theory of differential social control. *American Sociological Review, 59,* 365–390.

Henry, S. (1981). *Can I have it in cash?* London: Astragal Books.

Hewitt, J. P. (1991). *Self and society: A symbolic interactionist social psychology* (5th ed.). Boston: Allyn & Bacon.

Hirschi, T. (1969). *Causes of delinquency.* Berkeley CA: Free Press.

Hochschild, A. R. (1979). Emotion work, feeling rules, and social structure. *American Journal of Sociology, 85,* 551–575.

House, J. S. (1977). The three faces of social psychology. *Social Psychology Quarterly, 40,* 161–177.

Huesmann, L. R., & Eron, L. D. (1984). Cognitive processes and the persistence of aggressive behavior. *Aggressive Behavior, 10*, 243–251.

Huesmann, L. R., Eron, L. D., Lefkowitz, M. M., & Walder, L. O. (1984). Stability of aggression over time and generations. *Developmental Psychology, 20*, 1120–1134.

Jessor, R., Donovan, J. E., & Costa, F. M. (1991). *Beyond adolescence: Problem behavior and young adult development.* New York: Cambridge University Press.

Jessor, R., & Jessor, S. L. (1977). *Problem behavior and psychosocial development: A longitudinal study of youth.* New York: Academic.

Kahneman, D., & Tversky, A. (1984). Choices, values, and frames. *American Psychologist, 39*, 341–350.

Kaplan, H. B. (1980). *Deviant behavior in defense of self.* New York: Academic.

Kinch, J. W. (1963). A formalized theory of the self-concept. *American Journal of Sociology, 68*, 481–486.

Kornhauser, R. R. (1978). *Social sources of delinquency.* Chicago: University of Chicago Press.

Langer, E. J. (1989). Minding matters: The consequences of mindless-mindfulness. In L. Berkowitz (Ed.), *Advances in experimental social pathology* (Vol. 22, pp. 137–173). San Diego: Academic.

Lattimore, P., & Witte, A. (1986). Models of decision making under uncertainty: The criminal choice. In D. B. Cornish & R. V. Clarke (Eds.), *The reasoning criminal: Rational choice perspectives on offending* (pp. 129–155). New York: Springer-Verlag.

Lemert, E. (1951). *Social pathology.* New York: McGraw-Hill.

Lichtenstein, S., & Slovic, P. (1971). Reversals of preferences between bids and choices in gambling decisions. *Journal of Experimental Psychology, 89*, 46–55.

Luckenbill, D. F. (1977). Criminal homicide as a situated transaction. *Social Problems, 25*, 176–186.

Luckenbill, D. F., & Doyle, D. P. (1989). Structural position and violence: Developing a cultural explanation. *Criminology, 27*, 419–436.

Matsueda, R. L. (1988). The current state of differential association theory. *Crime and Delinquency, 34*, 277–306.

———. (1992). Reflected appraisals, parental labeling, and delinquency: Specifying a symbolic interactionist theory. *American Journal of Sociology, 97*, 1577–1611.

Matsueda, R. L., & Heimer, K. (1987). Race, family structure and delinquency: A test of differential association and social control theories. *American Sociological Review, 52*, 826–840.

———. (1997). A symbolic interactionist theory of role-transitions, role-commitments, and delinquency. In T. P. Thornberry (Ed.), *Advances in Criminological Theory* (Vol. 7, pp. 163–213). New Brunswick NJ: Transaction Press.

McCall, G. J., & Simmons, J. L. (1978). *Identities and interaction.* New York: Free Press.

274

McCord, J. (1979). Some child-rearing antecendents of criminal behavior in adult men. *Journal of Personality and Social Psychology, 37*, 1477–1486.

———. (1995). Introduction. In *Coercion and punishment in long-term perspectives* (pp. 1–5). New York: Cambridge University Press.

Mead, G. H. (1934). *Mind, self, and society.* Chicago: University of Chicago Press.

———. (1938). *The philosophy of the act.* Chicago: University of Chicago Press.

———. (1982). Class lectures in social psychology. In D. L. Miller (Ed.), *The individual and the social self: Unpublished works of George Herbert Mead* (pp. 27–105). Chicago: University of Chicago Press. (Original work published 1914)

Menard, S., & Morse, B. J. (1984). A structuralist critique of the IQ-delinquency hypothesis: Theory and evidence. *American Journal of Sociology, 89*, 1347–1378.

Miller, D. L. (1973). *George Herbert Mead: Self, language and the world.* Chicago: University of Chicago Press.

———. (1982). Introduction. In D. L. Miller (Ed.), *The individual and the social self: Unpublished work of George Herbert Mead* (pp. 1–26). Chicago: University of Chicago Press.

Newman, J. P., Patterson, C. M., & Kosson, D. S. (1987). Response perseveration in psychopaths. *Journal of Abnormal Psychology, 96*, 145–148.

Olweus, D. (1979). Stability of aggressive reaction pattern in males: A review. *Psychological Bulletin, 86*, 852–875.

———. (1980). Familial and temperamental determinants of aggressive behavior in adolescent boys: A causal analysis. *Developmental Psychology, 16*, 644–660.

Patterson, G. R. (1982). *Coercive family process.* Eugene OR: Castalia.

———. (1996). Coercion as a basis for early age of onset for arrest. In *Coercion and punishment in long-term perspectives* (pp. 81–105). New York: Cambridge University Press.

Patterson, G. R., Reid, J. B., & Dishion, T. J. (1992). *Antisocial boys: A social interactional process.* Eugene OR: Castalia.

Piliavin, I., Gartner, R., Thornton, C., & Matsueda, R. L. (1986). Crime, deterrence, and rational choice. *American Sociological Review, 51*, 101–120.

Piliavin, I. M., Hardyck, J. A., Vadum, A. C. (1968). Constraining effects of personal costs on the transgressions of juveniles. *Journal of Personality and Social Psychology, 10*, 227–231.

Rains, P. (1975). Imputations of deviance: A retrospective essay on the labeling perspective. *Social Problems, 23*, 1–11.

Robins, L., & Rutter, M. (Eds.) (1990). *Straight and devious pathways from childhood to adulthood.* New York: Cambridge University Press.

Rotton, J., & Frey, J. (1985). Air pollution, weather, and violent crime: Concomitant time-series analysis of archival data. *Journal of Personality and Social Psychology, 49*, 1207–1220.

Rule, B. G., & Nesdale, A. R. (1976). Emotional arousal and aggressive behavior. *Psychological Bulletin, 83*, 851–863.

Sampson, R. J. (1987). Urban black violence: The effect of male joblessness and family disruption. *American Journal of Sociology, 93,* 348–382.

Sampson, R. J., & Laub, J. H. (1993). *Crime in the making: Pathways and turning points through life.* Cambridge: Harvard University Press.

Schachter, S., & Singer, J. (1962). Cognitive, social, and physiological determinants of emotional state. *Psychological Review, 69,* 379–399.

Schafer, W. E., & Polk, K. E. (1967). Delinquency and the schools. In *Task Force Report: Juvenile Delinquency and Youth Crime* (pp. 222–227). Washington DC: Government Printing Office.

Schur, E. M. (1971). *Labeling deviant behavior.* New York: Harper & Row.

Shaw, C., & McKay, H. (1969). *Juvenile delinquency and urban areas* (Rev. ed.). Chicago: University of Chicago Press.

Shibutani, T. (1955). Reference groups as perspectives. *American Journal of Sociology, 60,* 562–569.

———. (1961). *Society and personality.* Englewood Cliffs NJ: Prentice-Hall.

———. (1986). *Social processes.* Berkeley: University of California Press.

Shiffrin, R. M., & Schneider, W. (1977). Controlled and automatic human information processing: Pt. 2. Perceptual learning, automatic attending, and a general theory. *Psychology Review, 84,* 127–190.

Short, J. F., Jr., & Strodtbeck, F. L. (1965). *Group process and gang delinquency.* Chicago: University of Chicago Press.

Shott, S. (1979). Emotion and social life: A symbolic interactionist analysis. *American Journal of Sociology, 84,* 1317–1334.

Simon, H. A. (1957). *Models of man: Social and rational.* New York: Wiley.

Smith-Lovin, L. (1989). Sentiment, affect, and emotion. *Social Psychology Quarterly, 52,* v–xii.

Stinchcombe, A. L. (1964). *Rebellion in a high school.* Chicago: Quadrangle.

Stryker, S. (1968). Identity salience and role performance: The relevance of symbolic interaction theory for family life. *Journal of Marriage and the Family, 30,* 558–564.

———. (1977). Developments in "Two Social Psychologies": Toward an appreciation of mutual relevance." *Social Psychology Quarterly, 40,* 145–160.

———. (1980). *Symbolic interactionism.* Menlo-Park CA: Benjamin/Cummings.

———. (1983). Social psychology from the standpoint of a structural symbolic interactionism: Toward an interdisciplinary social psychology. In L. Berkowitz (Ed.), *Advances in experimental social psychology* (Vol. 16, pp. 181–219). New York: Academic.

———. (1987). The vitalization of symbolic interactionism. *Social Psychology Quarterly, 50,* 83–94.

———. (1988). *The interplay of affect and identity: Exploring the relationships of social structure, social interaction, self, and emotion.* Paper presented at the annual meeting of the American Sociological Association, Atlanta.

———. (1989). The two psychologies: Additional thoughts. *Social Forces, 68,* 45–54.

Sullivan, M. L. (1989). *"Getting Paid": Youth crime and work in the inner city.* Ithaca NY: Cornell University Press.

Sutherland, E. H. (1947). *Principles of criminology* (4th ed.). Philadelphia: Lippincott.

———. (1949). *White collar crime: The uncut version.* New Haven: Yale University Press.

Sutherland, E. H., Cressey, D. R., & Luckenbill, D. F. (1992). *Principles of criminology* (11th ed.). New York: General Hall.

Sykes, G. M., & Matza, D. (1957). Techniques of neutralization: A theory of delinquency. *American Sociological Review, 22,* 664–670.

Tannenbaum, F. (1938). *Crime and community.* New York: Columbia University Press.

Tedeschi, J. T. (1983). Social influence theory and aggression. In R. G. Geen & E. I. Donnerstein (Eds.), *Aggression: Theoretical and empirical reviews* (Vol. 1, pp. 135–162). New York: Academic.

Tedeschi, J. T., & Felson, R. B. (1994). *Aggression and coercive actions: An interactionist perspective.* Washington DC: American Psychological Association.

Thoits, P. (1989). The sociology of emotions. *Annual Review of Sociology, 15,* 317–342.

Trasler, G. B. (1960). *The explanation of criminality.* London: Routledge & Kegan Paul.

Vigil, J. D. (1985). *Barrio gangs.* Austin: University of Texas Press.

Wiatrowski, M. D., Hansell, S., Massey, C. R., & Wilson, D. L. (1982). Curriculum tracking and delinquency. *American Sociological Review, 47,* 151–160.

Wilson, W. J. (1987). *The truly disadvantaged.* Chicago: University of Chicago Press.

Zillmann, D. (1988). Cognition-excitation interdependencies in aggressive behavior. *Aggressive Behavior, 14,* 51–64.

Zillmann, D., Katcher, A. H., & Milavsky, B. (1972). Excitation transfer from physical exercise to subsequent aggressive behavior. *Journal of Experimental Social Psychology, 8,* 247–259.

Subject Index

Author Index